IN SACRED MEMORY

"Tell ye your children of it

And let your children tell their children

And their children another generation" (Joel 1.3)

"Dedicated to the memory of Xavier Piat whose drive and inspiration
led to the publication of this book"

ISBN 0-620-19074-4
Published by Holocaust Memorial Council
Cape Town 1995
Editor Gwynne Schrire
Project Initiator Xavier Piat-ka
Project Co-ordinator Myra Osrin
Design and Layout Artist Lauren Morris
Cover design Esther Surdut
Cover illustration by one of the Survivors in this book
Printed by ABC Press, 21 Kinghall, Ave, Epping,
Cape Town
Cover Reproduction by Castle Graphics
165 Bree Str, Cape Town
Reproduction by Fairstep, Station Road, Woodstock

IN SACRED MEMORY

Recollections of the Holocaust by survivors living in Cape Town

Edited by
Gwynne Schrire

עלייה לבניכם ספרו ובניכם לבניהם ובניהם לדור
אחר

The publication of this book
was made possible by a grant
from the
**MAX & ROSE
LEISEROWITZ
FOUNDATION**

FOREWORD

The Cape Town Holocaust Memorial Council is proud and gratified to be associated with this unique publication.

In Sacred Memory is unique in that, unlike other Holocaust testimonies, it does not focus on any particular theme nor does it comprise stories from selected individuals. The publication contains testimony from every known survivor presently living in our community who was willing to share their painful memories with us.

Whilst significantly it is being published on the 50th anniversary of the liberation of the concentration camps and the end of World War II, the project was mooted over 6 years ago by members of the Cape Town She'erith Hapletah and, in particular, by its secretary Xavier Piat. We thank Mr Piat for his vision, tenacity and perseverance which in no small measure encouraged the eventual publication of this book.

We also thank John Simon, Dr. Frank Bradlow and Dr Richard Mendelsohn for their assistance and guidance in the early stages of the project.

It was however the editor's great passion for, and total dedication to, this project which ensured its successful completion and we are indeed indebted to Gwynne Schrire for her meticulous attention to detail and sensitive judgement in producing this book.

We acknowledge with sincere thanks the support and encouragement of Jeff Borstrock, Nicky Fintz, Raphael Israel, David and Ettie Korzuch and Bella Silverman, whose generosity enabled the project to be initiated.

Last, but by no means least, we record our gratitude to the Trustees of the Max and Rose Leiserowitz Foundation for their understanding and most generous support which made the publication of this important book finally possible.

Myra Osrin
Chairman
Cape Town Holocaust Memorial Council

ACKNOWLEDGEMENTS

This book could not have been compiled without the help of so many people - of Xavier Piat and the She'erith Hapletah who conceived the idea of recording their experiences in sacred memory of their families and who persevered with the project until it came to fruition, and Myra Osrin chairman of the Cape Town Holocaust Memorial Council who took the project under her wing, smoothed out obstacles and turned the dream into a reality. I also wish to thank Ian Sacks Executive Director of the Jewish Board of Deputies for his assistance; Dr Richard Mendelsohn for the guidance he gave to Julia Eppel, Matty Joffe, Claudine Franco and myself when we had to interview the survivors; Julia, Matty and Claudine for the time, patience and consideration with which these interviews were conducted and the memories transcribed; Meyer Druker for the dictaphone which made the job so much easier; Prof Paul Hare of the University of Beersheva for his advice and encouragement with the draft manuscript; Leonie Twentyman-Jones of U.C.T. Manuscripts and Archives Department and the Jessie and Isaac Kaplan Centre for Jewish Studies and Research for transcripts; Evan Robins who helped put these interviews on to the computer; Farrel Atlas who helped to fix the computer when it suffered indigestion from the unhappy stories it had to process; Shula Rabinowitz who turned the disc to a photostatted manuscript; Dorothy Kowen, Eunice Peisach and Mary Schrire who proof read and corrected the manuscript; Dr Azila Reisenberger for help with the Hebrew; Esther Surdut for her advice and assistance with the cover and layout; Lauren Morris for her desktop publishing skills, reliability and enthusiasm; the management and staff of ABC Press; HADDONS Paper Merchants and SAPPI; Evan, Estelle and Roy who had to share me both with survivors and a computer and managed to stay patient and loving, and to the wonderful people now my friends who agreed to recall these traumatic nightmares. And lastly, may I dedicate my own efforts in sacred memory of my own dear father, Dr Louis Schrire, a very special person.
Gwynne Schrire

Gwynne Schrire is a social worker who has studied Jewish history. She has researched and written articles about the immigration of Eastern Europe Jews to South Africa. She edits the magazine of her Hebrew Congregation and has also edited "The Graven Image: The Life and Work of Moses Kottler" by Ute Ben Yosef. She works for a senior's organization and enjoys the opportunity to learn about the past from people who were there. The present she learns about from her children Evan, Estelle and Roy.

CONTENTS

INTRODUCTION

IN SACRED MEMORY
Recollections of the Holocaust

Recently the Oxford historian, Martin Gilbert appealed to survivors of the Nazi Holocaust to **"set down in writing, whether it is just a single sentence or a paragraph, a page or a chapter or a whole book (for) people like me (to) publish and make known so that future generations can read and ponder."**

The members of the She'erith Hapletah, the Jewish Survivors' Association in Cape Town, have long recognized the historical importance of their experiences and that they should set down their memories in writing for future generations to read. The Cape Town Holocaust Memorial Council under the joint auspices of the Cape Town Jewish Board of Deputies and the Western Province Zionist Council have decided to publish these memories as part of the Cape Town community's commemoration of the Fiftieth Anniversary of the liberation of the concentration camps and the defeat of the Nazis.

This book is the result.

In a South Africa in which racism is now outlawed, it serves as a record to the suffering racism has caused. It is a memorial wreath of words recalled in Sacred Memory of those who did not survive and is a unique record of life during the Holocaust from survivors who live in Cape Town, South Africa, and who have recognized that one day there will be **"nobody left to speak in the voices of the millions who could find no haven."**

Although now living in Cape Town, the contributors originally came from different countries and backgrounds, home languages and experiences. Some were born in snowy Poland, some in sunny Rhodes Island: nowhere in Europe were they safe from the Nazi determination to eradicate the Jewish people, not Holland in the West, Rumania in the East or Greece in the South. The stories in this book are not only from survivors of the extermination camps. anti-Semitic persecution also affected those Jews who were victimized in Germany in the 1930s, those who fled before the German advance, those who went into hiding and those who were trapped in the tentacles of the Nazi machinery and became slave labourers and prisoners in ghettos, labour camps and concentration camps.

The interviews on which this book was based were often traumatic for the participant. Reliving these painful years was difficult, often bringing back night terrors, depression and survivor's guilt. Claude Lanzman (who filmed Shoah) said that even survivors cannot relate the full tale. How can one tell the story through the eyes of the living when the essence of the Holocaust was industrialized slaughter? This creates a special burden for those who would tell any part of the history. It is a heavy burden but the members of the She'erith Hapletah believed it was necessary, as did the famous Jewish historian, Simon Dubnow, who, in 1941, called out as he was about to be killed in Riga, **"schreibt un farschreibt"-"write and record."**

History is more than the story of the heroes and the hitmen, the doers and the done-to. The Holocaust is more than the story of Hitler, Himmler and their many victims. It is the story of the lives of all the people living at that time whose combined experiences make up the history of the period. The chapters in this book give us an insight into what it must have been like to be a Jew in Hitler's Europe.

The **first chapter** contrasts the lives of the Jews in a Lithuanian village before and after the rise of Nazi Germany.

The hatred and persecution of Jews went to absurd lengths even to the extent of burning books by Jewish authors. As anti-Semitic legislation in Germany became more and more severe, Jews tried to leave but fewer and fewer countries were prepared to take them in. Some of the German Jews who fled from Germany in the 1930s describe their experiences in **Chapter Two.**

The anti-Semitic germ became an epidemic that swept through most of Europe along with the advancing German armies. A few Jews from these conquered countries managed to survive by escaping - fleeing from country to country, West through Holland, France, Spain and Portugal or East through the Russian forests. **Chapter Three** depicts what life in flight was like for them.

Others survived by concealing their origins with forged identity cards and peroxided hair or by hiding themselves away in places from which they seldom emerged. In **Chapter Four** people from Holland, France, Greece and Poland describe their insecure lives in hiding.

Most Jews did not manage to escape but were caught in the web of the ruthless administrative network carefully spun for the bureaucratic slaughter of millions of Jews. This was carried out by faceless civil servants working industriously to eradicate Jews as efficiently and economically as possible. The outcome of this Final Solution is so enormously horrific as to be difficult to comprehend; impossible to believe.

How can one come to terms with the figures quoted by Raul Hilberg, that when the Soviets moved into Auschwitz they found that the Germans had burned down twenty nine out of thirty five store rooms in an effort to cover their crimes, that in SIX of those remaining store rooms the liberators had found 368 820 men's suits, 836 255 women's coats and dresses, 5 525 pairs of women's shoes, 13 964 carpets, large quantities of children's clothes, tooth brushes, false teeth and pots and pans, and in the tannery the Soviet investigation commission found SEVEN tons of human hair!!

Chapters Five and Six give the experiences of people trapped within this nightmare, as prisoners in ghettos and labour camps, as slave labourers in factories and coal mines, in concentrations camps like Mauthausen, Buchenwald and Dachau and in extermination camps such as Auschwitz.

The recollections of some of the Jews from Rhodes Island who were swept off their island paradise to the hell of Auschwitz can be found in **Chapter Six.**

Chapter Seven has an article by a soldier and an interview with a partisan who describes the organized resistance in the ghetto and in the forests.

The defeat of the Nazis did not represent freedom. Liberation did not mean the end of the suffering. Where could they go when liberated from the camps?

Home? Where was home? What was home without a family? What was home if their occupation of it and their very existence were still threatened by citizens reluctant to return former possessions to unwanted ghosts from the guilty past. Life as a displaced person, free, but still in camps, feeling unwanted in Europe and desperate to get out is described in **Chapter Eight.**

Certain themes recur in these reminiscences - memories of love and friendship, the pain felt for the suffering of one's family, the need to give testimony to what they saw, strong religious beliefs and Jewish identity. We read about a barmitzvah in Theresienstadt, festivals in Auschwitz.

Survival was influenced by the total lack of choice and the utter unpredictability of chance. Survival itself was affected by the senselessness of the Nazi brutality and the powerlessness of the victim. It was chance, not heroism, that determined survival. Heroism played no part. The film *Schindler's List* has recently focused attention on Righteous Gentiles. Some of the survivors give credit to these brave people to whom they owe their lives. However the book also contains stories about a kindly farmer who betrayed the contributor's parents in retaliation for rejected sexual advances, or about panicky peasants who called in a hired killer when they grew reluc-

tant to shelter the fugitives any longer.

The Nazi persecution changed the lives of the contributors irrevocably. Along with the numbers tattooed on their arms, their personal identity and the values and morals associated with humanity were lost. They lost their homes, their families, their possessions and were sometimes plunged from wealth to a poverty in which the possession of life itself was a wealth that could not be taken for granted; to a poverty in which a slice of bread became a treasure.

Hunger stalks through all the stories.

The experiences left indelible scars.

They cannot forget.

They cannot forgive.

They believe strongly NEVER AGAIN.

Never again should the world allow such things to happen.

They have recorded some of the things that happened to them in **SACRED MEMORY** of their loved ones who did not survive.

Writing about Auschwitz, Lord Russell of Liverpool, a legal adviser at the trials of German war criminals in the British zone of occupation, said;

"Were everything to be written, it would not be read.

If read, it would not be believed."

Read and believe these stories and honour the memories.

Gwynne Schrire Editor.

Today, as every day,
I bow my head in silence while my heartbeat slows its run
To pay tribute and pay homage to all those for whom a gun,
Or revolver placed behind the head,
Or cruel beating meant the end.
The days of horror nothing can erase,
The nights of constant fear, the scent
Of burning flesh alive cremated,
The march of doomed, the march to death.

Today, as all those days before,
I miss my nearest,
All of those who were alive but are no more.
In an avalanche of Nazi hate and terror
The earth has swallowed young and old.
Only a few of us, a miracle behold,
were saved to tell the world of the cold
blooded murder of my people.

"Why me," I have asked a thousand times,
"To have survived?" But full of memories and pain.
To have to go through life again,
While still the pictures in my mind
Screen dreaded nights of cruelty to men
And children slain
And women who are not able to give birth.

Am I the bearer of the torch of Remembrance?
The witness whose eyes saw all,
Whose ears heard the screams,
The million cries of innocents,
Whose fate proclaimed them - being Jews.

Let no one dare to spread the views
To say it did not happen. For it did,
It shamed a nation, shocked the world,
But with the passing time a mist has spread.
"Bygones" became the word, and "should we not forget"?

Forget the crime! Erase the Holocaust! Dismiss it?
I can not! Nor must you.
REMEMBRANCE is a MUST
To all who are honest,
To all who are just.
Remember and warn that NEVER AGAIN
Should a Holocaust of this nature happen to men.

XAVIER PIAT-KA

Chapter 1

LIFE BEFORE AND AFTER THE NAZIS

CHAJE BASE ALLON
(BETTY DIAMOND)
Josvainia, Lithuania

My father, Hirschel Allon, was born in Josvainia, Lithuania. My mother, Esther Fine, came from another village called Yalok. Her father's real surname was Greenblatt but he also had a brother. If a family had two sons, the one had to go into the army, so my father was registered as Fine, his brother remained Greenblatt.

I was born and started school in Josvainia. School was also held on Sundays when I would feel afraid to walk to school as the Lithuanian children would throw wooden crosses at us. During the day we would go to school, and ride on sledges, but in the afternoons we would go to cheder. I did not want to go but the Rabbi, Rabbi Rapeika, would shower money on me when I went, to encourage me to learn the holy letters, so I attended. I was frightened to go because next door to the cheder was a little room in which the coffin was kept. As the community could not afford a coffin for everyone, this same wooden coffin would be carried to the Jewish cemetery outside the shtetl when needed and would then be returned to the shul. The boys used to stand at the door of

the little shed and push us into the room and lock us inside with the coffin, so you can imagine why I was hesitant to go to cheder. I have a photo of my cheder class.

Only two in the photograph survived the Holocaust, myself and Rabbi Rapeika's son, Shimon, who after having been in the Kovno ghetto and Dachau, managed to get to Israel.

Socially there was very little to do in the village. In the cold winter evenings we would go from house to house "flicken federing"-cleaning the feathers to make peroners - eiderdowns. The whole winter we did this - this was our outing. We had no toys, no dolls. Our only dolls were little tins that would be placed in an old jersey and would be carried by the sleeves as a toy. This was the only toy I ever saw.

I had great excitement when relations from Germany arrived in Josvainia by bus. This was the first motor vehicle I had seen. We gathered outside to look at it and I felt very proud that as a relative I was allowed inside.

We children would stand outside the two shops and collect the gaily wrapped bonbon papers which would be thrown away when the sweet was eaten. We would stick them in books and look at the pictures. One day, as I was bending down to pick up a discarded paper, a dog chased a cat. I got a terrible fright and ran home crying. My mother wanted to know whose dog and whose cat had frightened me. I did not know. She asked the neighbours. It was a small community and it did not take long before the offending animals had been identified, and hair had been snipped off each one. A sheet was put over me, and under the sheet

I am standing in the front row with a woollen cap holding hands with a little girl with white pom-poms. The only other survivor is Shimon Rapeka, back row, 4th from the right.

the hair from the dog and the cat was burnt with a candle flame and I had to inhale the smoke to chase out the "shrek"-the shock that I had had.

Josvainia had a rabbi, a schochut and a communal bath. There was also a mill. The Greenblatts, my relatives, lived near the mill and when we visited them we would first pass fields full of green peas and we would slip in and pinch some peapods and eat them on the way. Then we would stop on a hill and pick schava, a green leaf that we made into soup. The mill was fed by a river on whose banks ducks nested. We would arrive at Aunt Greenblatt with duck's eggs and schava and she would make us soup and eggs which would be our meal for the day.

In the summer we went down to the "rovick" - the river- Schussver - and went swimming - nude - we did not possess costumes. The cathedral owned the field near the river. Sometimes the cows from the church would find our clothes which had been placed under the bushes and would bite them, carry them off, or eat them, and we would then have to remain in the water until someone could go to our homes to fetch some more.

Life was so quiet in the village that there was great excitement when one of the inhabitants decided to commit suicide. The whole village closed everything and followed him down to the "vald" to watch him shoot himself. There was disappointment when he reached the vald, put down his gun and changed his mind.

In 1931 my father's sister sent us money to come to South Africa to join my father who had come 2 years earlier. We got our things together and the residents of Josvainia gave us dried bread, which they had made into rusks for us to eat on the ship, presuming that we would all be seasick. From Josvainia we went by train to Hamburg from where we sailed on the ship "Ubena" with many other women and children from Poland and Lithuania. There were very few men because South Africa was clamping down on visas and were only issuing them to wives and children joining their families. Our clothing was fumigated and doctors examined our eyes. When the clothing was returned we found that the heat had caused the elastic to shrink so that we could not hold up our stockings. We were also told that it was not fashionable in South Africa to wear galoshes with vollekkes - black fibre linings that fitted into our galoshes - so we left behind our vollekkes and our galoshes and just put on our shoes without stockings as our suspenders had shrunk.

When we reached South Africa we settled in Grabouw where we became known as the "Allens". We occasionally received letters from Lithuania but after 1939 all contact with the family stopped.

We never heard again from our family in Josvainia, nor in Yolok, nor in Tels, where my mother had family and no one could tell me what had happened to them or to the shtetl, Josvainia.

Betty Diamond was born in Josvainia in Lithuania in 17.4.1923. She came to South Africa in 1931 and settled in Grabouw. She married Max Diamond and has a son Benjamin and a daughter Reeva.

Letter to Ruth Green, Cape Town

Merano Sanatorium ATDC,
Italy.
September 1945.

My dearly loved cousins ,

I kiss you and hold you. I feel as though I can see you. I cry. I cry for our suffering and I cry with joy. Believe me, until I came to Italy I did not cry, not even when I was in Lithuania four months ago. I went all over and I did not cry and now I can't hold back my tears. They are pouring from my eyes. Don't be cross with me for what I am going to write about, crying as you can see. They are tears of joy - soft tears. My dears, I lived in order to get that first letter from you telling me that my dears are well. I have read your letter hundreds of times.

I have cried, suffered and suffered and re-suffered, my dear ones. There was so much suffering it is no wonder I became ill. It is a wonder, a miracle, that I managed to arrive in Ponedel, my birth town, in May.

I came to your house. It still stands there, just the same as it was before - the little yatka, the butchery, is there, the stable is there, the garden is there, the brunem well where you got the water from is there. Our house is also there but almost the whole town has been burned down from Mr Meliz up to our house. From our house to the end of Birz street remains and the other side of the street from the Shammas's house down to the end of Simcha Shmuel Shies's house is also still there.

But my dearly beloved father, Joseph, my mother, Freda, my sister and brother-in-law, Chaya and Rachmiel and their small children - all, all are gone!

It is a miracle that my heart did not collapse. I felt happy to think that my dear ones were safe in South Africa. Ruth, even the colour you and I painted on the floor before you left for South Africa is still there. Then I got hardened and started to investigate the facts about the Lithuanian bandits, about everything and everybody and I am going to write briefly about what happened.

When the War started nobody realized that Germany would soon over-run Lithuania. They thought that they had time to get out - first the children, young women and old parents. But it was not to be that way. The Red Army was good for nothing - they too ran like the devil himself. The Lithuanian Catholics started against the Russian "Savetsky Vlest" but as they could not fight the Russians, they started with the Jews instead.

All roads were blocked and only a few Jews managed to escape. My father and Rachmiel with his two horses and the family and all the Jews from Ponedel drove to the border of Sevenishick but the Lithuanian Catholics closed the road. They robbed and beat the Jews so they had to go back to their houses in Ponedel.

After a few weeks in their homes, instructions were issued that all Jews were to gather at the big market place. The Lithuanian Bandits shot the Rabbi, Berka, the

8

son of Moses, and Rufka, the son of Ichick. Once all the Jews were gathered together, they were pushed into the big stone house belonging to Simcha Shmuel Shies. They were locked in for days. After this they were driven on foot to Rakeshik 28 kilometres from Ponedel.

From Rakeshik about 13 000 Jews were driven to Melumel, 3 Km away, to the big forest there. There the young Jewish men had to dig a big hole. They dug not knowing why. Then the Lithuanian Bandits started shooting. They shouted **"Kind und Kerk."**

The last to be shot was Jankel Shreiberg. The bullet hit him on the shoulder. He fell on top of them. He was not dead. The Lithuanians covered them with just four inches of soil. The cries from the grave were enough to kill. Jankel soon pushed away some soil so that he could breathe and waited until darkness set in. Then he pushed away enough soil to get out. He knew Rakeshik and had a friend who had a bicycle. He went to the house where the bicycle stood at the back of the house and rode to the border at Dvinsk. The Russians still held the town. He rode at night, ate grass, and hid in the forest during the day time. It happened about the 13th October. He escaped deep into Russia.

Now I will write about whom from my family has remained alive. My brother Iserke is alive and well and has a wife and child. He was a great general in the Russian army and lives in Klapeda near Memel. He is a Director, but would love to get out - it is difficult with a small baby. His sister Chaya ran with him to Russia at the beginning of the war. After the war they came to Lodz in Poland where she met a young man, Meyer Shumaker, and got married. Eliyahu walked through Czechoslovakia and Austria, and over the mountains into Italy where he became so ill that the authorities sent him to a sanatorium run by the the Joint in Milan to get well.

I myself am sick with lung trouble. All the tragedies I went through and the sufferings in the Russian Army broke my health completely. I have been here for two months - who knows how much longer I will have to be here. The doctors and the sisters are very nice to me. They want me to get fatter. I must eat more but I have no appetite and the food does not always taste nice.

Thank you for the two pounds you sent me. I bought something that I like. I cannot always manage to eat. Don't get cross with me. The doctors and sisters beg me to eat. Oh! I want to get well, I so want to see you all. Please you must all write to me. My dear, I cannot write any longer although I have a lot to tell. The Sister will not allow me to write any more as I am bleeding and I must lie flat. I will write again later.

Regards to all those who are from Ponedel.

Your cousin,

Abras Smidt

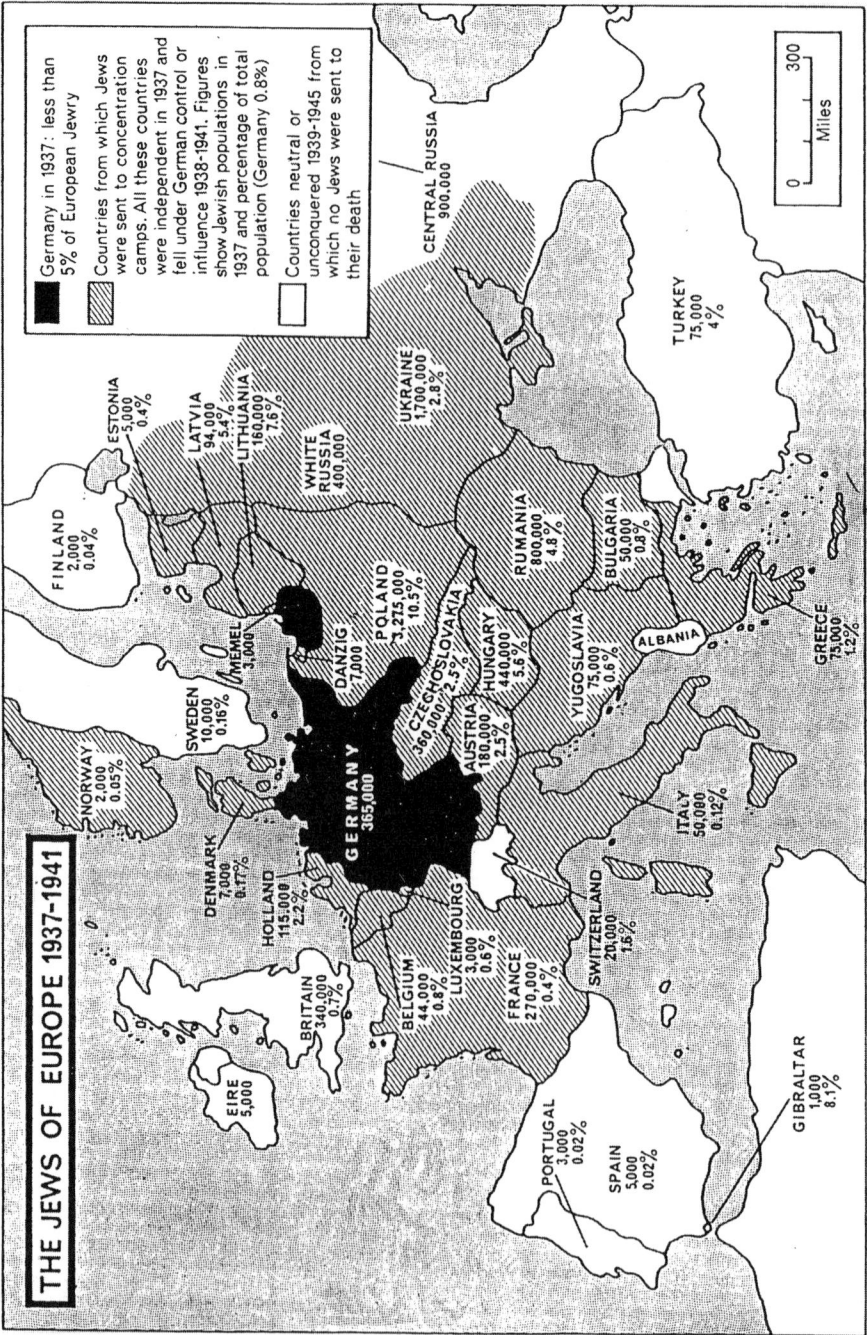

THE JEWS OF EUROPE 1937-1941

Germany in 1937: less than 5% of European Jewry

Countries from which Jews were sent to concentration camps. All these countries were independent in 1937 and fell under German control or influence 1938-1941. Figures show Jewish populations in 1937 and percentage of total population (Germany 0.8%)

Countries neutral or unconquered 1939-1945 from which no Jews were sent to their death

0   300
Miles

CENTRAL RUSSIA
900,000

TURKEY
75,000
4%

ESTONIA
5,000
0.4%

LATVIA
94,000
5.4%

LITHUANIA
160,000
7.6%

UKRAINE
1,700,000
2.8%

WHITE RUSSIA
400,000

FINLAND
2,000
0.04%

RUMANIA
800,000
4.8%

BULGARIA
50,000
0.8%

POLAND
3,215,000
10.5%

DANZIG
7,000

MEMEL
3,000

CZECHOSLOVAKIA
360,000 2.5%

HUNGARY
440,000
5.6%

YUGOSLAVIA
75,000
0.6%

ALBANIA

GREECE
75,000
1.2%

SWEDEN
10,000
0.16%

NORWAY
2,000
0.05%

GERMANY
365,000

AUSTRIA
180,000
2.5%

DENMARK
7,000
0.17%

HOLLAND
115,000
2.2%

BELGIUM
44,000
0.8%

LUXEMBOURG
3,000
0.6%

FRANCE
270,000
0.4%

SWITZERLAND
20,000
1.6%

ITALY
50,000
0.12%

BRITAIN
340,000
0.7%

EIRE
5,000

PORTUGAL
3,000
0.02%

SPAIN
5,000
0.02%

GIBRALTAR
1,000
8.1%

The Jews of Europe 1937-1941

From the Jewish History Atlas, Martin Gilbert

Chapter 2

LIFE IN GERMANY

SYLVA GUTTMANN
Baden, Germany

Hitler came to power in 1933. Already in 1934 when we were going to get married, the anti-Semitism was such that we felt uneasy about having to go to the shul for our wedding. We were scared that it would be risky and that when all the people came together something would happen. So we went privately to the house of the rabbi for the wedding and then about 20 people had lunch in our house.

One day when my husband went to close the gates of the shop the Nazis were marching past and they spat on him and said, "Bloody Jew! Get out of the country."

When we were sleeping at night we could hear them marching in our street.It was too terrible and frightening. They were singing,

"Schmeisst fie raus die ganze Juden bande
Schmeisst fie raus aus unserem Vaterlande"

My father used to play cards with a German friend of his, a school teacher who lived in the same building. My father was scared to let him come to visit as Germans were not allowed to associate with Jews. My father told him that it was too dangerous for him and for us to play cards together and he had better stay away. This man's wife later committed suicide because her son was a Nazi.

We left Germany in 1936 with nothing. When my parents came to join us in Cape Town in 1939 they told us that my husband's best friend had come to the train to say good- bye and had told them that he had just been released from the Nazi concentration camp.

He looked too terrible. His hair had been shaved off and he had been released with the message that if he could leave the country within ten days he was allowed to go, if not, he would be returned to the camp. He could not leave - he could not get a visa although we tried to get him one. So he was taken back and killed there.

After the war we would send food parcels to a very religious Catholic man who had given food to my parents-in-law. We had written to Pretoria requesting permits to enable them to join us in South Africa. These were refused because my father- in-law had been born in Katowitz and the Polish quota was filled.

My poor mother-in-law committed suicide in 1938 and my father-in-law perished in Auschwitz.

SYLVA GUTTMANN was born in Kippenheim, Germany in 1908. She was educated in Mainz, Germany and emigrated to South Africa in 1936 with her husband Willy. She has a daughter Florence.

HENNY SAUER
Brakel-Erkeln, Westphalia

Time was running out. I had seen the Nazis marching in Cologne singing their anti-Jewish songs and there I stood in front of the burning synagogue in Bochum. I had been going with friends to the Chilean consulate to try to get papers.

That night the German thugs came to the house where we were all staying and smashed everything downstairs - not a piece did they leave intact. We stood shivering with fear upstairs in the dark pretending that we were not there.

I had been working in Bochum for a former lawyer, now a "consultant" because as a Jew he was no longer able to practise law even though he had been an adjutant with a high rank in the First World War. I watched the shul burn, went back and gave notice.

It was time to make use of my papers for London and then to try to get my mother out from there.

My father had a shop and my grandparents lived with us. When my grandfather saw the SS man outside our house on April 1st 1933, the day of the general boycott of Jewish shops, he told my father to invite the man in and give him a schnapps. He was in his nineties and never realized what was going on.

We had to close down the shop because there was no more business. My father died of a broken heart. People would come round to the back of the house in the dark to give my mother some food.

I never succeeded in getting my mother and brother out although I tried. After they were deported in 1942, I never heard from them again.

I arrived at Victoria on May 1st 1939 in the dark of night, alone and feeling quite forsaken. I had a domestic job and worked for a Jewish couple with one child. War was imminent and the mother and child evacuated themselves to Devon. I went with them and felt very much the outsider. The husband stayed in London.

The nightmare began then. The lady was afraid to give me food, she thought she might run out herself. She resented me - I had a better education than her, and better clothes and linen - I had been allowed to take nothing else out from Germany. The English couple where we boarded saw this and made up for it and told me to regard their house as my home in England. They were ordinary working-class people.

After some months we went back to London, where we could not find jobs, because people were afraid that we might be German spies. I packed my things and returned to Devon. I found a job in a Nursing Home in Torquay and later with a family of Quakers who were kind and considerate. Devon became a protected area and back I went to London.

HENNY SAUER was born in Brakel-Erkeln, Germany in 1913. She was educated at Kloster Brede, Brakel and was an office worker. She left Germany in 1939 and arrived in South Africa in 1949. She was married to Max Sauer and has a son, Julian

CHANA OBERNDOERFER
Fuerth, Bavaria

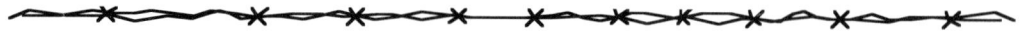

I was a teacher in Fuerth, Bavaria, at the Jewish school, one of the oldest Jewish schools in Germany. Henry Kissinger, then called Heinz, was one of its pupils. All our teachers were Jewish; many of them had had to leave government schools because they were no longer allowed to teach German children. I had applied for a student's certificate at the University of Jerusalem and had had no trouble getting it as I had already passed matric at the Oberrealschule in Fuerth and had a teacher's certificate from the Jewish Teacher's Seminary in Wuerzburg. However I had been refused an exit visa on the grounds that I was needed as a teacher in a Jewish school!

On the 10th November 1938, I came home from school as usual. We had heard about the shooting of a German diplomat in Paris over the radio but we had not thought that this would affect us any more than all the other troubles we had from the Germans had done but in the middle of the night we were woken from our sleep by glass being broken and people entering our flat. We had no idea what was going on. Our flat faced the town square, already renamed Adolf Hitler Platz. We were very frightened. We quickly threw on some clothes and were taken outside. There we were comforted by the fact that we were soon joined by many other Jews. Not everything was terrible - how one was treated was a matter of luck. We were allowed to return to our flat to fetch my glasses and warmer clothing, as it was an icy cold morning. There we found a high school professor watching our flat to prevent theft.

When most of the Jews in Fuerth had been assembled on the square - it was one of the oldest communities in Bavaria - the men over 16 years were gathered together and brought to what was ironically called Berolzheimerianum, the City Library. This had been established by a Jew. The street along the square in which we were gathered was also called after a Jew - Koenigswarter. Another Jew, Mr Sigmund Nathan, had given a lot of money to build the nursing home where I had been born - the Sigmund Nathan Stift. Of course all these buildings were soon renamed.

After the men had been taken away, the women were allowed to go home. Naturally we were very worried about what was going to happen to them. My father who was over the age of 60 came home soon as did the other men that age. The Jews in other towns were not treated as considerately. My twin brother had to stay. The younger men were loaded roughly onto lorries and sent to Dachau. My brother returned home just before Xmas. They had been told that they were "lucky" that this had happened in winter because had it been summer they would have collapsed in the heat. He had told the other men that whatever happened they must eat, even if the food were not kosher.

We were lucky that in our place the treatment was not as bad as it was in other places. A cousin from a village in Wuerttemberg had to kneel down and pluck grass with his teeth. Our town did not go that far and we had loyal non-Jewish friends. The worst off were the people from smaller places where the Nazis did not use the local population to deal with the Jews but brought in people from outside. The German attitude to the Jews at that stage had not yet hardened to the extent that they became really as cruel as they were to become later. Nevertheless some people were beaten - my sister's fiancee developed a kidney infection from which he later died.

I went on teaching and was even obliged to attend special continuation meetings for Jewish teachers. I was not really interested in doing my work for this kind of meeting. The inspector in charge of these had taught me in my first 4 years of school and I can still hear him saying "Miss Oberndoerfer, if you don't do your work properly it is because you do not <u>want</u> to do it and not because you <u>cannot</u>." How right he was - I was already thinking of Aliyah. He was a fine man and obviously not a Nazi but unfortunately there were not enough like him.

In between my teaching I went to Berlin to try to get my brother's papers in order. A cousin of ours who lived in Palestine (whose mother had helped me get my certificate) paid for my brother to get a Yeshivah certificate - luckily we had rich cousins. My brother was the first to leave. He went to Palestine where he joined a religious kibbutz; he did not go to a Yeshivah - this was just arranged to enable some young people to get to Palestine.

My sister got to England. A woman from Fuerth arranged for Jewish girls from Fuerth to get jobs in England as domestics and quite a few lives were saved this way. She now lives in Israel.

I was the last one to remain as I could not get an exit visa. Then we were told that we could not go on living in our flat because it faced onto the square which was being used for Nazi demonstrations and no Jews were allowed to stay there. We now had to share a flat with a Jewish doctor and were forced to sell many of our belongings very cheaply.

In Berlin I had got all my papers in order. A friend of mine who helped me very much was Dr Joseph Burg, who subsequently became an Israeli government minister. He and I had been together at Jewish summer camps, although he was much older than I was. I remember peeling potatoes together with him. We were youngsters and had had a wonderful time then - who could have forseen the future?

Tragically war broke out at that time and only people who already had exit papers and the necessary photos had a chance to leave immediately. Luckily I was able to catch the second last ship to leave Germany for Palestine. To do this we had to go to Trieste via Switzerland. I was put in charge of a group of children. We had a certificate for one child who never appeared - I do not know what could have happened to this child, or what the future for that poor child was, but in the end I decided to leave the certificate at the Swiss border in the hope that he or she, would get it. Another tragic case was of a youngster who developed appendicitis and had to be put off the train in Wuerzburg.

We stayed in hotels in Trieste and then were put into cramped quarters on a large Lloyd Triestino ship. We had to sign that if we could not get into Palestine we would be returned to Germany and would go straight to concentration camps. Only one more legal boat left Germany for Palestine after that.

Unfortunately my parents remained behind in Fuerth. My father had been a Zionist all his life but had turned down the opportunity to leave with my mother on one of the illegal boats, because he felt that he was not well enough to risk the journey. At that time this was regarded as more of a health risk than was remaining in Germany! We got the last letter from them via the Red Cross in June - July 1943 from a small concentration camp, Icbica. That was their end, but if you had asked them, they would have said that the main thing was for the children to leave and they would join them later. But that did not happen - life is like that.

So I was one of the lucky ones.

Chana Oberndoerfer was born in Fuerth, Bavaria, where she attended school. After training at the Jewish Teachers' Seminary in Wuerzburg, she taught at a Jewish school in Fuerth as principal of the lower classes until leaving for Palestine in 1939 on a student's certificate for the Hebrew University. She came to Cape Town in 1950 and after completing her M.A. in German at the University of Cape Town, she lectured there in the German and Hebrew departments. She is married to Dr E. Benjamin.

LOTTE LIEBRECHT
Altenburg, Germany

Hitler's misdeeds before World War II are often down-played and this has prompted me to relate my own experiences which I witnessed and endured between 1933 - 1939.

I was born in 1920 in a small town called Altenburg, 35 km from Leipzig. My brother Hans was the oldest, then came Ruth, then the twins - my sister Lore and myself - then Renate the youngest. My Father was a most astute and successful business man, who owned a large department store. My Mother lived for books, music and her children. There was great harmony between them as each respected the other's interests. They were very popular in Altenburg and were the patrons of our theatre which was of a very high standard even though it was only in a small town. My father was very charitable to all who needed help.

My first thirteen years were blissfully happy. Although we lived in a very large house with many servants, we were brought up with good values and our parents set a perfect example. Instead of being driven by our chauffeur, my Father walked to work every day and we children had strict instructions to go on foot anywhere that was less than 3 km away and were forbidden to ask our staff to do anything for us which we could do ourselves.

There were too few Jews in our town for a synagogue so my Father arranged for a Hebrew teacher to come from Leipzig every Sunday to teach us Hebrew and make us aware of our heritage. Under the guidance of our Mother, we played a lot of music together. She also taught us the importance of reading and often said,

"Tell me what you read and I shall know what you are."

Her library - her holy room - was filled with books with personal inscriptions to her from Stefan Zweig, Franz Werfel, Jacob Wasserman and most of all, from Thoman Mann, with whom she corresponded and who had sent her pictures of himself and his

Drawing of our house. My twin and I are portrayed in the room on the left, Ruth and Renate at the window upstairs, my parents and grandmother on the right and our governess at the bottom window.

sons. All her books had a bookplate of a linocut reflecting her personality which an artist had drawn and which was also featured on her writing desk. We often went on trips, to places like Italy or Switzerland. The memories of these happy, fulfilling days can never be taken from me and I am grateful to have them.

This happy life changed rapidly in 1933 when Hitler came to power. Gradually our school education changed and academic teaching became secondary. The emphasis on the importance of the Aryan Race became a daily subject. The Hitler Youth became a compulsory movement. All the children wore uniforms and hands had to be raised in salute to Hitler. This clever strategy to give these young people authority over us Jews was abused by most but some were passive and looked at us with compassion. My sister Ruth and we twins were often called Christ Murderers.

One day I was told to read a piece of paper aloud to the other pupils. The content was *"What Jews consist of"* and I was forced to say that we Jews were greedy, dishonest cheats, only interested in making money. When the children went on outings or to swim, we had to stay behind. I had been chosen to represent our school in an inter- school art exhibition. When the exhibition started my six paintings were torn up. I was to play Red Riding Hood in the school play. When I arrived for the dress rehearsal wearing my new costume, the children got up and said,
"No Jewish Red Riding Hood!"
They had waited for me to get my costume before humiliating and excluding me.

The three of us were the only Jewish pupils at the school. We were spat at, slapped and could not defend ourselves. My nose was broken when a girl kicked me in the face. We were physically separated from our classmates and things went from bad to worse.

One day a German teacher told me to go to the office of the principal, a friend of my mother's. When I entered, I found him hanging from the ceiling. On the desk was a note stating that he was not prepared to

My mother in her study. On the wall is a photo of Renata doing ballet.

treat Jewish children the way he had been instructed. Ultimately our parents were forced to take us out of school and our Mother, who was intellectually well-informed took it upon herself to teach us at home.

The Nazi newspaper, "Der Sturmer", was displayed everywhere and living in such a provincial town all the anti-Semitic articles and pictures were aimed directly at us. Pictures of my family and the interior of our house and derogatory articles about us were featured. Life became difficult to endure; invasions by the SS became a regular feature. I can remember in 1936 going on my knees and begging my father to leave Germany, my instincts telling me that we would all lose our lives. My father took me to his bedroom and showed me the Iron Cross which he had been awarded during the First World War and said:
"Look what I did for Germany. They will not touch us."

My Mother was a close friend of Thomas Mann's intimate friend, Fiedler. She received a letter from him which was intercepted as Mann was then banned. They came to fetch my Mother and took her to prison for "High Treason." Later they came to the house and went into my Mother's library and tore the books to shreds, throwing them at me. I noticed that they walked right past literature like Karl Marx and unfortunately took at random her most

The Schoolroom. Renate being taught by my mother (left), Lore at the piano, Ruth at the back and myself at the organ (right)

precious books with the personal inscriptions.

All kinds of discriminatory legislation was passed, like the termination of mixed marriages. A cousin was married to a Gentile and had a blind child. She looked for the easiest way out for everyone concerned and committed suicide. In parks only one bright yellow bench was put aside "**For Jews.**" In 1937 all cinemas, theatres and places of entertainment were closed to Jews.

That very day while we were having supper in the upstairs diningroom, I heard music coming from the downstairs music room. I went to investigate and found about 25 members of the theatre orchestra playing Bruch's *Kol Nidrei*. Not a word passed between us, they simply wanted to show their feelings of compassion for us. Every year on the eve of Yom Kippur I am reminded of this touching experience.

In 1934/35 my Father sent my brother to several countries to find a new home for himself. He chose Port Elizabeth, South Africa. My future brother-in-law, Ruth's fiance, went along with him. My brother visited Germany periodically as long as it ws possible. After 1938 it became too dangerous. Ruth went to P.E. to get married at the beginning of 1937.

1938 was a particularly bad year for us as so many horrific things happened which I tried to forget. On Krystallnacht we were all pushed on to the floor and trampled upon. Many SS men were stationed in front of our store with banners saying "**DON'T BUY FROM JEWS** " and consequently business came to a standstill. I shall never forget that at the age of 17 I went to our store to find my Father in his private office with his head on the desk feeling demented. I took him by his hand and slowly walked him down being aware of his desperate feelings of despair, his depression at seeing his hardwon success go to ruin. That was the last time he went to the business. As for my Mother - we had not heard from her since she had been taken to prison for high treason and we did not know where she was.

Things escalated and we lived in fear of what would happen next. To leave Germany became more and more difficult and we were not allowed to take money out of the country. Our lives became isolated, stones were thrown through the windows and many incidents happened too horrendous to relate.

One morning at the end of 1938 there was a loud knock at the door. It was 5 a.m. Uniformed SS men pulled my Father out of his bed and made him walk in his night shirt through the town to a truck which took him to Buchenwald, one of the notorious concentration camps. For many weeks Lore, myself and Renate had to fend for ourselves as we were not allowed to keep on any servants. Adolescence passed me by and from a child I became an adult, never to experience the "fun" of a young girl.

Unbeknown to me, my Father had applied for emigration to Holland. We had Dutch relations there who managed to get permission for us to settle in Holland. My twin and I went with the official Dutch papers to Buchenwald to try to get my Father's release. This was only granted on condition that my Father agreed to sign over our house to the German army.

Of all the unfortunate experiences, this was one of the worst. The man who was taken to camp and the man who came out to me was not the same person. My fastidious father was still wearing the very same clothes in which he had been arrested. He was dirty, hungry and scared. To communicate with him was almost impossible. We took him home, helped him to clean himself and he then literally threw himself on the food and still would not talk. When we managed to quieten him down, we put him to bed and night after night he would scream fearfully and we would take it in turns to sit with him. When we asked him about his weeks in the camp, he never answered us. This had an enormous emotional impact on us girls, Renate being 16 and we twins 18.

The day came when we left for Holland together with my Mother's parents. The train journey was a nightmare as my father went on his knees to pray and kept asking us for reassurance that we were going in the right direction as he was so frightened that we might be returning to Germany. On the border the Nazis gave us a last push, by pulling us off the train and demanding every cent that we had in our pockets, which was about the equivalent of R20.00 to buy something to eat. When we got to the Netherlands border my Father looked for a Jewish name in the phone book and a man came and loaned my father some money to buy some food and my Father insisted on signing an IOU to repay the man the moment he got to Amsterdam. When we finally arrived there I could not believe my eyes when I saw my Mother at the station. Our Dutch relatives had managed to rescue her. The reunion was emotional and tearful.

We first stayed in the summer house of Jacques v.d.Velde - it was unheated and we froze. Later my Father rented a house in Amstelveen about 15km from Amsterdam selling jewellery and our car to enable us to buy necessities. Holland and its people were a haven to me. To walk about without being molested, to see rehabilitation centres for German Jews being established and even a street collection being held for us remain vivid in my memory. Gradually my Father told us some of the incidents which he experienced in camp, which I find difficult to relate. I soon learned to speak Dutch and accompanied my Father to business meetings - he became a partner in a plastic factory.

My father then told us that he had tickets for a boat for America and South Africa to see my brother and sister, so, at the beginning of 1939, having become Dutch residents, we arrived in Port Elizabeth. We were all in a bad state psychologically and needed a holiday badly. I was very keen to learn to speak English and was subconsciously afraid to go back to Holland as it was so close to Germany. I asked my Father to let me extend my visiting permit in South Africa for a further two months. He agreed to do this as he always encouraged anything to do with education - which saved my life!

My family returned to Holland and we said a casual goodbye as I was to rejoin them when we went to visit America. This was not to be, as war broke out. After a few letters from them, I heard nothing more. My instinct told me that they came to a bitter and sad end.

Later my brother, after nearly 6 years in the South African army, managed to get a passsage to Holland in 1946 where he found out that our family were taken to Auschwitz during the German occupation of Holland where they were murdered. My grandmother, a wonderful blind woman, died during the horrific journey to Auschwitz. Her body was thrown out of the window of the cattle truck.

My brother also visited Altenburg which was then in Eastern Germany, and documented all my Father's properties which had been taken from us. In 1991 he phoned me from London with the surprising information that he had been approached by a bank in Cologne with the request to sell them our bank building. It appeared that since the unification of Germany all properties were being returned to survivors, if there were sufficient proof of ownership. This was comparatively easy for us as we were well known. We were well compensated and my brother is still busy with the negotiations for other properties. I received a newspaper from our town which mentioned that my Father was such a respected and charitable man who had died such a tragic death with his family that they wanted to name a street after him, which was duly done. Our own large private home which is still recorded in the deeds as belonging to the German Reich, was badly in need of repair. We have decided to leave it to the town to be turned into an orphanage or such like to be named after our Grandmother.

Having lived through Hitler's strategic ways which slowly but surely escalated into a nightmare, I should like to state categorically that not all Germans were Nazis. I have forgiven but I can never forget and the experiences I have written down will leave a scar on me forever.

LOTTE LIEBRECHT was born in Altenburg, Germany in 1920 and was educated there until forced to leave school. She arrived in South Africa in 1939 and is widowed with three sons

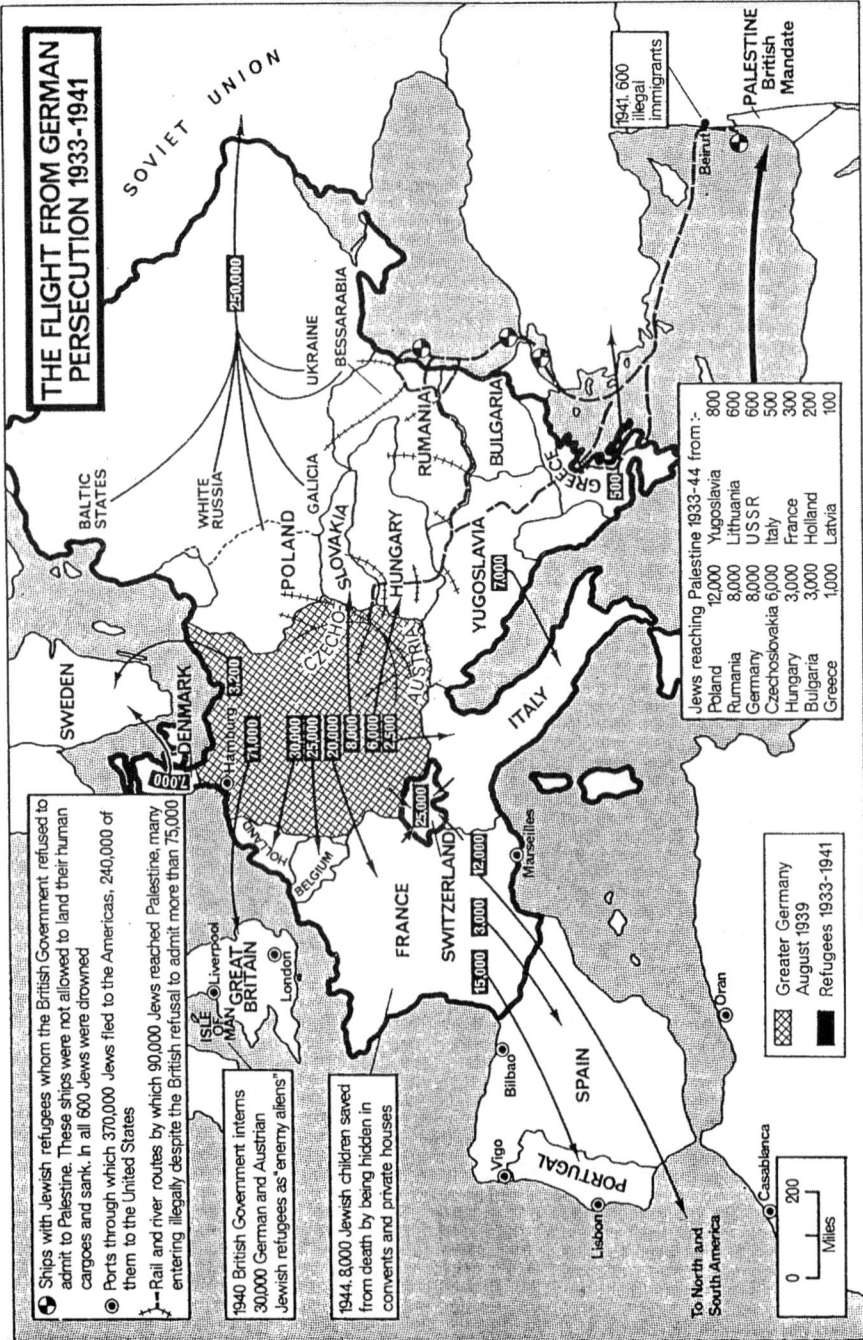

THE FLIGHT FROM GERMAN PERSECUTION 1933-1941

SOVIET UNION

PALESTINE British Mandate

1941: 600 illegal immigrants

Beirut

250,000

BALTIC STATES

WHITE RUSSIA

UKRAINE

BESSARABIA

RUMANIA

GALICIA

POLAND

SLOVAKIA

HUNGARY

CZECHO

AUSTRIA

YUGOSLAVIA

BULGARIA

GREECE

500

7,000

SWEDEN

DENMARK

Hamburg 3,200

70,000

30,000
25,000
20,000
8,000
6,000
2,500

7,000

ITALY

Jews reaching Palestine 1933-44 from :-			
Poland	12,000	Yugoslavia	800
Rumania	8,000	Lithuania	600
Germany	8,000	USSR	600
Czechoslovakia	6,000	Italy	500
		France	300
Hungary	3,000	Holland	200
Bulgaria	3,000	Latvia	100
Greece	1,000		

HOLLAND

BELGIUM

25,000

Marseilles

SWITZERLAND

12,000

FRANCE

3,000

15,000

ISLE OF MAN

Liverpool
GREAT BRITAIN
London

Bilbao

SPAIN

Oran

Vigo

PORTUGAL

Lisbon

Casablanca

To North and South America

Ships with Jewish refugees whom the British Government refused to admit to Palestine. These ships were not allowed to land their human cargoes and sank. In all 600 Jews were drowned

Ports through which 370,000 Jews fled to the Americas; 240,000 of them to the United States

Rail and river routes by which 90,000 Jews reached Palestine, many entering illegally despite the British refusal to admit more than 75,000

1940 British Government interns 30,000 German and Austrian Jewish refugees as "enemy aliens"

1944, 8,000 Jewish children saved from death by being hidden in convents and private houses

Greater Germany August 1939

Refugees 1933-1941

0   200
Miles

The Flight from German Persecution 1933-1941

From the Jewish History Atlas, Martin Gilbert

20

Chapter 3

LIFE IN FLIGHT

A.R.
Belgium, France, Spain, Portugal, Belgium Congo

My father and mother came from Poland. They emigrated to Belgium in 1929 or 1930 as there was no future for young Jews in Poland. They built up a big business on the main boulevard in Brussels and we lived in a large flat above it. As children we had many private teachers. Apart from having to go to school we had a "professeur" who would come every evening from 7p.m. to 9 p.m. Two or three times a week an old professor of music from the Conservatoire of Brussels came to teach me how to play the piano. He taught me more than how to play the piano - he taught me how to create music. He was a fantastic guy and I enjoyed it. Then we had a Hebrew teacher who came twice a week for my brother and myself. He loved Russian tea and would sip it noisily through a hard sugar lump. The lesson was 45 minutes but he would stay for ever and ever. I think he liked our maid. With all those teachers, there was not much time for play but most of our free time was spent playing in my father's shop.

Every year we were sent for a two months holiday in a Pension Mayer at the beach in Blankenberg and we loved it. We had very little opportunity to enjoy the outdoors except on the occasions when the pro-fesseur would take us to the Bois de la Cambre or La Forest De Soigne and we really enjoyed it. So our days were full - but I hated school!

On the 10th May 1940 Germany invaded Belgium. Brussels had not yet been invaded. My father organized our escape from Belgium - not only for the direct family but for quite a number of relatives as well. In fact it is amazing how efficient, calm and resourceful my parents were on what must have been one of the most traumatic days of their lives. My father called us all in the morning and said we had to leave in a few hours. He told us that each child had to take just one suitcase and pack into it what he wanted. At first I put in my toys, then my

hobbies, then eventually I packed in what I felt was really necessary - the shirts, trousers, underpants. While we were busy packing, one of the biggest textile manufacturers in Belgium who was a great friend of my father came to the flat and told my father,

"Look, I have a big farm. You can go with your wife and children and live on the farm and I shall look after you and you do not have to pay a cent for the whole period of the war."

My father always made good friends. People liked and trusted him. However he did not want to take such a chance.

My father then gave each of the three children a belt in which 12 gold sovereigns were concealed and he explained to us that we should never change more than one at a time if it were necessary and he gave us an idea of the value of those sovereigns. It was impossible to take any money out of the bank that morning so he could only take what there was in the tills of his business. He also contacted one of his customers in Argentina who owed him some money and instructed him to keep back payment.(That money was paid to us in the Belgian Congo the following year.) So certain was my father that the war would be over in a very short period that on the door of his business he hung a big sign -

"Back in three weeks."

As for me, I was so happy that I did not have to go to school. It was marvellous. That was what I was thinking about - that I did not have to go to school - how I hated school!

Eventually we left by car for a "holiday". At Knox on the border of France we spent one night and the next day we went to Paris to a beautiful hotel. Paris was in complete chaos and my father was arrested by mistake. After 3 or 4 days we went to a little town not far from the French border called Dax, a well known spa, absolutely beautiful and calm. We were so sure about France being able to repulse the German army that I was even sent to school in Dax. I remember walking and seeing for the first time an aeroplane, a German plane, far above. Life was very peaceful and my parents seemed very happy. I made quite a few friends - there were lots of refugees there - obviously we did not feel the pressures of our parents.

When Paris fell on June 14th, it was a shock. No one had believed that the German army could conquer France so easily. We left Dax and went to the Spanish border to the town Hendaye. There were thousands of refugees. In order to go to Portugal you had to obtain a visa but the Portuguese consul in Bordeaux, Aristides de Sousa Mendes, gave everyone visas without having the authority to do so. Afterwards he was severely punished although Israel subsequently gave him recognition in Yad Vashem among the Righteous Gentiles.

I remember seeing those very brave French soldiers ripping off the jewellery from poor ladies, wedding rings, all that they had with them - it was terrible. I remember seeing people hiding their jewell-ery in tea and coffee tins. All they had was what they had on themselves and in their suitcases. I remember seeing people selling their cars at the border for a few francs.

Spain at the time was under the dictatorship of Franco and when we went through it by train we could see the great poverty. Eventually we arrived in Portugal and went to a holiday resort, Curia. My parents organized the most complex problems without any difficulty. I don't know how they managed it and with very little money on them. The whole world was in complete chaos, and yet we were calm and at peace.

From Curia we went to Oporto and rented a room or two in a very small house. My mother was a top flight business woman who had never done domestic work before - yet four weeks after leaving her smart Belgian apartment she was living in a few rented rooms, cooking and cleaning without complaint.

Refugees were not allowed to work. My father discovered that there was a small difference in the rate of exchange in Oporto and Lisbon, so on Mondays he would exchange his total amount of money in Oporto into escudos and on Thursdays he would go to Lisbon and would change them back into dollars. The small difference that he got enabled us to survive.

The Portuguese were very good people and went out of their way to be kind and nice. I would walk with my brother and they would invite us to lunch - we had never seen such kindness before - or after. There was great poverty. In Oporto we lived for about 6 months and we felt that the war would not last long - in fact some of the refugees went back to France and Belgium because they had heard reports that the Germans were behaving in an honourable manner in spite of the fact that my father and mother and other refugees tried to dissuade them from going back.

I went to school in Oporto. I learnt to speak Portuguese. It was a very interesting school because several standards were taught in one classroom all at the same time and I remember learning how to extract cubic roots. When you think about these poor people who were going to become shoemakers or tailors, having to learn to extract cubic roots - one realizes how impractical their whole school system was.

Despite the pressures my parents must have been under, they were very composed and efficient. This time in Portugal was probably one of the happiest periods that we as a family have experienced. I understood my parents much better at this time than previously, perhaps because they spent more time with me.

My father used to tell beautiful stories in Yiddish. He had such a skill at telling stories that he used to go to coffee places and sit at the table with other refugees and me, the little boy next to him, to drink coffee for a few hours and tell stories and every one would come to listen to him.

Twice a week we would go to a small grocery store and send "pekelach" - parcels - to my mother's large family in Poland. Each child could chose something that was needed or useful and we sent perhaps 12 parcels at a time not in our own name, but through a Portuguese firm. If we asked my mother what happened if the pekelach did not arrive she would say,

"That is not our business. Our business is to send."

But the parcels did arrive intact and we found out after the war that these parcels made the difference between life and death, or between life and starvation

Eventually we left Oporto and took a boat to the Belgian Congo, the "*Muzino*", 8 000 ton. It took 2-3 weeks and went through Madeira.

So in these six months I was in Belgium.

I was in France - where I attended school.

I passed through Spain.

I went to Portugal - where I attended school.

(I even wrote essays in Portuguese.)

And I went to the Belgian Congo.

A.R. was born in Lodz, Poland in 1929. He escaped with his family from Belgium through France, Spain and Portugal to the Belgian Congo. He came to Cape Town in 1945. He has a wife, two sons and a daughter.

FREDA GLEZER
Poland, Russia, Uzbekistan

When Poland was divided between Germany and Russia, Dubnow fell into the part taken over by Russia, so even though we heard about what was happening to the Jews in Germany, we felt safe. We lived for over a year under Russian rule and their propaganda made us think that their army was invincible.

On the 22nd June when Germany declared war on us, the German planes immediately started bombing, three or four times a day. For three days we were bombed incessantly and many people were killed.

My brother had been mobilized straight away and my mother insisted that I go away for a few days. I was 18 and good looking and we had heard stories that the German soldiers were not gentle to young girls.

So I left home without a suitcase, just in the clothes I was wearing. My mother gave me jewellery which I kept in one pocket and in the other I had roubles.

I never saw my mother again. She was killed 10 days later.

I went to Zhitomir, the Russian town closest to us, to people whose address I had, Russians whom I had met while we were under Russian rule. I had difficulty getting into Russia because my passport indicated that my father was a businessman - he had an oil factory and owned much property. The Communists only wanted to help the workers so every one else except me was allowed across the border, until I bribed them with the jewellery.

I spent three or four days in Zhitomir and slept at these people. The news had spread that the Germans were in Dubnow and were advancing and doing terrible things, so I realized that I could not return home. Then the Germans started bombing Zhitomir. I do not know if my friends survived the bombing.

I met up with some other refugees from Dubnow - there were ten of us. We could not turn back, but had to go on to be safe. I had no change of clothes, nothing - I was still wearing the clothing that I had left home in. After three weeks we were full of lice and dust. That was the way it was and that was how I had to stay.

From Zhitomir we walked through forests to Kiev. We could not use transport because the incessant bombing made this impossible in the daytime and in the night time we could not travel. We walked in the day and at night we used to sleep in the forest holding hands so that we would not lose each other because it was so dark. We did not even have matches. We could survive in the forest because they were bombing the streets and railway lines, not the trees.

Three or four weeks after leaving home we reached Kiev where there was a very nice Jewish population. They found us and asked,

"Are you amichai"? (Jewish?)

They invited us to come and wash ourselves, gave us food and advised us to look for a particular school being used as a refugee centre where we would be helped and put on a train to go further into Russia. In the meantime for a few days we could sleep in the school instead of in the street. We were told that there was transport available for Harkov on cattle trains - but one had to be strong to go in those trains!

At every station they would throw us out of the train because there was no room for us. In Russia the trains often broke down or would run out of water. We would sit for three or four days out in the field waiting for the next train. This went on for weeks and weeks and weeks.

When we finally arrived in Harkov I met Gala, a very nice Russian woman with two children whose husband, an army officer, asked me to help her on the journey to get water for the children. She told me that she was going to join her sister in Namangaan, in Asia - first Tashkent, then Samarkand, then Namangaan. She advised me also to go to Namangaan because it was a very nice town. She joined our group of ten, which included other mothers and children.

The train stopped, they threw us out, we waited for another train, and so it went on until we arrived in Tashkent, where we slept in a public garden for four days until someone came and told us that there were trains going to Samarkand and Namangaan.

We came to Namangaan. For weeks we slept in the street. I still had my money but there was no food by that time although there was a little fruit. Although Tashkent was famous for its bread and its fertility, it was one of the most popular countries in Asia.

In the daytime we would try to find news - there were no radios - and would go into the streets and one day I saw Gala with her two children. She was really pleased to see me and told me her address so that I could go and visit her and said that she might be able to help us with a little bit of bread or something - but she looked so embarrassed (she was already washed and dressed and I was still in the same clothes in which I had left home) that I thanked her and went away to hear the news which was very bad.

I decided to find work. We all found work in Namangaan - at first I selected dried fruit and later worked in a big factory making boots with wool for the Russian army - a terrible thing to work with, but it was a job.

Then we looked for somewhere to stay. We found a little shack with goats and asked the owner if she would let us stay there. She said,

" No! It is for the goats; it's dirty! How can you sleep there?"

I said, "We shall sleep."

At least we now had a place to go to with a yard and did not have to sleep in the street. We could not sleep without being bitten by the lice - we used to brush them off with our hands. For four years I was in the same clothes that I had left home in and for that whole time I went without a pair of shoes. We made ourselves clothes from sacks that we washed. We looked like beggars.

There were food shortages and you needed a ration card which enabled you to get a half a kilo of heavy black bread a day - and this was finished before you even looked at it. Once a day we got a soup of potatoes and pepper at the factory - and after the soup

you got tummy cramps. My weight was then 42 kilos. The pay was very poor.

Every day things got worse and worse. They hated the refugees; they blamed us for everything, for taking away the food, even for the bad weather - for the first time in 50 years there was snow - and rain. The atmosphere was so tense - you were scared you would be arrested if you made a criticism. You dared not complain that anything was bad or that you were short of anything.

Problems did not exist in a communist state.

Meanwhile one of our group got typhus and died, then another. I had a very close friend from home in our group of ten who also got ill and she was told that she had to go to hospital.

I said, "You must not go to hospital. They will throw you out of the window while you are still alive and bury you."

But someone reported her illness so she had to go. I made an arrangement for her to jump out of the hospital window and I took her back home and looked after her. I did not get typhus because I had had it as a child.

We remained in Namangaan until the end of the war and met many people who had been sent to Siberia before the war. Many rich people had been sent there.

Then somebody wrote a letter to Israel and I asked if they would include a message for my sister, whose address I could not remember, saying that Sonia Steyn's sister was there, in case my sister got to hear about it. After four or five weeks I received a card from my sister who wrote carefully that she would do everything possible to help me.

She sent two parcels to me via Teheran, through the American Joint and after weeks and weeks the parcels arrived and saved my life. They contained soap, clothes and things. I had to pay duty for the clothes with money that I did not possess, but a nice older man from Riga with a daughter lent me the money and said,

"Freda, take out these parcels and sell everything inside and use the money to buy two more ration cards for bread. If you use the soap, it will last for one or two weeks, and you will still have no bread but if you sell it then at least you will always have bread."

With three cards you could get one and a

half kilos of bread, you would not be so hungry and you could sell the surplus. The Black market was in the hands of the Uzbeks, Moslems, and it was so strong that you could get anything for money including ration cards. Sometimes there would be no bread for 8 or 10 days on the open market but the Uzbeks could get all sorts of things.

So I sold all the clothes in the parcel and I repaid him. I bought two more ration cards. Then we had more bread. It was already a very big thing. It was like buying a big business - you had another half a kilo of bread.

Then the war ended. What were we to do? A Polish organisation promised to repatriate all Poles who had lived in Poland before 1939. We went to register, but you had to be able to speak Polish and in the past four years I had forgotten my Polish, I had only spoken Russian, so for a few days I tried to think only in Polish and the language came back to me and I was able to get myself organised. I wrote to neighbours at home to try to find out what had happened to my family.

The answer was that **no one** had survived, that I was welcome to come home, and that they would help me.

I knew that this was not a solution and I must go somewhere else.

Then I got a letter from my niece who had arrived in Israel. She had survived the whole war hidden in a potato cellar in a field with my brother and sister-in-law. They had given away all their jewellery and possessions to the Polish farmer who had hidden them.

They wrote that I was not to go home to Poland as I might be killed. We had left an oil factory, big properties, and a very good home, all of which had been taken over and the Poles were so anti-Semitic that it would not be safe for me to return. I should instead go somewhere with the refugees from where my sister would be able to get me out to Palestine. I listened to her and decided to join the other refugees.

My sister-in-law wrote to tell me that my brother was in hospital in Berlin. He had been mobilized and there was still fighting in Berlin. My niece asked me to come home to investigate selling the property.

I wrote back that I was not going to go home where I would be lost or killed.
I was going to go where the rest of the refugees wanted to go.
To Palestine.
I was not going to go backwards.
I was going to go forwards.
(Continued in chapter eight)

FREDA GLEZER was born in Poland in 1920 where she was educated. She spent the war years in Russia and afterwards was in displaced persons camps in Poland, and Germany before going to Israel, arriving in South Africa in 1952. She is widowed and has a daughter, Batya.

LUCIEN FEIGENBAUM

Warsaw, Bialystock prison, Northern Dvina Corrective Labour Camp, Samarkand, Uzbekistan, Sudetenland, Poland.

I was born in Warsaw on 24th August 1914, just after the start of the First World War.

My aunts came to visit when I was born and said,

"This child will not see another war because this is the war to end all wars."

My mother's family owned the first shoe factory in Poland and Russia; my father's family ran a big shipping business in Warsaw. I had a happy loving childhood. I went to a progressive school, half Jewish, half gentile but I never had a gentile friend. Like me, my friends came from assimilated homes yet there was no danger of us not staying Jewish - the anti-Semitism of the Polish population saw to this. At home we only spoke Polish. My parents spoke Russian, German and French. My father, a socialist, was a devoted Yiddishist and belonged to the Yiddische Wissenschafte Institute in Vilna which promoted the Yiddish culture and language.

We regarded ourselves as Polish citizens of the Mosaic religion. Two years before matric, pupils from a Yiddish school joined us because they had been deprived of the right to attend their school. They were surprised to discover that in our registration books we had put 'Polish' down for 'Nationality.'

I first came across violent anti-Semitism at a pre-matric lecture on Polish literature for combined schools. My friend was being taunted by boys from a church school who were sitting behind us. We did not pay much attention to this but when we were going home these boys lay in wait for us and suddenly hit him with iron knuckle-dusters. My friend had to spend a few days in bed with a bad wound. Our headmaster insisted that these boys be expelled from the church school, which was done, even though their principal pleaded with him because one boy was a good sportsman and in matric.

I matriculated in 1931. We inscribed on our matric certificate "1931-1941" because we planned to have a reunion then - but there was certainly no reunion. Already in 1931 my father would tell me that there was no future in Poland for a young Jew and would encourage me to emigrate. From a socialist Bundist he had become a Zionist - Poalei Zion - and suggested that I study agriculture in order to go to Palestine, but I was not interested in agriculture. Another idea was that I should study abroad, perhaps commercial engineering in Brussels. I was too young to do that, so I decided to study law.

I enjoyed my four years at university although anti-Semitism was on the rise. The gentile Polish students would beat up the Jews who would fight back, but as we were a small minority we could do little. The fighting was serious, the university would be closed for a month because of the disturbances, but every year the same pattern would be repeated.

After obtaining my law degree in 1935 I had to register for military service but was not conscripted because I was Jewish and a lawyer. I became an articled clerk to the Ministry of Justice, where I stayed for three years. Unfortunately it became illegal for Jews to be in private practice as lawyers, so I studied for and passed the Judges Exam. This too was, for Jews, only an honorary title. So my legal career came to an end.

A few months later the Germans attacked Poland. On 7th September 1939 all able-bodied men were ordered by the Government to leave Warsaw. I left on foot with a group of friends and walked eastwards. On the 15th September I joined the Polish army in Kovel. Two days later the Russians army over-ran this part of Poland so I caught a train to Bialystock to be closer to Warsaw. I contacted my parents through private couriers and they advised me not to return to Warsaw under any circumstance. They wrote that there was no place for a young Jew under Hitler. Nevertheless, most of my friends returned.

In 1940 my father wrote that he had been able to get me an Italian visa. He advised me to return to Warsaw, for a short time only, to collect it. Unfortunately as my large group of illegal returnees led by a young peasant guide was crossing the new Polish frontier, we were caught by the Germans. It was 4 a.m. and my biggest worry was that if I were interrogated, would I betray my nation and deny that I was Jewish? What would happen to my self esteem if I were to do so? My Jewish identity was a strong part of me. The Germans never even asked me - they took it for granted. They did not even keep us long - they just took my money and returned me to the Russians who arrested me. I stayed in prison in Bialystock for six months till July 1940 when I was moved to Witepsk. Then after being sentenced, I was sent to a labour camp near the town of Kotlas in Northern Russia - we saw no court, there was only a piece of paper read by the security man. For a year I remained at the Northern Dvina Corrective Labour Camp. During that winter a third of us died.

In June 1941 the Germans attacked the Soviet Union which then joined the Allies. One of the conditions of this agreement was that Polish citizens were to be released under an `amnesty'. There were a million Polish citizens in the labour camps. The formalities for release took several months. Winter was coming, and our conditions in the camp were very bad. We were released in October 1941 to join the Polish Army which was to be made up of the ex-prisoners.

I went with four friends to Samarkand, mostly because of its warm climate, while we waited for the formation of the new Polish Army. The money we were given in the camp soon ran out and I had to find work. With all my degrees, I became a donkey driver - a good job because I worked for a food shop called "Gastronom". For six months I delivered food to the shop with a donkey called Mischa. Then I finally managed to join the Polish Army at Kermeney, near Samarkand. I had no rank and I was a Jew, but the Polish Army was not fussy at this stage. I sold all my possessions and went to the Samarkand station to entrain. At the last moment I developed typhus and was sent home. The next day I was taken to hos-

pital. I was discharged early as the bed was needed for other patients. There was an epidemic in Samarkand, even the wounded soldiers were evacuated to make room for the typhus patients. When I was released from hospital, weak and very hungry, I was unable to get food because I had no ration cards. I persuaded my landlady to take me back. Some friends helped me. Two weeks after my discharge I returned to work. I was still too weak to be a driver but fortunately I was appointed to be the man in charge of transport - transport being one horse and three donkeys. This involved a lot of walking but somehow I survived.

The Polish Army had a disagreement with Stalin and moved to Persia. As the opportunity to leave the Soviet Union was at a premium, the Poles decided that they did not want to share this perk with Jews, so I remained on in Samarkand. I was by then in charge of delivering bread, a skilled job - getting the bread from the bakery was a profession!

By then Polish relief committees with good supplies from America had been established for Polish citizens. My friend was responsible for the committee outside Samarkand, in Juma, and asked me to join him which I did. When the Polish Government in exile fell out with Stalin over the massacre of Polish officers in Kettyn, all the relief committees helping the Polish citizens were closed by the Soviets and we were supposed to take Soviet identity cards or passports. My boss was a Warsaw advocate and had a Polish consular passport. I did not. As an important Pole in the district I was supposed to be the first to take Russian documents. I refused and was sent to prison. I remained there for a few weeks until I agreed to take the papers. My friends persuaded me to do so by suggesting that it was not a passport but only an identity document. There was no hope of an alternative although we were afraid that if we took a Russian identity, we would never be able to leave.

Fortunately another Polish Army was started, this time under Communist rule. This new army was also made up of people from camps as well as other Polish refugees. By bribery we managed to get conscripted. It is interesting to note that if my papers had stated 'Jewish' as nationality, the Russians would never have allowed me to join the Polish Army. We went by train to Ryazan near Moscow. By then we were properly conscripted and were sent to a part of Poland that had already been liberated by the Russians. We got our military training near Lublin and were sent west to replace the front line troops. I participated in the Battle of River Neisse which was one of the last desperate stands of the Germans.

When the war had ended I tried to find my family although I did not expect to find anybody. This fear was confirmed by my friend, Hala Hermelin, who survived the war on 'Aryan papers.' She knew my whole family well - everybody had been taken away. Hala directed me to my mother's grave in the Warsaw Jewish Cemetery. My Mother died on the 6th November, 1941, in the Warsaw Ghetto, therefore she has a grave. The only other member of my family with a grave is that of my Grandfather, Elias Feigenbaum, who died in 1913. I had to take my revolver with me to visit this large empty Jewish cemetery because Polish masons were destroying the Jewish graves for the marble.

It was very difficult to get demobilised. I succeeded in January 1946. In the same year my South African relations managed to trace me and helped me to get a visa to this country. In December 1946 I left Poland and, after a year in Italy working for the American Joint Distribution Committee, I arrived in South Africa in February 1948.

> Lucien Feigenbaum was born in Warsaw, Poland on 24.8.1914 and was educated at the University of Warsaw to be a lawyer. He spent the war years in Bialystock, in a Russian gulag labour camp and in the Polish army and after the war went via Italy to South Africa arriving here in 1948. He is married to Shirley and has a son Leon Andrew and a daughter Annette.

ZOFJA ROSJANSKA
Wilno Ghetto, Kaunas

Zofja with her parents

The Wilno where I was born and grew up in a comfortable settled home was a city which for centuries had been the very heart of Jewish learning and culture. Suddenly, in a nightmare of confusion and reality, it became a trap containing the Ghetto into which we were herded from 1941 to 1943.

Two families stand out of the shadows of my past; they risked their own lives that I might become the person I am today, still able to help others, perhaps by the very telling of these examples of selflessness beyond understanding.

I owe to my parents my escape from the Ghetto the night before its liquidation. My father, **JACOB ROSJANSKI**, spoke both Lithuanian and German and was friendly with Jacob Gentz, Jewish head of the Ghetto, also with many others, both Jewish and Gentile and so was able to find out about the impending liquidation. He was a mild and gentle man who I guessed was doing a lot of `illegal' things for others; some of these deeds I heard about later by chance, many I shall not know for he did not talk much either then nor afterwards. In the Ghetto it was safer to be silent and after liberation he never boasted.

It was my mother, **JULJA ROSJANSKA**, who had the daring to lead us out at three o'clock in the morning past the Lithuanian police who knew my father, into empty streets under curfew. As we passed the cathedral I could make out a gallows with the bodies of three people hanging there; later we heard they had been caught helping Jews. We walked in the dark, street after street for one and a half hours to get to mother's Polish schoolfriend, who had been supporting us by selling some of the possessions we had left with her and bringing the money to us at the gate of the Ghetto. We stayed with her a few nights but she was terrified because her daughter had recently married a Radziwill, a man from a famous aristocratic and infamously anti-Semitic Polish family. He was staying in the house at that time and she was afraid he would denounce us and thus implicate her as well. She, too, was anti-Semitic although some Jewish people were not '*Jewish*' to her, such as my mother who had been one of the only two Jewish girls at a Russian Imperial Gymnasium, where they had met.

Tense, unwelcome, we could stay there only a few nights before sheltering with different families who would demand money from us and then, having taken all we had at the time, would no longer be prepared to keep us. Day after day, for six months, we kept moving; it could not last. Desperate, we returned to mother's friend to plead with her; no, not in her house, the risk was too great but yes, she had heard of a priest from a nearby church who might be willing to help. I was then seventeen or eighteen. My mother took me there and we spoke to him. A very helpful man who said that certainly he would take me but not my mother, and keep me in the convent providing I became a Catholic. My mother asked what would happen to me afterwards if I survived the war. The priest answered that I would remain Catholic. We simply turned on our heels and left. I still wonder if he realised the risk to which he was willing to put the twenty or so nuns in his care. Was it to gain an extra soul or to be as decent as he could within the limits of the vows that bound him?

We felt trapped. We could think of nothing else to do but to go back to mother's friend. Wilno was full of suspicion and rumour. She had heard there was a certain Lithuanian man who was supposed to be a very fine person and helpful to anyone. We went there, without our yellow stars of course, not knowing him, and simply knocked on the door. They received and kept us, my parents till the end of the war.

DANIEL JURKUS was an agricultural instructor, utterly fearless, an enormous man and a moral giant who respected no authority. Throughout the war he insisted on taking my parents out for a walk every day because, as he said, "even animals need exercise and fresh air."

We stayed in a room in their house and once when someone came unexpectedly, he locked us all in the bathroom.

It was an unreal existence being cooped up in a part of their house, eating their rations, unable to repay them except by trying to be a bit helpful and not being noticed publicly for we did not `exist', at least not officially. If we could trust this strange man what of his wife? Would his young son not let a word slip out to some friend in an unguarded moment? Any day ...

I still cannot explain this, not fully. The bond between husband and wife was strained, that I could sense. Perhaps she, a devout and narrow-minded Catholic, hoped to win back his affection by supporting his stand for right in a time of wrong. And the son? Well, I owe him my life for keeping his young lips shut.

Daniel Jurkus was not the kind of man to give a damn about the likelihood of becoming a martyr. A complete stranger, a Gentile, a professed atheist, he simply knew what was the decent thing to do, and he did it, without hesitation; a man without doubts. He was awarded no medals; no monuments have been erected to honour him.

Later, after the Russians had come and we were again staying in our house, a young Jewish policeman brought him to us under arrest. He had been caught near a military installation with a pair of very powerful binoculars so was presumed to be a spy, and that meant execution. Typical of Daniel Jurkus, being curious to see what was going on, he would defy any restriction, had nothing but contempt for uniforms and orders. In his defence he claimed to have sheltered a Jewish family during the Nazi occupation. Luckily we were able to vouch for him. `A life for a life' can also be positive though we did not have to risk ours to save his as he had done for us.

Before the war Gdansk (Danzig) was part Polish, part German; there was a German `head of city' and **JULIAN DEIMART** had been the Polish one. When the war started he felt threatened and moved to the east, eventually landing in Wilno. There my uncle who was a lung specialist had treated his wife taking no fee. In return Mr Deimart decided to shelter my uncle. Again `a life for a life'. My uncle was already in hiding though he did not survive. The people who kept him handed him over to the German police a few days before the Russians liberated us.

Julian Deimart

Through the Polish underground movement we managed to get in touch with Mr Deimart. He was willing to take me instead. It was one of those odd chances on which so much depended in those days. The underground supplied me with false documents. My name was changed to Janeczka something - I can not still remember the surname. With a fair complexion, green eyes and a small nose I did not look Jewish

Deimart's house in the forest

and I spoke a fluent and correct Polish. Still, it was a very dangerous journey from Wilno to just outside Kaunas, where the Deimarts lived. I spent the rest of the war there.

It was quite a different setting from the claustrophobia of an overcrowded Ghetto or of one room in the Jurkus' house in Wilno itself. Here was relative comfort, it felt like luxury, with no shortage of food in a house divided into two, the Deimarts' home and a holiday flat belonging to their friends. At that time Mr. Deimart was working for the German ministry in Kaunas. Quite often high German officers came to the house to listen to the BBC; I would then be sent into the other part.

To this day I still do not understand what forces were pulling in which direction. Was Mr. Deimart an agent? A double one? A collaborator or a superb example of humanity itself? How could he work for the Nazis, be connected with the resistance, have under his roof at the same time men in those grey uniforms who themselves were committing treason by listening to 'enemy' broadcasts, together with a hunted girl of whose very existence he had been unaware before the world went mad? I could not afford to think about it then; it still doesn't make sense.

Imagine, here I was, at the very centre of the most violent storm the world has ever known, with the worst brutality and butchery, with a bedroom to myself, pretty curtains and clean sheets, learning from Mrs. Deimart in the kitchen how to put the fine touches to various delicacies while a maid attended to the everyday routines.

The Deimarts were a very different couple. He, handsome, a gentleman of bearing and authority, sophisticated with the formal and somewhat haughty manners of the Polish upper class, rather too friendly with the wife of a fellow-officer away on service. Mrs Deimart a disappointed and unhappy childless wife, very correct and wonderful to me. When I arrived, malnourished, with lice in my hair, it was she who helped me get rid of them; I remember rinsing her comb in paraffin not to spread the infection.

An incident shows up both her tension and my freedom. I had been out in the forest picking mushrooms and when I came back into the room where she was standing, me with a knife still in my hand, she gasped,"Are you going to kill me?"

It was bizarre, unreal, this surface suburban life, orderly and lacking in nothing, together with this underlying strain. Not once throughout the war was a hand lifted against me, never did I see any violence man-to-man. Even when the Germans evacuated the place we lived in they left without firing a shot.

For us the war was over. I rejoined my parents in Wilno; after some years we were brought out to Cape Town by relatives. I married, have children, grandchildren. Probably most others see me as `in control`.

And yet even now, when I look out across the sunlit lawn of the garden at flowers and fruit-trees and it all seems so calm, so peaceful, I see the shadows. Always there will be a shadow over me, wherever I turn, together with a spot of brightness as I remember those who braved the darkness so that I might still feel how warm the sun can be.

ZOFJA LURIE nee Rosjanska was born in Wilno in 1925 and was educated there until war broke out. She spent the war years in the ghetto and in hiding in Wilno and Kaunas being liberated there in 1944, when she went to Lodz, and Paris until moving to Cape Town in 1949. She is married to Edward Lurie and has a daughter Heather and a son Jonathan

SANTA PELHAM
Knapsack, Germany, Spain, France, Rhodesia

My parents were born and married in Poland. In 1916 my father went to work in Germany. Two years later I was born in the village of Knapsack (some 14 kilometers from Cologne) in the German Rhineland. Later we moved to a village nearby, Berrenrath, where my brothers, Levi (1921) and Chaim (1922), were born. My mother, Maita, sold soap from a pushcart. Later she opened a shop, and Shimon, my father, handled the wholesale side of the business.

We were the only Jews in the area. However, around 1923/1925, I recall my first encounter with anti-Semitism: one cold winter day the teacher was ladling out hot milk into the mugs of the children - she ignored me, saying that I did not need any.

On another occasion when I was five a girl at school, with whom I used to play, said: "Don't let's play with Senta"-because Senta had killed Christ. I couldn't understand what she meant. My mother tried to explain.

Until 1933, I enjoyed a good life as part of a warm, loving family. We were an observant family and religion played an important part in our lives. When I was 10, my parents decided that my brothers and I should go to a Jewish Day School. I was to go to Yavneh, a High School, my brothers to Moriah a Junior School. The Schools were about 14 Kilometres from Berrenrat. What a long and tiring journey it was as we had to walk to the station, catch a train, then several trams, followed by a long walk to the schools. I was in charge of my brothers and I felt it a very tiring responsibility. I cannot look back to my school days with affection because they were so exhausting.

After 1928, we began to hear about National Socialism for the first time and we heard that the word "Jude" was beginning to appear on shop windows - although not in our village.

In 1933, Hitler came to power (my parents were still Polish citizens). Late one night in June 1933 there was a loud knocking at our door. An acquaintance of my mother came to tell her that her husband had attended a meeting that night of the National Socialist Party at which speakers had spoken of the Jew in Berrenrat who had become rich on their misery. The woman had come to warn my father to leave immediately. My father refused to leave. He was liked and respected and did not believe anything would happen to him.

On Friday 16 June 1933, while my father was saying the Shabbat Kiddush, two members of the Gestapo turned up with the only policeman in Berrenrat. The latter, unwilling to arrest my father, had deliberately became drunk. However, he was not given the choice and the Gestapo dragged him along. My father was accused of being a Communist! He was taken to prison in Mulheim. The following day my mother visited him there - he had been very badly beaten. A few days later, my mother urged me to visit him.

He was in a very bad state; I was devastated. He told me that during the nights he was terrified that he would be taken out and shot because he heard shots at night - Communists were being shot. (I remember one day when I was about 15 and I think had just visited my father in Mulheim, overhearing some Nazis talking about Hitler as the Messiah.)

After about a week, my father was transferred to a penitentiary. My mother tried to get him released. She approached my father's two brothers in Cologne. My father had brought them to Germany in 1920. Samuel, the elder, had been in the theatre as a young man where he had become very friendly with a German, now a high ranking SS man who managed to get my father's release on condition that he left Germany within a week.

Where were we to go? The Spanish Republican Government granted permission to our family to come to Spain as German refugees. My father had become a nervous wreck. My mother decided that he and the elder son, Levi, aged 12 were to leave at once. My father was permitted to take with him 1000 marks. On the train from Paris to Spain, they met a Russian Jew married to a Spanish Catholic woman who suggested that my father settled near him in Barracaldo, a village near Bilbao where he could be of assistance. My father bought a derelict shack, a bit of ground and an incubator: he had decided to breed chickens.

My mother, helped by Samuel, managed to sell our shop but received very little for all her assets. Like my father, she was only allowed to take out 1000 marks. My mother and my younger brother, Chaim, left Germany for Spain in November 1933.

I was to remain to finish High School. I went to live with my uncle and aunt in Cologne but I was not happy there. My father wrote that I ought to learn hairdressing so I would be equipped to earn money in Spain.

In November 1934, I left Cologne. The chickens had not done well; my father's morale was not good. My mother had been selling linens of all kinds, travelling from station to station carrying heavy suitcases. I started as a hairdresser. I was doing very well until I was stopped by the authorities - I had no licence to work. I became ill and had to go to the outpatients at the hospital in Bilbao with an ulcer.

We were not known as Jews but as refugee Germans. We kept our surname (Erder) but adapted our first names - I remained Santa, my mother was known as Maria, my brothers, Levi and Chayim became Leon and Jaime, my father, Simon.

However, we practised our religion secretly, like Marranos. My brother Levi (Leon) had a Barmitzvah, taught by my father. About three or four other Jewish refugee families came to celebrate with us.

Then in July 1936 the Spanish Civil War started in the South. Franco had the help of Spanish Moroccans and we had heard that he had promised them that, for their help, they could, when capturing a town, loot and rape as they pleased. As Franco moved northwards, we began to hear the sirens; by 1937 the situation had become very dangerous and people started to stream towards France. My father, meantime, had been bartering chickens so we had plenty to eat and wear. Leaving our house and most of our possessions behind but carrying sacks with our perrenes and clothes, we left for the station. Thousands flooded the station of Barracaldo, all fleeing; Bilbao was being bombed.

Finally, a train arrived and as thousands of us crowded on, we were separated from my father and Leon. At one stage, the train stopped and again there were rumours that the Moors were attacking. Then the train started again. After a while it stopped and everyone had to get off. As we walked we were strafed and took shelter in the ditches. The road was littered with the carcasses of animals; there was panic everywhere.

Lorries were passing in both directions but none was willing to give us a ride. Finally a lorry stopped and took us to a village where arrangements had been made for the refugees. We were directed to the church where we took shelter with hundreds of others. Somehow we slept that night on our sacks. The following morning, more lorries turned up and in one of them were my father and Leon!

We were all taken to San Sebastien where we were lodged in a small house vacated by a priest. My mother became very ill. We had to call in the doctor who prescribed nourishing food so we were able to get plenty to eat. We stayed there for about 14 days while my mother recuperated.

One day, Chaim brought the news that an English boat was in the harbour; it was unloading coal, and he had heard that it was willing to take on 2000 refugees. Those wanting to leave were to be at the harbour that night. It was extremely short notice but we were there in time. My father and elder brother were not allowed to embark because they were both of military age and had to remain behind.

After an uncomfortable journey of a few days, we arrived in Brittany on the North West coast of France. I remember being greeted by the notes of the accordion, so discordant to my ears after the melancholy strains of the Spanish guitar.

We had to queue in the square, where we gave our names and were given food and were broken up into groups. Our group travelled by bus to Locmine, a little town where we were taken to a farmhouse. Of the twelve of us, ten were women and girls, only two were boys, Chaim and another. They slept downstairs. I had studied French at school and found that I was the only one who could communicate so that I became important as the spokeswoman for the group.

We were able to get in touch with Paris and heard that my father and brother were there. I applied to the friendly and helpful Mayor of Locmine to learn typing. He agreed and allowed me to use the typewriter in his office. I was making good progress until, one day, the police arrived and thought I was a spy - that was the end of my typing days.

After about 3 months, we applied to go to Paris but we were told that we had to return to Spain from where we had come. My father came to Locmine and appealed to the Prefecture. Permission was finally granted because we had Polish passports and we went to Paris. My father had rented a small apartment for us in Aubervilles a suburb to the North-West of Paris. Father had arranged with ORT that Leon be trained as a machinist. He finally got a good job in the Hispano-Suiza car factory. Chaim worked in a restaurant. I did a 6 month ORT course as a manicurist. My mother charred. So we were all working.

It was 1938; we had to report regularly to the Prefecture. As German refugees we were allowed to live in France but not to work so there was a constant fear of being reported.

My father's Polish passport expired and he had to have it renewed at the Polish consulate. After waiting for a while for this to be processed, his name "SHIMON ERDER" was called out at which point a man came up to him and asked whether he was the Erder who had once lived in Knapsack near Cologne. He was Simon Puterflam who as a young man of 18 had boarded with us in 1918. He had become wealthy, was living in Aubervilles and had married a beautiful young woman, Renia Weinstock, and had a little daughter. That evening, our family went to visit the Puterflams. Later, Renia was to tell me that when she saw me she immediately pictured me as the wife of Jack Pelham, her sister's brother-in-law. Renia, my mother and I became very close.

Life became difficult - my father and Leon were both reported for working illegally and taken into custody in Paris for 4 days. They found new jobs, but were reported again

Renia had been trying to get me interested in the young man, and with the problems we were having - no emigration papers, constant employment problems - I began to think that it might be a good idea to make contact with Pelham in Rhodesia. My mother persuaded me to marry him. I agreed after some correspondence with him because I thought that he would be able to bring my family out of France to Rhodesia. Enclosed in letters, Jack sent me eight pounds, in one pound instalments. With these, I bought my trousseau.

Before leaving France, I went to Besancon to meet his brother who was a Rabbi; the other brother, married to Renia's sister, also lived in Besancon. Finally, on 15 May 1939, I sailed for Africa. What a terrible leave taking from my family the night before I left!

I would never see my parents or Chaim again.

One month later I arrived in Salisbury where I married Jack Pelham with whom I had been corresponding, a man I barely knew. I wrote and told my parents that I had found happiness. When war broke out we were able to correspond through the Red Cross, but our letters were limited to ten lines only. From mid 1940, letters to my parents were returned "ADDRESS UNKNOWN".

I heard later that they, together with Jack's family, had fled Paris for the country, where they worked on the land and were safe. Unfortunately my mother developed bad toothache and insisted on returning to Paris to see a dentist. They first visited my cousin Reuben's parents and then went to their own apartment. The next day Reuben's father went to see them. He found the door to their apartment open, my parents missing. They had been caught and had been taken with many other Jews first to a cinema where they were held for some days and then possibly to Drancy before being sent to Auschwitz in 1942.

Both were gassed there.

In 1940 Chaim and Reuben decided to leave Paris and make their way to Spain. They walked through France and were apprehended by the Vichy Government who handed them over to the Germans. They were sent to a camp in Oberschlesiengen in Germany near the Polish border. For six months he wrote to Leon through the Red Cross.

Then he was never heard of again.

Leon was drafted into the French army, where he became an interpreter because he could speak both French and German. His regiment was captured and he was sent as a prisoner of war to a Stalag but survived. He wrote regularly to me from there and it was from him that I learnt about Chaim. When the war ended and the Stalag was liberated, Leon walked to Paris and found our apartment but it was occupied by strangers. He made enquiries and discovered the fate of our dear parents. He met a Polish girl who had been in a concentration camp, married her and settled in Australia.

When I learnt from Leon after the War that my precious parents and brother had perished and I realized that I would never see them again, this terrible loss and all the events leading up to the horrors of the Holocaust caused me to become extremely ill.

However, in defiance of Hitler's insane vision to exterminate the entire Jewish race, we brought three wonderful daughters into the world. We lavished love on them, surrounded them with peace and security and concentrated our energies on giving them everything that was denied us.

Santa Pelham was born in Knapsack, Germany on 26.3.1918 and was educated at the Jawne Gymnasium, Koen am Rhein, Germany. Having fled from Germany she went to live in Southern Rhodesia, coming to South Africa in 1974. She is married to Jack and has three daughters Ruth, Naomi and Aviva.

JONY MARKMAN
Belgium, France, Shanghai

I was a child refugee during the Holocaust. The word for refugee in Russian is 'byeszenyetz' which means 'with nothing' and this typifies my early years. I am sorry that I did not ask my parents questions when they were alive because so many details of our experiences have been lost.

My story starts in Belgium where I was born in Brussels on the 10th September 1939 to my parents Leijb (Louis) and Gita (Genia) Markman. I was named Yona after my maternal grandfather who had a small mill in Shadeveh in Lithuania. Grandfather died tragically, strangled to death by his tie which caught in the milling machinery. When my grandmother was told the news, she became paralysed and died the following year. My mother was a concert pianist who had studied music in Berlin. Because of the restrictions on Jews in Germany she had to continue her studies in Brussels at the Belgium conservatorium. She and her sister Luba lived with their married sister Frieda. My mother met my father who had come to Brussels from Vilna to study engineering - the number of Jewish students allowed to study in Poland was limited.

The war started just before I was born and some time later as the German army advanced, my parents decided to escape to France. They took me and a bundle of napkins and fled. Aunt Luba and her husband came too. Aunt Frieda had gone to Prague some months before. In France at a railway station they had to go through a health inspection. The nurse realizing that I was a Jewish child warned my mother not to believe the rumours that it was safe to return to Belgium. Many of the refugees were returning home now that the initial panic had subsided but my parents heeded her and decided to continue into France which was under a Vichy Government.

Life was very difficult.
We fled on trains, we fled on foot.
We had no food, we had no shelter. We had nothing.

Food was rationed. There were long queues for the little food available.
Sometimes we would sleep in barns amd make a fire on bricks, sometimes on a little primus stove.

I do not know where my parents got the strength from. Once my father was pulled out of bed in the early hours of the morning by the Vichy police. He was released later because he had a Polish passport and they felt sorry for him. Another time when we were in a park it was surrounded by police who were rounding up Jews for deportation. My father was very softhearted and took me in his arms to kiss me goodbye. The gendarme saw us, looked at him and walked away. Some power must have been watching over us.

Eventually we ended up in Marseilles; homeless, penniless refugees. Fortunately we found out about an association that

With my parents in Marseilles

helped Jewish refugees like us and eventually we managed to get some papers to enable us to leave the country. These, ironically led us onto a Vichy troop ship that was leaving Marseilles to help the forces in Indochina.

There were five of us on the troop ship - my family, my aunt and uncle - and the troops threatened to drown us. The voyage lasted SIX months without disembarking anywhere. We even sailed passed Cape Town. We arrived in Saigon but the ship was not able to land there so we landed instead in Shanghai, China and that was the first time we got off the ship. I was now about two years old and I began to be aware of what was happening.

Although it was in China, Shanghai was a modern metropolis with sky scrapers. There was an international community and each group lived in their own area of the city. By 1940 there were twenty thousand Jewish refugees in Shanghai. The five of us stayed in the French section with earlier refugees, who had come from Russia before the war, and had settled down well.

My Dad was religious and became involved with members of the Mir Yeshivah who had escaped to Shanghai. I remember Cantor David Bagley who was also one of their students. They were a fantastic group of people with wonderful rabbis - as a little child I can remember the atmosphere there. My father would often take me with him to the discussions he enjoyed attending. They got him work as an engineer and he constructed a mikvah for them. The Yeshivah did not have any money to pay him so they gave him a set of books, chumashim, Rashi, targum inscribed by the Rosh Yeshivah which I still treasure. In 1947 the whole yeshivah moved to Brooklyn, NY.

We were in Shanghai for five years, some of it under Japanese occupation. I remember this started off with a lot of bombing. My mother became very anxious and this anxiety was passed on to me. Whenever my Dad went out to look for something to eat or to find work she would be besides herself worrying whether he would return. I remember very vividly the bombing, the destruction of the buildings and the people blown up in the air. Being White barbarians and Jews we suffered very badly under the Japanese occupation. There was no food, there were many arrests, my father was

The five of us in Shanghai

picked up a few times and taken to the police station. The Japanese were so short that they used to get up on chairs in order to beat up people. They had been well indoctrinated in Anti-Semitism by their Axis friends and they started to put together concentration camps for Jews. Documents released after the War showed this. David Bagley was incarcerated in one of them.

Then the Americans liberated Shanghai. They were regarded as such heroes that people flocked to see them; it was as though they had come from outer space. My Father and my uncle were employed by the American army. It was the first time we were able to enjoy life because we were no longer oppressed although we did not have much money or food. I was sent to three or four schools - a French Roman Catholic convent, followed by a Russian school, a Chinese school and then to a Jewish school which was subsidized by America. There I learnt English.

I remember the day my parents received a telegram from relations in England telling them that my mother's family, Freda and her three children, had been wiped out, killed in the crematoria. It was a catastrophe. My mother was inconsolable. Many Jews lived in our block of flats and they came round to see her. We also learnt that my father's family had perished in the Vilna ghetto. With the threat of a Communist revolution, there did not seem to be much future for us in China so we decided to leave and join relatives in America. The first ship available was going to Australia so we went there instead.

When we arrived in Sydney, I discovered that even here I was not free from anti-Semitism. I was the only Jew in my school. I was called names and if anything went wrong, it was blamed on me. When a pair of glasses was stolen, I was sent to the principal. After seven years in Australia my father decided to join his only surviving sister in Cape Town and we moved here in 1954

Jony Markman was born in Brussels, Belgium on 10.9.1939. He spent the war years in Belgium and France before escaping to Shanghai, China where he was liberated in 1945. After some years in Australia, he moved to South Africa in 1954. He has a wife Myrna, a son David and a daughter Amanda.

Chapter 4

LIFE IN HIDING

KARL LANGER
Vienna, Utrecht

MY REMARKABLE MOTHER

I wish to pay tribute to my Mother, to whom I owe my survival. Her name was
HELENE LANGER
but everyone called her ILUS. Her father Joseph Goldberger was a goldsmith who came from Austria.

She was a remarkable woman.

Helaine Langer

I was born in Vienna to a Jewish mother and a Catholic father and was brought up as a Catholic. In 1938 after the Anschluss, all Jews had to register with the authorities, had a J stamped in their passport, had to surrender their possessions and were told that they had 14 days to leave Austria, or be sent to a concentration camp. My parents decided that it would be best for my mother to go to Holland with my sister and me while my father would remain behind to look after his hotel.

We were allowed to take only ten guilders and a small suitcase. A gold bracelet and a diamond ring were hidden among the toys in the suitcase. I was 5 years old and I remember saying goodbye to my father at the station. We had trouble on the train when my mother was arrested at the German border. At the last moment she was allowed to board the train and we arrived safely in Holland. We went to relations of my father who ran a Catholic boarding school called Groenestein, so although my mother could not take money with her, she did at least have family to whom she could go.

Unfortunately she had no visa for Holland so the police ordered us to leave within 24 hours. Luckily my Mother remembered that a Dutch Minister, a Mr Van Buren, had stayed at their hotel, so she located him. She went to his house in The Hague. He was away but my mother told his wife that we were Jewish refugees from Austria and that the police wished to send us back there where we would be killed. Mev Van Buren spoke to the police and as soon as her husband arrived, he arranged for us to get residents' visas. So we have to thank Mr and Mrs Van Buren for this kindness which saved our lives.

My sister and I stayed at the boarding school while my mother looked for work. The money from the sale of the diamond ring gave us sufficient to cover our living expenses for a month. (The gold bracelet I still have and it will go to my daughter who is a schoolgirl at Herzlia). My mother was from a hotel family and soon found work as a cook.

Then, in May 1940, the Germans invaded Holland. All Jews were ordered to move away from coastal areas to either Utrecht or Arnhem. Luckily we decided not go to to Arnhem - most of Jews there were killed - and many others died in heavy bombing when the Allies landed there later. We chose to move to Utrecht where the Groenestein nuns had a brother order with a similar convent school which we could attend.

Soon afterwards the Nazis ordered the Jewish leaders to start a Jewish Council. At that time there were 140 000 Jews in Holland. With the Jewish Council as a buffer, the Jewish people were lulled into a belief of safety; as long as they did certain things, and then more and more things, they would be safe.

Soon everyone in Holland was told to register themselves as either Aryan - or Jewish. Failure to fill in those forms was itself an offence as was saying that you were Dutch if you were Jewish or vice versa. Some people only discovered then that they had Jewish parents.

My mother completed these forms and we were issued with identification forms with a large J inside. We also had to declare what possessions we had, what bank accounts we had. People should have realized where this was leading, but they were naive and completed the forms. So the Nazis got a list of all the Jews and to make things respectable they established bureaux where people could apply if they felt that they had been wrongly classified. There were divisions between full Jews, half Jews, quarter Jews. The Jewish Council was used, abused and misused by the Germans. The Nazis then started *"labour camps."* The Dutch might have become alarmed if their fellow Jewish citizens were to be sent to concentration camps but labour camps were acceptable because it was reasonable that with so many soldiers at the front, young people would be required to take their place. If one volunteered one was promised pay, holidays and visits from their families. Many Jews believed this. My mother did not.

After a while we were not allowed to go into grocery shops, into fish shops, to own telephones, radios, bicycles, or go on the tramways, which meant no transport was available for us. Jews were not allowed to hold certain jobs or to work in the government. The Jewish Council were also given the responsibility of distributing the yellow star at 4c a star.

My mother had to get her star, but she did not wear it because a miracle happened. Some people pretended that they were not Jewish. This did not save them, however. We could easily have done this because my mother was married to a Catholic, and both my sister and I had our baptism certificates, and had been brought up Catholic.

She decided to pretend that we were Germans, Aryans. She put on her fur coat, combed her hair - she was a beautiful woman - and went to the highest German Officer. She took her passport, destroyed the pages with the J on it, and said that she was a German on holiday visiting her sister, that her husband was a German officer fighting on the Eastern front in Russia, and that her passport had been damaged so that she was unable to leave the country to return to Germany, so would they please give her a new passport. She would never talk about the visit, but when she returned she had a new passport without the J.

We were now classified as Reich Germans and as such were even entitled to more rations. My mother looked as Jewish as any one else. If they had checked on her in Austria - and it only needed one phone call - they would have discovered the truth. It took great courage and it worked.

The convent school we attended also knew that we were Jewish. When the Germans ordered all the Jewish children to be kicked out of schools, the Archbishop of Utrecht, Dr J. De Jong, made an official decree that the Catholic schools were not to dismiss any baptised Jewish children despite German demands and threats to close the schools and execute the school principals.

Being `*Reich Germans*` we now had a certain measure of security, but there was still constant anxiety from second to second because we might be found out. My sister was now sixteen, and as a Reich German, she had to work in a German office. Luckily she was put in an office organizing transport of cars and things - nothing too oppressive and through this she made contacts that were invaluable to us later.

I was supposed to join the Hitler Youth movement and I kept getting notices that I must join and attend meetings. My mother would tell the organizers that I could not go because I had asthma and was weak, and I got out of it.

Having a safe address, my mother now hid Jewish people. We had some very good hiding places. One was in the attic behind the coal bunker. Another was my idea. We had a front door with a stoep going up. Above

The hiding place was under the floor, behind the window above the third door from the left, house 33 bis

the front door was a window, an open space about 80 cm deep and the width of the door. There was nothing up there except the glass in front and the glass at the back and an empty space just above the door. We cut the floor open and put two mattresses on top to deaden the noise. When there was a razzia and the Germans would start banging on the door, we would open the floor, the people would jump inside, 4 or 5 people could stand in there, we would close it up, put a cupboard on top and there I would sit playing with my toys. I was then about 10. (After the war I visited Holland with my wife and I showed her the hiding place. The people living there did not know of its existence and had wondered why the floor had been cut.)

We had several Jewish people staying with us. There were the Kaufmanns, an old couple who stayed with us right through the war. There were the Levs, a young couple, and individual people.

There was a tragedy. My mother got to know a hairdresser called Joop Danielson who came to hide. His family were living in Utrecht. As his brother had gone voluntarily to a work camp, his parents had felt that they were safe. My mother had warned them that this was not so and that they should go underground. Eventually Joop

decided to go underground in my mother's house. Later his whole family decided to do the same and came to our house one evening and were going to move the following day to a proper place in the country because my mother could not take so many people. All of a sudden the police came to our door banging and shouting. Everyone ran upstairs to the coal bunker. My sister quickly stacked the dishes together so that they would not see that we had had people for supper. My mother opened the door saying:
"What is all the noise?"
The Nazis stormed up with their guns.
"Where are the Jews? Where are the Jews?"
"What Jews?" said my mother
"We know that they are here!"
The Danielsons had been betrayed by the people with whom they had stored their possessions. They were found. This was before we had the other hiding place. The Danielson family were taken away by the Nazis and we never saw them again. They lined us up in the dining room and were going to shoot us all on the spot but my mother told them in German:
"How can you do this. I did not even know that these people were Jewish. Get out of my house"
She was formidable.

The Kaufmann family were in bed. My mother said:
"Don't go in there. They are Germans, they are old people, they are in bed, they will have a heart attack."
and the Nazis left them alone. My mother was amazing.

A few days later on Sunday morning the Nazis came again. This time it was the Dutch security police and they took my mother and me away to check up on her papers. We were not allowed to take anything with us - I was about ten. My mother fainted in the street. We had to walk and I rushed into a shop to try to get some water. We arrived at the police station. There was a big office and my mother threatened to commit suicide and jump through the window. I held her back and they quickly grabbed her. Then they told us that we were to be sent to a concentration camp. We were sent downstairs to a big bus which was waiting. There were German guards and lots of people and we were pushed onto the bus.

My mother and myself in the front.
At the back l to r. My sister Lies, Joop
Danielson and my sister's friend. Joop was
betrayed. The Nazis raided our house and
took him away.

There were Catholic nuns in the bus, but because they had Jewish blood it did not help. The bus took us to Amsterdam.

We arrived at the Jewish Theatre. Hundreds of people had been assembled there for transportation to concentration camps. Again a miracle took place. My sister who had not been arrested because she worked at a German office had contacted the underground and the following evening we were released. One of the very few. Perhaps my mother talked her way out of it, persuading them that she was innocent, although she was arrested as a German hiding Jews, a terrible crime. We had no money, nothing, but my mother went to a house, knocked on the door, explained the circumstances and the people gave us food and money to return to Utrecht.

We had many more razzias from the Germans, but we were able to hide the people in time. We had many more people coming to hide, sometimes we would send them over the balcony to neighbours - all sorts of schemes. I was the messenger boy.

Feeding these people was a problem as there was a food shortage and the people in hiding could not go out in the streets, so my mother had to manage to get food for every one. Behind us was a big garage, the Garage Honders, occupied by the Germans where petrol tanks and cars were kept and the guards of the garage lived right next door. They had to deliver bread to the German soldiers in different places in Utrecht. A little van would go each day to the bakery and then to the various army units to deliver the bread. I would go with the soldiers to help them to fetch and deliver the bread. For my trouble I would be given one or two loaves for ourselves and this helped. We had to be very careful with the Germans next to us.

My mother helped to rescue non- Jews as well. Young Dutch boys were ordered to report to the Germans for work. I remember seeing hundreds of them coming to Tivoli with their suitcases on their way to Germany. Nearby there lived a Dutch couple who later moved to the Congo. Dr Pino was a dentist and my mother and Mrs Pino were friends. At night they would put on their fur coats and go to Tivoli during curfew when no one was allowed on the streets. They would walk past the guards speaking German to each other and chatting as though they were prostitutes. They would go past the young men and say:
"Drop your suitcase and come with me. Keep quiet and don't talk."

Then they would grab them and would walk past the guards talking German as though they had gone to meet a boyfriend or to pick one up. They would make jokes to the guards as they went past and then bring the boys to our house. Then they would go back and fetch other young men. These boys would stay with us for a few days and would then be sent to the country as farmers. In my childish handwriting I would sent a postcard to their parents saying,

"Dear Aunty So and So,
I am having a wonderful
holiday in Utrecht, don't
worry about me. The weather is beautiful here and I
shall be home soon.
Your loving son,
Whatever."

45

and would post it. Many of these Dutch boys were saved.

My mother was a very courageous woman and rescued people despite the risks she ran. She died a few years ago in Highlands House.

To this day I find it difficult to talk about these times although I feel that I have a duty to do so. Our experiences are only a small part of the things that happened in the Holocaust. The Holocaust was more than just concentrations camps. The transports started in 1941, but the organized system of persecution started long before. The suffering of people before the transports began must also be taken into account when assessing the horrors of that period.

Why should we record what is long gone? Never ever must it be forgotten, even in a thousand years time and it should be discussed and written about because the basis of the Holocaust is anti-Semitism which is a universal sickness that has still not been eradicated from this world. Any anti-Semitism or racism is a disaster for the Jewish people. They must not ignore it.

They thought in Germany that it could not happen to them. They had lawyers, they had educated people - till the last minute when they were loaded into cattle trucks, they still could not realize what was going to happen to them. Jews all over the world must protest if there is any flare up of anti-Semitism. I was not in a concentration camp but I still experienced the Holocaust and that was bad enough.

KARL LANGER was born in Vienna in 1932 and educated in Utrecht, Holland where he was hidden until 10.5.1945. Afterwards he lived in Switzerland, and Namibia, arriving in Cape Town in 1956. He went on Aliyah in 1979 coming to Cape Town in 1985 to be near to his mother who was ill. He is married to Sandra and has a son, Benjamin and a daughter, Mirah.

ISRAEL AND RAY KETELLAPPER

Amsterdam, Westerbork, Bergen Belsen

Mr.KETELLAPPER

When the War broke out in Holland we stayed in Amsterdam for a few months .One day near the beginning of the German occupation, I was walking on the Jonas Daniel Meyer Plein near the Great Synagogue and in front of me were the Gruene Polizei (the Order Police who did the work for the Gestapo) who were putting about fifty young Jewish boys against the wall. When I saw this I realized that we must leave Amsterdam and go into hiding. This was very difficult but my father-in-law, who had a piece goods business, had a friend in Haarlem half an hour away who took us to stay with him.

After a few weeks they put us up with an elderly couple in an attic. My name was changed from Israel to John because Israel was too dangerous a name while we were hiding with a Gentile couple so it has been John ever since. We stayed there a year and never saw the street, never went out, just stayed inside in the attic. They brought us food and sometimes we went down and ate with them at the table.

One evening there was a knock on the door. We heard it upstairs where we were hiding behind the wall in the attic. The Gestapo came and said,
"You have Jews in hiding."
The old man said,
"No! We haven't got any. If you want to go through the house, you can go through the house."
So they went all over the house, about four or five of them, and we heard them walking all over the place and we heard them say,
"You _have_ Jews in the house"
So he said, "Well, look around."
They went away without finding anyone. When they left I said to myself,
"Look they are an elderly couple. I cannot endanger them. We shall have to go back to Amsterdam."

My wife's aunt was still in Amsterdam. She told us that if one had diamonds, one could buy a special stamp for one's pass which would enable one to go to a special camp to go eventually to Palestine. My father was a diamond dealer but my father-in-law collected diamonds for his wife. My father-in-law had already been sent to a working camp at Westerbork. My aunt said that she knew where my father-in-law kept his diamonds and she was sure that he would not mind if she got them out for us. So we went to the SS in the Euterpenstraat in Amsterdam. A Scharfuhrer was sitting inside who said,
"Have you got the diamonds?"

We each had to pay 100 000 guilders in pure diamonds (which today is a few millions) plus 6000 guilders hush money for the Gestapo themselves - the rest went to Germany. We got the pass and they told us that nothing would happen to us but that we would go to Palestine. We stayed in a small flat and in the meantime thousands of Jews were being picked up and sent to internment camps.

Mrs KETELLAPPER

The Germans would take a street in the ghetto where they had all the Jews in one place and they would put a tank on the one side of the street and a tank on the other side of the street and all the males that were milling around there and had a Magen David or a J on their jacket were taken away whether they were three years old or sixty years old, that whole bunch, because it was easy. The Jews could not get out and they transported them somewhere, where exactly nobody knew at the time. This was the end of 1941.

Mr KETELLAPPER

We heard rumours that first they were sent to a special camp in Holland from where they were transported in cattle trucks. The Germans said they were going to working camps.
(Continued in Chapter Five)

47

KLARA VAN KLEEF
Amsterdam

I was born in Amsterdam where I lived with my father Isaac, my Mother Leah, two brothers and a sister. My father had been brought up in the Jewish orphanage which was very strict. He was unhappy there and afterwards didn't want to know anything about religion and became a socialist. He worked six days a week making kapok mattresses.

When I was young I never realized that I was Jewish. It was never pumped into me. It was a big country and I knew there were Jews and Roman Catholics and Christians and things. Later I was told that I was Jewish, my grandparents were religious but that was all. It was only when I was about 16 that I was made aware of being Jewish. The Germans came in to Amsterdam and the people started splitting up into Jewish and Non-Jewish and we had to wear a star of David, sewn onto our clothes, not put on with safety pins, and have an identity card with a big J on it. Even people who were your friends before separated because they could not go out with Jews and it was a very, very nasty feeling. We were very scared.

A week after Holland was occupied, in May 1940, there were German soldiers all over the street. We had neighbours, the Englanders, opposite, (we did not even know they were Jewish) who put their heads in the gas oven and committed sucide. Many others did the same at that time.

My father was picked up and he had to go to a labour camp and work there digging trenches and all sorts of things. He didn't get any money for it but he came home in the evening. We began to prepare for being sent to the labour camp. People would take down their curtains and make them into big jackets for warmth. Then people all had to go to a certain theatre, people whose names started with A or with B, but when we were told to go, we didn't. We said,
"No, if they come, they must come and fetch us."

When the razzias began we would hide or not open our doors, pretending that we were out. The Nazis would knock on everyone's doors because they did not know who was Jewish. Collaborators would tell them, "There's a Jewish family living there!" They had guns and would hit you if you didn't answer them properly .

Then I was picked up. They came to the clothing factory in town where I was working and they picked up everyone with the star, and put us in a corner. There were a whole lot of people already standing in the street and they put us all together in a big column with SS soldiers around the three to four hundred of us and we had to walk for about an hour. Those who fainted or didn't want to walk were kicked in the ribs.

They marched us to the Euterpenstreet school which the Germans had taken over and had built gaol cells inside. We had to stand there on the field and it was raining. Twenty four hours a day we had to stand in the rain without food. One man said something to the Germans and they took him to a corner and we all had to come and watch him being beaten to death. We had to watch it and if you didn't watch they came at you and made you watch.

For four days I stood there and one night I slept in a cell with about twelve people. There was one cot but no blankets. The guards were terrible. The best thing was just to keep quiet and walk around when they told you to. Twice in those four days we got food - the Red Cross or some such organisation arrived with dirtbins containing stew and they dished it up and we all got a soup-spoon full of it.

On the third day that I was there, they called out names and those whose names were called were allowed to leave. I asked why those people could go - apparently they had a certificate showing that they were working for the Germans. They didn't count them, would just call out their names, and as the people walked out in line, the Nazis

would say
"Run! Run! Run!"
and would hit them with the butts of their guns and they would go out of the gate so when the same thing happened the following day I took a chance and joined them and when they said
"Run! Run! Run!"
I never ran so hard in my life and I ran home!

Then of course I <u>had</u> to go into hiding. I had a friend whose parents lived in Enschede on the German border. My brother was in the Resistance and they were already making false IDs. The Resistance had stolen a whole lot of false blanks and stamps and would put your photo in it. My brother was good at fine precise work like making false documents. I got new papers and was put on a train to Enschede. I could choose a new name and I chose the name *Barendina Dykstra.*

We tried to get false papers for my parents but unfortunately they were picked up before the papers were ready. One day my father failed to come home and the rest of my family were picked up one by one.

My parents were sent to Westerbork and from there to Sobibor where they were gassed.

For six months I worked in Enschede as a housekeeper for my friend's parents. I had false papers, I was blonde with blue eyes, and I lived with them like one of the family. Then I returned to Amsterdam. My parents were gone but I rented a room and got myself involved with the Resistance as a courier and I stencilled newspapers and went into the country on a bicycle smuggling identity cards and guns to the resistance network. We all had code names,

mine was Babs, which I am still called. It was well organised but we had to be on guard all the time.

In the meantime I was staying in a safe house where we were printing illegally and doing all sorts of things we should not have been doing. When the neighbours downstairs lost a bicycle, they said that I had stolen it and I was picked up by the police. That was very nasty because there were a lot of questions I couldn't answer. The police were all bad. But one bigshot knew another bigshot from the Resistance and one of the police bigshots who was OK let me go after a day, but my G-d how I sweated!!

After the war I continued to work for the Resistance and we got the collaborators and put them in camps in Utrecht. I became a camp warden for the women. It was not a nice job. The poor girls had all their hair shaved off, they were a bit hard on them, but they all went to Court and were tried, and those found guilty were sent to prison.

I then went to Belgium, married and settled here. My brother became a chemical engineer and later worked for the Dutch mint, this time printing real money!.

KLARA VAN KLEEF was born in Amsterdam in 1923 where she was educated and worked as a seamstress until the war. She was in hiding in Holland until liberated on 5.5.1945 after which she stayed in Belgium and Rhodesia until coming to South Africa in 1984. She married W. Visser and has a son Raymond and a daughter Joan.

LOUIS THEEBOOM
Amsterdam

My parents were divorced and my mother, brother and I stayed with my grandparents in a large flat. I was 6 and my brother was 4 years older. During the day my mother worked and we went to school. One day we came home to discover that my grandparents and all my uncles and aunts had disappeared. We went to stay in another flat with a family called Bloch. Then it happened again. While we were away, the Bloch family was taken away. When we returned we found that we had the flat to ourselves. We stayed on there because we were not registered as living there. The Germans had been given the names and addresses of all the Jews so they knew where they lived and just went around methodically picking them up.

In 1943 we were picked up by accident by the Dutch police one night in what they called a razzia organized to pick up Jews. We were taken away to the theatre having been caught in a trap. The grownups had to sit in the chairs as though there was a performance going on while the children ran around.

What I most remember the first night was that another group of people was brought in, amongst whom was a famous singing group of two Jewish boys called Jonny and Jones, who went straight onto the stage and started to perform and sing and make music. A sicherheidtsdienst hero came and kicked them bodily off the stage.

One funny incident occurred when we were in the theatre. Our names were called and my mother said,

"You must not go because they take you to the gas chambers."

They kept on calling us and only afterwards did we find out that we were being called because friends had sent us a parcel of rabbit to eat - the rabbits had been stolen from German collaborators and cooked and sent to us, but we did not collect it.

It is a strange thing that everyone said that they did not know that they were gassing the Jews but I clearly remember my mother saying,

"Don't go because they will put you in the gas chamber!".

So people did know! In the theatre all these thousands of people were sitting waiting to be taken away to be killed. They could not believe it - they were convinced that they were going to be resettled in Poland. The only thing that kept them in their seats was an old German soldier, with a wonky leg and an old rifle, who was at the front of the theatre by the ticket booth. Anybody could have just got up and walked out and nobody thought of it.

One day our underground friends managed to get my mother out over the wall of the theatre. At night the children were taken off to a creche in the theatre where they slept. They were only accompanied by two nurses as the Nazis did not expect them to run away from their parents. One morning we came back from the creche and all of a sudden we heard the shout,

"JOPIE, LOU, RUN!"

My brother grabbed my hand and dragged me along. We were picked up and put on bicycles and were taken back to our flat because we were not registered as living there.

We stayed there undercover - they called it diving under - and started getting help from the Communist Underground who would bring us food. You needed stamps for food. The Underground would steal the food stamps and give them to us.

My mother never came out on to the streets during the day, only at night to stretch her legs and then only between two six-foot blokes from the underground. We also stayed inside and only came out in winter when it was necessary for us to go out to look for food and firewood.

One day the whole street where we lived looked on in amazement when my brother and I appeared with our hair changed. Instead of jet black it was now a beautiful blonde. This had been achieved by putting 30% peroxide on our hair, eyebrows and eyelashes which hurt like hell. Everybody laughed and the people living above us also laughed - they were German collaborators but they never gave us away.

My brother and I had to be on the streets, especially near the end of the war, to look for food, and firewood for our little stoves which gave tremendous heat. Everything disappeared. We lived around the corner from the station and the trains used to come and dump their coals there and the whole of Amsterdam used to come and dig there for coal. A year after the end of the war we were still using coals which my brother and I had dug up.

There used to be little wooden blocks between the railway lines like bricks which vanished overnight. The houses in our street were four storeys high. One day the last family left in one building was taken away. The house was empty and as soon as the Germans disappeared the whole street including my brother and I came out with saws and axes and within one hour this 4 storey house disappeared. It was the most amazing thing. We sat upstairs on the fourth floor sawing off the wooden beams to take them home for firewood. In those days this was normal.

We had an alcove through which you could walk, with a wardrobe on each side and between the two we made a special place where my mother would hide at the first sign of trouble. She would climb in and hide away and we would just stay inside the house. We were safe because we were blonde and when the police came to look, which would often happen, my brother would guide them around and show them the rooms. My brother would try to speak in what he thought was a very Aryan Dutch although friends after the war assured us it sounded very Jewish indeed.

The sicherheidstdiens who would come in were never in uniform but were vicious. The Gruene Polizei were not the vicious type, just ordinary guys doing their national service and they didn't like what they were doing. I know that because downstairs lived a Jewish man married to a German woman - he had been sterilized which is why he was allowed to stay alive. Her brother was in the Gruene Polizei and he would visit her and told her that they did not like doing what they were doing.

I shall never forget the razzias. The doorbells would ring, someone would pull a rope and open the door and someone would shout :
"Are there still Jews there?"
If we said "No", they would go away. On the third floor there was an old gentleman and his wife, his daughter and three grandchildren. One day he answered,
"Yes, gentlemen".
He answered very politely not knowing that he was condemning his whole family to death. So they had to go all the way up and took them away and I saw all my friends with rucksacks on their backs marching away. I never saw any of them again.

Thousands were voluntarily taken away to be "resettled" in Poland including my aunt. At the last moment she must have got wise because she gave her baby of eight or nine months to someone in Friesland. He grew up there and his father's name, Leendert Schyveschuurder, is on the Dockworker's memorial to the heroes of resistance.

This baby was the only one in the whole family who escaped. My grandparents, my mother's sister and four brothers, their wives and all their children - none of them ever came back, not one. We were the only ones left - we, and klein Jopie, my mother's sister's little boy who grew up on the farm. He is in Holland now. I recently found papers belonging to my mother giving details of where our family was murdered - mainly in Auschwitz and Matthausen. Those creatures actually kept records of their murders.

We stayed hidden in this flat until the end of the war. Living in Amsterdam we were the last ones to be freed, the rest of Holland was freed 6- 9 months before.

We went through the Hunger Winter as it was called when 100 000 people in Amsterdam died of hunger. They ate rats, there were no dogs left, no cats and people used to take their sheets and towels and anything else they possessed because money had no value and go to the farmers and exchange these for potatoes and wheat. Unfortunately when they came back they had to cross over the river called the Y where the German and Dutch police would wait for them and take everything off them.

At the end of the war, my mother after years and years of hiding, battling it all out had to get the tension out of her system. A couple of days after the capitulation of Germany we heard a raucous noise outside and my mother came into the house - my mother was all of 4ft 11 - and her legs were bleeding and her hair and face! What had happened? Well, she met the girl from upstairs who was in the Hitler Jugend in the street and she had dragged her from one end of the street to the other twice, and that was that. Nobody said a word, nothing was ever said about it. It was never held against her and everybody just went on living and that is basically what happened.

Our story is like that of Anne Frank only with a better ending.

LOUIS THEEBOOM was born in Amsterdam in 1935 and was educated at the Rosh Pinah Jewish School. He spent the war years in hiding in Amsterdam until liberated on 5.5.1945 after which he stayed in Australia before moving to South Africa in 1967. He is married to Ashna and has two sons Daniel and Elan and a daughter Simone.

SIPPORA (SIPPY) LOCKITCH

Amsterdam, Hengelo

I was born in Amsterdam in September 1924. I was an only child, much loved and indulged. My maternal grandparents lived with us.

In April 1940 I wrote my exams. In May the Germans invaded Holland. It was frightening to see them march into Amsterdam. I was fifteen and a half. From about July, Jewish children were not permitted to attend school, so that was the end of my education. Within 6 months, all Jews had to wear yellow Magen Davids with the letter "J"; Jews were issued with new identity cards. These had a Magen David as well as a "J"; we were not permitted to use public transport, or ride bicycles; a curfew was instituted: in summer we had to be indoors by 8 p.m., in winter by 5 p.m.

From about November 1940, the Germans started picking up young Jewish boys in the street. These boys were told that they would be sent to work in Germany to take the place of the Germans who were in the army. Resistance on the part of the boys or their family resulted in instant shooting. Within a few months, mothers would hear that their sons had died of pneumonia - all these boys seemed to die of pneumonia!

Towards the beginning of 1941, Jewish girls were being called up to work in Germany. Notices in the newspapers informed us of this and also carried the threat that failing to obey the call-up would result in the arrest of members of their family.

About August 1941, I received my call-up paper. I was instructed to report on the 8th August at the Amsterdam Theatre. I was to bring with me a knapsack containing a few items of clothing and enough food for 3 days. I went to see a doctor, in the hope that he might provide me with a certificate indicating that I was not fit to leave home and work in Germany, but I was unsuccessful.

My mother was in a terrible state at having to part with me. My father took me to the Theatre. There I had to sign that I was going to Germany "*of my own free will.*" I said "*goodbye*" to my father and went into the theatre.

We sat there, having been told that we would be transported to Westerbork, a transit camp in Holland near the German border from where we would be taken into Germany. I became aware of a young couple sitting next to me with two very young children. I thought it strange that such young children had been called up to work in Germany and I became suspicious.

At that moment, I heard my surname being called. It was a man whom I had never seen before. He was Jaap, an old boyfriend of my aunt who was now working for the Jewish Council. He told me that my mother was waiting to say goodbye to me once more in the foyer of the Theatre. She had made the excuse that she had to bring me winter boots which I would need in Germany. I said *goodbye* to my mother.

I told Jaap about my suspicions and that I had no intention of going back into the Theatre, but intended to run away. He tried to dissuade me from taking this dangerous step but my mind was made up. He led me to a dressing room from where I managed to get out and scale a wall. Fortunately, I knew the area; my grandmother had been living in an old person's home nearby since the death of my grandfather, and I had often visited her.

I made my way to the home of my mother's sister and her husband. They had 2 daughters: one was married to a Pole who had escaped from a camp and was stateless and therefore she had also become stateless. They were in hiding. The other daughter was married to Jack, a half- Jew, who was running my uncle's livestock business. Because he had been involved in the black-market, the Germans were looking for him.

I stayed the night with my uncle and aunt, sharing a room with their German house-

keeper, Julie. I had a pullout bed. I was supposed to get into a cupboard if there was any search.

During the night, there was a search for Jack. I got out of bed, put it back and hid in the cupboard, sitting on top of the gas meter. Julie pulled me out and told me to get back in bed. Each time, she pulled out the bed and each time I put it back. At last, I warned her that if she opened the cupboard once more and pulled out the bed, I would hit her.

That night, they took my uncle away. The next day, my aunt went to tell my parents where I was. Then my aunt got in touch with the Resistance. They arranged hiding places in safe houses.

Until the War ended, the Resistance found about twelve houses for me. A member of the Resistance would make the arrangements, take me to the house and provide the owner with money for my keep. (One of the places I stayed at was interested in keeping the money and there I starved.) I had false papers, my name became Kitty.

Then my parents went into hiding also. It was arranged by the Resistance that my parents and I go to the same place, Hengelo, where we lived in different houses but in the same street. My mother worked as a servant as did I. My father never left his room.

One Sunday a farmer took me to see my parents. He tried to force himself on me and I threatened to tell his wife and his pastoor. At the end of 1942, my parents were taken away to Auschwitz. Only later did I discover this and that they had been betrayed by this farmer in an act of spite. At the time, however I had no idea of what had happened to my parents.

After the war I reported him to the police and he was arrested for a short time. On release he tried to run me over in his lorry. I shall never forget his leering face, coarse laugh and yellow teeth as his truck bore down on me.

Still in Hengelo, where I remained until the end of the War, I had to move once again. This time I was placed with the elderly parents of the local Resistance agent (Gert). They had a daughter, Jannie, several years older than I; we shared a room and became great friends. This was the period of constant air- raid warnings. We were

close to the German border and the British were bombing. During times of danger, I would hide in the cupboard but when it was necessary to go to the shelters things became very difficult and I felt that I was putting the elderly couple's lives in jeopardy.

So, once again I moved, this time to Uncle Wim, Tante Mien and their daughter Lyda, a year younger than I. Tante Mien's sister was married to a German soldier. Although he knew I was Jewish, I was safe as far as he was concerned because he was not a Nazi but a Social Democrat. Uncle Wim had a wireless and listened to the BBC news three times a day. He was a highly-skilled train driver who was involved with sabotage and would steal materials from trains for the Resistance and hide it under the landing along with the wireless. Tante Mien's brother, Uncle Herman, was also involved with the Resistance. He used to make up the weekly packets of maintenance money for the wives and families of Resistance workers. He would do this in the day in our house but for safety would sleep in the church at night.

One day Lyda's boyfriend came to stay in order to be safe. At that stage, the Germans had begun to pick up non- Jewish boys for work in Germany. Now Lyda and I shared a bedroom, and Gert had a room to himself.

One woman, angry that her maintenance money was late, reported the courier to the Gestapo and they came for Uncle Herman. I had been playing chess with Uncle Wim and as I went up to bed and checked the black out curtains I noticed that we were being surrounded.

We quickly got a message to Uncle Herman not to come round the next day and Lyda rushed out with the briefcase of money. Gert climbed into the hole above the landing alongside the sabotaged goods and I hid in the small hole at the entrance hall that contained the water main.

The hole was covered by the wooden floor boards, the underfelt and the carpets. There I suffocated and froze. Above my head I could hear the stamping of the Gestapo boots and I shivered.

Lyda was caught outside with the briefcase but she told them that a man in the street had given it to her. The Gestapo sat in the lounge to wait for Uncle Herman. Uncle

Wim stoked up the fire to make the room stuffy and when they fell asleep he smuggled me upstairs to share the secret hiding place with Gert between the top of the staircase and the kitchen ceiling.

The Gestapo sat and waited in the lounge for two days. For two days Gert and I hid in the hole. Sometimes Uncle Wim managed to get food to us.

I returned to live with Jannie and her family and there I remained until the end of the War. We were liberated in April 1945, officially in May. I wrote to Tante Annie in Amsterdam (her husband had been my father's best friend) who advised me not to return to Amsterdam until things had settled down a bit.

Of my father's family of 144 people, only five survived - two in America, one who escaped to Spain, one who survived Auschwitz and myself.

Finally, Jannie and I hitchhiked to Amsterdam, arriving there at the end of September 1945. Walking in the street I heard, for the first time in many years, my real name being called -

"Sippy, Sippy!"

It was my cousin who had returned from Spain.

Sippora Lockitch "nee Croonenberg" was born in Amsterdam in September 1924 and was educated at the Amsterdam Commercial School. She spent the war years in hiding in the Netherlands being liberated in Hengelo, in April 1945. She came to South Africa in 1948.

HANNAH JOLES
Amsterdam

I was born in 1919 in Amsterdam where my father had an insurance company. Four years later we moved to Bussum a friendly village nearby. My brother Jacob, my sister Esther and I were very privileged. We had everything - we went to Switzerland for winter sports, we had bikes, a car, a yacht. When I finished school I got a job in an antique book shop in Amsterdam owned by a Russian Jew where I worked for 4 years.

The Nazi influence became stronger and stronger in Holland. My brother belonged to a Hockey club and at a certain stage Jewish members were excluded. The 3rd of May 1940 was a cousin's birthday and we had a party. That was seven days before the invasion. My aunt who was married had a premonition and said, "This crowd will never be together again. I feel that something is going to happen."

I remember a beautiful spring in May. I was at home. In the middle of the night we woke up as it was beginning to get light and we heard the heavy droning of many aeroplanes. We put the radio on and learnt of the bombing of Rotterdam. And then we heard that the Germans had landed and war had broken out!

When the Germans entered Amsterdam, they marched past the Dam square near the palace. I stood on the sidewalk with hundreds of people and watched tanks and armoured cars and column after column of singing, marching soldiers with grim faces and those horrifying boots. The crowd watched in dead quiet with drawn faces; you could feel the hatred around you.

All the Dutch flags disappeared. Soon after, the decrees started to come out and the rationing, but these came drop by drop and that's why it was a poisonous way. The indoctrination, the killings. Every time the Nazis went a little bit further, watching to see how people would react.

Jews were not allowed to have bicycles, or own a radio, they had to wear a yellow star. There was a curfew between 8p.m. and 8a.m. so you could never visit anybody unless you slept over. If you were found at an address which was not on your card, you could be arrested, so you could actually not go anywhere. At one stage there was a decree every day. Jewish people had to go to the synagogue office to have a J printed in the identity books. I should have had the foresight to realize what this meant.

The idea of going into hiding began to prevail, and people tried to make contact with non-Jewish neighbours - a gardener or a remover, a tailor or an upholsterer, a carpet man or anybody who had contacts in the non-Jewish world. My father got false identification papers, with another name, without a J. He hid these inside books on a certain page. We all knew where they were.

One of the first things the Germans did when they occupied Holland was to block all the Jewish accounts so nobody could get money. My father sold paintings and some of my mother's rings. You needed identification papers for ration cards, so if you were not registered and had a false surname you could not get ration cards, and without them you could not get food. Poor people with large families would sometimes sell one or two for a lot of money to the underground movement who would distribute them to Jews if they paid.

Then after 1940 raids on people began. Young men were taken for labour. My parents decided not to let Jacob, who was 19 or 20, go to Amsterdam to work, and found him a place as a farm hand with a farmer in Putten in the east of Holland. The mayors of all the towns were replaced by Dutch Nazis, and the Putten mayor was very cruel and powerful. My brother made friends and one day when they were skating together someone said,

"You don't look like a farmer's boy, who are you?"

He trusted them and told them his real name.

Jacob was betrayed. He was arrested by the police, taken to prison and was never seen again. He died in Auschwitz in 1943.

In the bookshop were the boss, Mr Horodisch, a Russian Jew, his partner, my best friend and myself, both Jewish girls, a non-Jewish girl and a messenger. There were three storeys in that shop. The first floor was separate. Very soon Jews were not allowed to own businesses anymore and the shop became Aryanised. One morning around that time the non-Jewish girl said to us when we came to work,
"I am a bit worried because I haven't got my identity card, nor has Cornelus, the messenger."
I said: "Why haven't you got your identity card?"
"Well Mr Horodisch said he needed it for administrative purposes, so we gave our cards to him."
My girlfriend and I looked at each other, and we said,
"Well, we had better phone him then."
But there was no reply from his home.

A week or two later, a registered letter came from Switzerland with their two identity cards with which my boss and his wife had escaped. They had put other photos in.

We were left with this Aryan caretaker. My Jewish friend and I were not allowed to sell books downstairs because we were wearing a star. We could only work on the first floor.

Then came the time that we had to tear up books by Jewish authors or about Judaism. We had an enormous department of Judaica. The first day we were crying. We had to break open every book and tear out the middle section. We had to destroy books letter by letter - Buber, Heine even Thomas Mann. Every day we put sacks of damaged books outside with the refuse. After a few days we lit a stove with the books, it was winter and very cold. Soon with the daily horrors around us, books no longer seemed so important.

Father got a registered letter stating that he could no longer have his own business so he could not work any longer. My mother became a school teacher again because Jewish children were not allowed to go to non-Jewish schools nor were Jewish teachers allowed to teach non-Jewish children. Little schools sprang up in the ghetto because the children had to learn; they had

to be out of their homes because conditions were too terrible at home.

We had no soap, no light, no hot water. Lots of children got lice at school. There were of course hundreds of very good Jewish doctors, not allowed to treat non-Jewish people. Jewish actors were not allowed to perform for non-Jews so Jewish theatre sprang up. That was actually the thing which kept the people alive and sane. A lot of music was being made, a lot of lectures, people were learning languages. People were reciting poetry and prose and singing. We also listened on the quiet to the BBC.

The Jewish Council were in direct contact with the German Administration of Amsterdam. They were told that the Jewish people had to go to Germany to work for the war effort. However, girls who sewed well could make uniforms, get an appropriate stamp in their identity book and would not be sent away - for the time being. We made shoes, helmets, equipment, batteries, all for the war effort. We just knew that we had to work, but we did not know that the final end was the Final Solution and we did not realize the danger.

About 1941 we all got notice at the bookshop. My mother had known Professor Cohen since childhood. Formerly Professor in Classical languages at the Amsterdam University, he was now in the Jewish Council. She phoned him one night and said,
"Can my daughter have a job please. We have already lost our son."

The following day he got me a job and I got a stamp. I worked there retouching photographs and making photostatic copies of the innumerable documents and reports needed by the Nazis.

I knew I was privileged to be working there and at the time I only felt relieved to have a job. I didn't feel guilty; much later I felt, 'why should it have been me and not some one else?'

I remember once as I walked through one of the poor streets - we had to walk everywhere, we were not allowed to make use of public transport - a very poor woman called after us,
"You! You won't have to go to Poland! You work for the Jewish Council! But we! We have to go! We haven't got the right con-

Hannah Souget at work in the Jewish Council Office retouching photographs

nections!"

The poorer people blamed the Jewish Council for collaborating with the Nazis, perhaps rightly so.

Once when working at the Jewish Council workshop reproducing copies, a co-worker said:

"It doesn't matter if we have to go to Poland, we shall go and work together. We can work on the land or we can work to make shoes, it doesn't matter. As long as we can work, we'll survive."

He did not survive.

I went to work every morning walking all the way from where I lived to the ghetto where the office was or the workshop with a little pot of food in a net, like potatoes or carrots. There was no bread. We warmed it up on a gas flame and then we walked back again at night.

In 1942 people who lived in the country were herded together in ghettos in Amsterdam and Rotterdam. We had to leave our homes and go to certain parts of Amsterdam. Our house in Bussum was very beautiful and it was taken as a home for German officers. Mother had to leave six of everything from chairs to teaspoons for six people, six beds and bedding for six, everything.

We lived for a long time with a remover and he stored a lot of valuables for my parents. But we lost a lot. So my family had to move into an attic above my father's office. I had a room on the top floor of his office.

Shortly before they left Bussum, my Grandparents were rounded up. My Granny was a very courageous woman. She said to the lorry driver,

"I have forgotten something, would you mind going back to my house?"

The driver was not a Nazi and agreed because he knew how awful their fate was going to be. Why did she go back? What did she forget?

A cushion and a children's game like snakes and ladders.

She wanted to take it because she knew there would be many children in the camp and she wanted a game to play with them. The cushion was with her all the time. My Grandfather died in Westerbork.

My Grandmother went on to Belsen, where she died, and that very cushion went with her. Everybody used it and it came back via Sweden through a friend of my mother's and it landed at last in Israel. When we visited my uncle in Tel Aviv in 1950 - there was grandmother's cushion! My mother wrote a short story about the cushion which was published in a Jewish newspaper.

At that time, 1942, my work in the Jewish council dealt with the administrative moving of people to the Amsterdam ghetto. The Germans are very bureaucratic. Everything had to go on typed forms. It was a big office and there were two young boys my age working there whose parents had been deported. There was nobody to look after them. I received a registered letter stating that I had to vacate my room in my father's office because it was outside the ghetto.

So I said to those two boys, "Shall I come and live with you? Then I can cook for you and look after you, and I can have a home." (and one that was in an area from which the Jews had already been removed.)

My boss said, "You will never get a licence to move outside the ghetto to that part of Amsterdam".

I said, "Well, I can try".

He said, "How will you try?"

I said, "I will go to the German office and explain the situation to them."

It was a very dangerous thing to do but I thought I would risk it. I went to the German headquarters with my forms and I said that I had been given notice to move out of my room and wished to apply to move in with these boys and here was a letter from the two boys who were now orphans.

The officer said "It was very nasty of the caretaker to send you this registered letter, wasn't it"

He gave me permission, knowing full well that we would be taken away by the Germans later anyhow, but I didn't know that. So he gave me his signature and I went outside where this boy was waiting for me and I said:
"I have got it. I shall come to live with you tomorrow".

He couldn't believe it and I lived there with them for seven weeks.

From that address I went into hiding. It was much easier for me to do this from there, because from my own front door I had to go out everyday with a star, but here I could walk out without one. I could get out without being noticed, without people looking at me and I looked Jewish. In the ghetto the German police were always patrolling, whereas in this quiet part of Amsterdam there was no police, nobody cared. The safety was artificial because the two boys did not survive.

I packed a suitcase with everything I could afford at that time like soap, toothpaste, bandages and clothing. I went to the central station where I met a non- Jewish girlfriend who was to accompany me so that I did not have to travel alone. We went first by tram, then by train. I had not travelled on either for two or three years. I went to my first address at Arnhem and became a servant under an assumed name, having to do domestic chores and sometimes I was not allowed to go outside when it was very dangerous.

My first madam was a trained sister. She was an unmarried woman, a horrible person who kept a boarding house. I had to serve all the boarders in their rooms. I would have to bring up every meal to them on trays. She took a risk in taking in a Jew. I was there three months. I hated the work and she compared me all the time to the previous servant. One day she told me that the baker's boy had remarked that I was not an ordinary servant and looked different, so I had to leave.

I went to Wassenaar near the Hague to a very rich woman, a lawyer divorced from her doctor husband with four boys. I was servant and governess to her sons. She was a very nice, intelligent woman who was dis-abled and walked with two sticks. I stayed there about three months but had to leave when a platoon of Germans moved into their enormous garden and put up their tents. I went to my madam and said, "Look, I have stuck it out for so long, if I stay here one of them might become suspicious."

One of them had said that I looked funny, not like a servant, because they tried to make contact with girls all the time.

She said, "Oh please, don't leave me because who will help me?"

I said, "I know that you need help but I am sorry, I must leave, I don't want to risk it now"

She let me go with one month's salary. One of her sons took me to the Hague, to a non-Jewish friend of mine. I thanked him and I said,
"Don't follow me and never talk about where you took me and forget the address."

I stayed with this friend for a week or two and then I got the address of a woman who was half Jewish. She hid her own daughter in her house in an attic for two years. The girl never went out. Her face was pale because she never had any fresh air. We ate together, slept together, played gramophone records together and became good friends - she lives today in America. Once I went out to the hairdresser but she asked me please not to do this again. But I left very soon afterwards.

Then I went to my aunt in Deventer, East Holland, who was married to a non- Jew and lived in a small house, which she had during the whole war. She kept people in hiding in an attic, in this room and that room. I also stayed there about three months or so. There were so many people in that house all hiding.

She got me a place around the corner from her with an English teacher, Mr Kruger, and I worked for them for some time until it also became dangerous. Mr Kruger was a very popular English teacher, very anti-German, and one day there were rumours at his school that he was hiding a Jewish girl in his home.

He said," I am terribly sorry, you will have to go. My children's lives will be at risk."

He had four or five children among whom was a son who was eligible to go to a labour camp in Germany and was also in hiding in his own house.

Then I worked for rich people who had an enormous mansion in Loenen. I was a servant everywhere because there was not much else one could do. It was easier for girls to be hidden than for boys because the girls could always do housework inside.

They had a very big family with many brothers and sisters and everybody who wanted to go on holiday could always go there. There was a big staff there - a gardener, coachman, whatever. There was a little coach house fully equipped, where this family lived during the war and I worked there for them. The big mansion itself was occupied by German soldiers. There was no water and no electricity and we had to pump water. For every bucket we had to walk into the forest, pump and walk back with the heavy bucket. Whenever I came in my clogs and my apron, looking like a dowdy servant, there was always a German soldier who pumped water for me. He saw that I was struggling, and he carried something back to the house for me. He had no idea who I was.

Fortunately these soldiers were not the SS or the Green Police, just ordinary soldiers. I didn't mix with them but if they saw people struggling they were sometimes helpful. They gave people lifts in the military cars, they carried things and chopped wood when they had nothing else to do.

My parents also went into hiding in Loenen. By then there were hardly any pupils for my mother, as all the children had been transported. Esther also stayed at Loenen, with a childless teacher and his wife. She survived and lives today in England. None of us was really hiding like Anne Frank as we were able to move about. We travelled by bus or on old bikes to farms to get bread or milk. My father had nothing to do so he started to learn Latin by correspondance under his assumed name. He sent in his work signed by his false name and got it back corrected in red ink. This really kept him from getting very depressed. He also kept on practising his violin and tried to play and invite people to come. My mother earned a little teaching the farmer's children. I saw my parents regularly because their house was about five to ten minutes' walk from the one I lived in.

We had no light. In order to have a little light we used an old bicycle frame which we put upside down on the floor in the room and somebody sat behind it and pedalled. Everybody had to pedal for twenty minutes, and that's how we had light.

At the end of April 1945, I was in the kitchen washing up. A girl from Arnhem burst into the kitchen, embraced me and said:
"Smell me! What do you smell?"
So I said: "Cigarettes".
She said, "Yes! They are Canadian cigarettes and we met the Canadians. They are here in Loenen and we are free!!!"

I couldn't believe it and we danced in the kitchen together! She said that there were posters in every public place in Loenen inviting all the girls who could speak English to come to a dance to meet the Canadian liberators.

Were we excited to be free!! We couldn't believe it! People cried and laughed. We went to the dance and my parents came along as well and sat on the side having tea. I danced with a navy sergeant and I said to my father that I introduced myself to people with my <u>own</u> name. That was something!

After liberation we had no home to go to, so I continued to work in that kitchen. Suddenly there was a knock at the door and in came an old friend of mine who had been with me in the Zionist Youth Movement and he said to me:
" What are you doing here? Why are you working as a servant? You are free! Why should you go on working here?"
I said: "Well I have nowhere to go, we have not been given a house or whatever".
He said: "I will try and see that you and your family get a house in Apeldoorn."

He had organized a soup kitchen and I became his secretary.

A little later we were allocated a big house in Bussum which had belonged to a Dutch Nazi. He and his family had to leave their house and were put in a Dutch camp for ex-collaborators. We started to search for our relatives, for my brother. There were a lot of bureaux set up. There were columns after columns of names in the papers because everybody was looking for relatives and also for their children who had been given to Christian neighbours.

When they were back in Bussum my parents decided to adopt a Jewish orphan who had lost his parents. They obviously wanted a boy having lost a son. One night there was a ring at the door. My mother opened it and there was a woman who said,

"Mrs Souget, we know that you have a big house and a big heart. I have in my car two sisters who have lost their parents and perhaps you could take them."

Mother said: "Please let them come in".

I can't remember how old they were, about seven and nine. That very evening there and then my parents decided to take them. So I actually have two step sisters. Although they always kept their own name they are really my sisters.

I joined the Dutch A.T.S. army. I was sent to the Hague and became secretary of the head of the Dutch army and through this job I eventually came to South Africa.

I have a feeling of terrible hatred towards Germans. I lost my brother, I lost my family, I lost my friends. All my aunts, my uncles and most of my cousins were killed.

I also have a feeling of frustration because I lost my youth which I spent scrubbing other people's floors. I never went out, I had no social life at all, it was a time of great boredom and loneliness and when the war was over, my bloom was over. But I should not complain, because I was at least fortunate to be alive. I never starved, I was not persecuted or tortured or put in jail. However, the war made an invisible crack in our lives cutting off our past and although this crack has healed the scar will be there forever.

Hannah Caroline Joles-Souget was born in Amsterdam, Holland on 13.1.1919 and was educated at the Hilversum Gymnasium. She was a secretary until she had to go into hiding in different places in Holland, being liberated in April 1945 in Loenen, Holland. She arrived in South Africa in 1946. She married Alexander Joles and they have three children, Lieske Bloom, Jacob and Benjamin.

MENNO DE JONG

Rotterdam, Amsterdam and farms near Alkmaar.

Children when they are small are seldom interested in what happened to their parents. They accept everything. Later, as they grow up, they hear what happened, find it interesting, but seldom ask questions or are really interested. Only when they have children of their own, do they begin to realise that what they say and do will influence their children as they in turn had been by their own parents. So they begin questioning and remembering. We must ask before our parents are gone and before they forget.

I was in a war when I was young, a war in which millions died. Forty million in fact of which six million were Jews. About thirty of my very close relatives died during the war.

I attended a Jewish High School for about a year and of the thirty five pupils in my class three returned after the war. How did it happen? Why did it happen? These are most difficult questions to answer because the world and the values in the world were different in those days.

I remember waking at 5 a.m. on the 10th May 1940 because I heard many low-flying planes. I was thirteen years old and had hardly had a party for my Barmitzvah because of the dangerous situation and the mobilization. It was already light and I heard some artillery fire far away. I got up about 5.30 a.m. Our house was opposite my school and some people were already awake. I hung out of the first floor window looking at the planes. I saw people slowly coming out of their houses, some in pyjamas, and they were standing around and talking.

Suddenly a boy shouted, "The radio is on" so I went downstairs and switched on. It informed the Army that so and so many planes were sighted flying here and there in such and such directions. I could not understand it. It was now 6 o'clock and I went to my parents' bedroom to tell them all the exciting news of the exercises. My father got out of bed and said

"THAT'S WAR!!!"
I never ever thought about that.

I dressed, ate, and went to a street nearby in Hilligersberg to watch the army which had commandeered a high school. Everyone was dressing and I saw two soldiers in pyjamas but wearing boots and helmets. They carried a big gun and crossed the street to a soccer field where they started shooting at the planes which were flying just above the tops of the trees. They were standing in the middle of the field with a big crowd of people around them shouting;
"SHOOT THE BASTARDS DOWN!!".

Everyone was very excited and encouraged the soldiers. No one thought how dangerously exposed the crowd was without protection or camouflaging. All of a sudden a parachute dropped from a high-flying plane. Something like a man was hanging from it. We could see that it would land in the field north of our house so I went there. From the end of our suburb where the meadows started I could see people, soldiers and a policeman with a revolver in his hand. By then it was known that Germany had invaded Holland. The paratrooper turned out to be a canister with straw arms and legs. I never found out why.

It was now after 9 a.m. A police car stood next to our house and our German neighbour was picked up. My Mother enquired whether I had to go to school. Well, for the first time in my life I had completely forgotten about school. I went across the road to see the Headmaster on top of the stoep saying that there was no school.

At 10 o'clock it became known that the school would be converted to a hospital. Two hours later the ambulance came with the first wounded soldiers who had been fighting in Rotterdam. The whole neighbourhood turned out putting the contents of the classrooms into the yard, carrying in beds, blankets and medical supplies from home; a painter was on the roof painting a big red cross and retired sisters and doctors offered their services. Like a miracle by 12 o'clock our school was a hospital.

At that time no one thought about the Jews. For the time being there was a togetherness as never before. There were roadblocks and the soldiers on duty got the most exotic foods as the central kitchen system had broken down. I remember a man going round with cigars. Our army had to be in top shape! That day I saw about 20 planes coming down. Later I heard that the Germans lost 300 planes that day, more than ever on one day.

My Father had a business importing secondhand tyres from England. He had an office in Rotterdam and a warehouse on the Wijnhaven which was near the bridge over the river which was in German hands. When he went to his office he encountered fire from the Germans in front of him and from the Hollanders at his rear. He put his car into reverse to get out and arrived home safely.

We then started clearing out the cellar. We made it into an emergency area. We carried in saws, hammer and tools, all the foodstuffs from the kitchen, makeshift beds and blankets, and the contents of the medicine chest. All this was on the advice of the "luchtbescherming", a civilian organisation. We were told to leave our front doors open, so that doctors and military people could enter our house. We covered the windows with strips of paper to prevent glass flying into the rooms. In the evening there was a complete blackout so that enemy planes could not find their target. Cars drove without lights. The moon was shining.

When we sat at supper we looked at the neighbour's windows in which we could see reflected the fires of the oil tanks 11 km away. The newspaper did not arrive. The radio was on the whole day but everything sounded all right. We filled our bath and pots with water in case the watertower was hit. We could not phone relatives as the phones were out of order but we knew my Oupa and Ouma were safe. They had moved 5 days earlier from Apeldoorn to Alkmaar.

On the fourth day of the war we packed our suitcases and all our valuables in order to try to reach England. For a long time my Father had wanted to live in England where he spent a fortnight each month buying tyres. He asked for a permit to stay in England but the permit came too late for us so all of us, including my sister Hetty who was 3 years old went to Amsterdam, zigzagging via small roads to avoid road blocks and aeroplane attacks. From there we went to Ijmuiden.

Once we had to jump out of the car when planes dived at us. The whole road was blocked by cars going the same way. One hour after we had left Rotterdam the city was bombarded by German planes. We never saw our house again. From Ijmuiden we drove a few km. south to Santpoort where my Mother's half-brother, Dolf Marcus, stayed. His wife was not Jewish and that saved his life during the war. They had two children called Hans and Grietje. We talked from early morning till late at night.

From Santpoort we went to Haarlem a few km. south where Uncle Nol (Arnold) lived with Auntie Stella and my cousin Fredie, aged 11, a beautiful girl and the only cousin of my age group. Little did we know that three years later the whole family would be wiped out.

Here too the radio was on the whole day. There was a special announcement. General Winkelman had decided to surrender to the Germans!

The announcement hit us like a bomb. We leapt to our feet and everyone started crying. We could not believe it. We were angry and frustrated. For days we had been told to listen to the voices of the announcers over the radio so that the enemy would not broadcast messages which were false and when someone shouted in the street that it was, hope flickered. But soon it was clear that it was true. Soldiers confirmed that they had the message from their officers. They were angry. Many threw their rifles in the moat. Years later the underground forces used these abandoned rifles. We had a terrible night.

The next day as the Germans had not yet arrived we decided to try to go to England by boat. We went to Katwijk on Sea which had a small fishing harbour. We made our headquarters in the local pub overlooking the harbour. Unfortunately a sunken fishing boat was blocking the harbour entrance and no vessel could go. We teamed up with an Englishman, a Frenchman, a Dutch officer and someone else to try to buy a small shallow fishing vessel. Part of the payment would be our motorcar. We could not find a captain so settled for a second mate who insisted that his wife should come along. She refused to join us so there was a "stalemate".

I still remember that we ate sandwiches and a boiled egg for breakfast. Our nerves were on edge. I could not eat anything and to me the egg smelled rotten. After lunch a message came that a fishing vessel had been lying a few km. outside the harbour entrance for several hours. How could we get there? We looked everywhere for a lifeboat and could only find an old leaking one. We bought material and tar and started repairing it.

"You will never make it" was the advice, "because tar has to dry for 24 hours." I started vomiting.
"It does not matter," said my father, "because we only have to go to the vessel and not back to shore."

Some workers helped us and a few hours later our vessel was hoisted on a trailer and pushed towards the beach. Before we pushed it up the dunes we looked for the fishing boat. It had gone and so was our last chance.

We decided to go to Alkmaar where Oupa Moos and Ouma Riek had been living since the 1st May 1940. Safe behind the Waterline!

This was a defence line of low land which was just under water. Too little water to cross with a boat, too much water to cross in a tank . Dutch artillery behind it ensured that the country was safe. No one ever thought that the Germans would parachute soldiers near the bridges so that the main German army could fight its way into the heart of Holland. Five days later Holland capitulated.

Safe for exactly 10 days.

After long talks my parents decided to stay there with them. My father realized that the Germans would confiscate his possessions so he went to our house in Hilligersberg, packed everything and sent it to A.B. Streng in Apeldoorn, a big warehouse, for safekeeping till after the war. Streng, an old school friend of my Father, later joined the Dutch Underground Forces, was caught and all the household effects, including ours,

were confiscated and sent to Germany.

My Father then went to a bulb merchant. We took a chance going by car as the Germans had prohibited our cars on the road. As we drove in Alkmaar the Germans arrived, in a whole column of warlike cars en route to Den Helder, the Navy base. My Father pulled his car off the road and we watched - terrible! Apart from the German vehicles there were no cars in the street, no cyclists, no people walking. No one was looking over the balconies. Some people peered from behind the curtains.

My Father's car was parked at the back of a bulb warehouse, and a wall built in front of it. It survived the war.

My Father then went to Apeldoorn where we had a few very old houses, some lockup garages and an old small warehouse where he used to have his furniture factory till 1936. He went to the Bank and took out as high a bond as he could get. He knew the Germans would confiscate his property. (It was not easy to get the property back after the war as it was sold because my my Father had not paid the interest on the bond but he was able to prove that the Germans had prevented him from paying the interest.)

He purchased a whole lot of "gouden tientjes" a gold coin similar to Kruger Rands. The gold coins went up and up in value and reached astronomical heights as the war went on. Later he sold them one by one, each one fetching more, and so supporting us throughout the war. Next we went on a buying spree in order to hoard food. We not only bought rice, chocolates, tins of food, soap, washing powder, but also textiles. As everyone had the same idea there was a run on the Banks so they restricted the weekly amounts of withdrawals. I did my bit and my parents used my savings account.

During the Five Day War and the following weeks while we were in Alkmaar, I did not go to school but I was supposed to sit for an entrance exam for the HBS, a medium High School. It was, however, useless to write an exam not having studied for several weeks.

After the holidays I went to the Mulo in Alkmaar, a lower high school, where no entrance exams were required. August 31 1940 was the Queen's birthday and we schoolchildren wanted to celebrate. But how? Just as the bell rang to go inside the inspector arrived. We started singing the National Anthem. Later in the morning in another classroom a boy asked the teacher if he could go around the classroom with sweets as it was his birthday. He said, "You have to sing Happy birthday (Lang zal hij leven) first". So it happened but the other classes, not knowing the reason for the song joined in. In no time the whole school was singing Happy Birthday. This was an enormous morale booster.

Then the Germans ordered the Dutch Jews to register. There would be heavy fines and imprisonment in the East (Poland) for those who did not. My Father advised everyone not to register although he did so himself so as not to endanger his Father's life with whom we lived. The instructions of the Nazis came faster and faster. It was very clear that the Dutch population as a whole was very anti-German. Winter came and the snow came down as usual. We made snowballs as always, maybe a little more compact than usual. This year the number of snowballs which went through the windows of Nazis was very high. So the Germans prohibited the picking up of snow to make snowballs.

On the 30th May 1941, after a year in Alkmaar, Oupa and Ouma went back to Apeldoorn. As we were living with them we had to leave too. We went to a furnished house in Bloemendaal, a suburb of Haarlem where I went to the Mulo and Hetty to a playschool.

During the school holidays there was a decree that Jewish children could not go to a public school. The decrees of the Germans were always before a weekend, a public holiday or a Jewish holiday so that they did not disrupt life too much. As there were plenty of Jewish teachers within one month there was a Jewish school established in Haarlem, in the Wilhelminastraat. Although I had been in the 2nd class of the Mulo, I went back to the first class of the Lyceum. In no time the school was the best school in Haarlem.

The Germans now started razzias. However, opposite the German barracks lived a Hollander who warned four or five people around him which direction the German cars went. (I met this man for the first time 45 years later at a Rotary meeting in Cape Town where he now lives.) So whenever there was a raid we were warned about 5 or 10 minutes in advance. A small overnight bag was always ready. In this way very few people were caught.

I went on a bicycle to the family Koedijk in Haarlem whose daughter, Annie, was our char. Our silver and other expensive things were transferred to the Koedijks for safe-keeping.

Now came the time for everybody to carry an identity document. On the Jewish document they printed a big J. My father tore his up and reported it stolen. He tried to get new documents without the J but did not succeed.

The bulb merchant in Hillegom knew an old farmer, about 80 years of age, living with his unmarried son and daughter. My father asked if he could come for a weekend's relaxation and fishing as a paying guest. The farmer was very poor, anti-German, and Catholic. My father went several times and once took my Mother along. In the beginning the farmer did not know we were Jewish.

During the bombardment of Rotterdam all my father's tyres went up in flames. As he could not import any more he had no more income. However, with one of his clients, Wijnperle, he started a tyre repair business in Amstelveen. There were official prices for tyres but black market prices were higher. One day my father did not come home from work. No one knew where he was. After two days he turned up and told us that they had been arrested for asking inflated prices. It was a very traumatic experience as people in Dutch prisons were often handed over to the Germans. My father's youngest brother, Jule, who had bought a lot of bicycles for investment during the war was sent to the police office in Apeldoorn, and from there to a camp in Amersfoort, then to Germany and was never heard of again.

My father decided to go into hiding. At this time Jews outside Amsterdam were forced to move to Amsterdam where the Germans created a Ghetto and before the move four "gentlemen" would come to your house and make an inventory of your goods because you had to leave everything behind. These four Dutch people had come to us but were not very successful as we lived in a furnished house. My father heard that the Germans had made enquiries about him at the Receiver of Revenue. This usually meant that they wanted your money and would arrest you.

My parents packed their suitcases. The food and clothing had already been transferred to the farm. Their basic ration cards had been given to a Gentile friend who was the only one who knew where they were staying. He sent us the coupon books and would occasionally sell one of my Father's gold coins for him to pay for their accommodation.

Accommodation was found for me in Amsterdam in the Jekerstraat with a Jewish family with two daughters from where I could go to school by tram and train. My grandparents also moved from Apeldoorn to Amsterdam and stayed one street away. I did not know the address of my parents and sister but could contact them via the Gentile man.

In the last week of April the Germans announced that Jews had to wear a yellow Star of David on all their clothing. I thought it was dangerous because it made one stick out like a living shooting target. My friends argued that you had to be proud as a Jew to wear it. I argued that there was nothing to be proud of if your enemy orders you to do this. The argument went on for several days. From the 2nd May we had to wear those Stars and I refused.

On the 1st May 1942, during lunchtime, my Father phoned me. After asking how I was, he said,
"I suppose you have heard that you have to wear a Star".
I said, "Yes, but I am not going to wear one".
He said, "That's okay. You don't have to wear one if you don't want to. Don't you think it is a good idea to come to the farm as that would be safer if you don't wear a Star?"
I said, "Yes, you are right."
He said, "Tell your teachers that your Mother is very ill. Take all your books and go home but you realise, of course, that you can't go to any school. Pack your clothing in Amsterdam and say goodbye to Oupa and Ouma."

I was quite relieved. For the first time here was someone who agreed with me. It did not worry me that my education would stop; the war would be over very shortly, wouldn't it? I said goodbye to the teachers and the pupils in my class.
"All the best with your Mother" they said. I was the first pupil in the whole school to go into hiding. Of all the teachers at the school only two survived the war. Of the 35 pupils of my class three survived including me.

In Amsterdam it was a very traumatic experience telling my Grandparents what had happened. My Grandfather blessed me and I never saw them again. They went into hiding themselves later.

Oupa died a natural death probably accelerated because he did not want to eat non Kosher food. A week after his death my Grandmother was picked up and sent to Westerbork where she met her daughter, Julchen, and they were sent together to a concentration camp.

My grandmother was gassed on arrival.

A few weeks after Siegfried Marcus, my Mother's half- brother married, he and his wife happily went to Westerbork and were never heard of again. Another of Mother's half- brothers, Manus, vowed they would never get him alive. When they came to fetch him he shot a few Germans dead and he was torn to pieces by their dogs.

The contact gentleman came to fetch me and we went by bicycle to the Heer-Hugowaard, about 12 Km. from Alkmaar to a small farm owned by an old man with his children Piet and Griet Beers. On the same plot was another farm where another son stayed. They had three children, one a few years older than me. They grew flower bulbs, grain and green cabbages. They had six cows, two sheep and a number of chickens and pigs.

It was decided that I should work for Bas who was the neighbour. He had one hectare of which a lot was under glass in which grew flowers, tomatoes, grapes spinach and cabbage. In the open he had brussels sprouts, chicory and seed potatoes. He was a Communist as was his opposite neighbour. They were enemies. Bas called his neighbour an anarchist and the neighbour called Bas a Trotskyist. I disagreed with both but learned a lot about whatever grows on the land. About 5 o'clock I went home, a mere three minutes away. The street was called the Rustenburgerweg.

There were six people in the street with the name Piet Beers so his nickname was Zwarte Piet, although he was grey.

Piet, Griet, Bas and family Waterboer and the neighbours plus the Catholic Pastor knew we were Jews. This kind of life went on for about a year. It was the first time that I ate non kosher food. We were not aware of any Jewish holidays for the next two years. My Father made a little bit of money by retreading bicycle tyres. He cut old inner tubes of motorcars into ribbons, made a solution of raw rubber and petrol and glued the strip on the bicycle and with a sort of electric iron he vulcanised the strip in four places on to the bicycle tyre. As the war would be over soon we decided I should have school lessons from a high school pupil. He came once a week and I studied dutifully.

We were in hiding for about a year when a policeman on a bicycle came to visit us. He said that the Mayor, who was also the head of the police, had received an anonymous letter that Pieter Beers was hiding Jews.
He said, "Well, I see no Jews here so I shall report that to the Mayor, but one does not know whether the letter was also sent to the Germans".

Off he went to "investigate" the other cases and report to the Mayor that everything was okay. Nevertheless we were very worried. I took a bicycle and went to sleep for about a week at the farm of my teacher. I could not stay there permanently so I was sent to the Catholic priest in the Wieringermeer with a letter. It was a 60 km. ride. All I got was the addresses of five farmers, a letter of recommendation from the priest, some food and one night's rest so back I went to my teacher in Oterleek, who took me back to the priest and I was sent to a 20 ha. experimental farm. They had sixty cows and milking and feeding was automatic.

Six weeks later, right above our heads, I saw a dog-fight between an English plane and three German planes. The English plane was hit and slowly circled down head over tails and a parachutist jumped out. We thought the pilot would land on our farm but the plane crashed several kilometres away. Immediately underground workers rushed to the pilot, tore off his uniform and gave him an overall and a cap and spirited him away. The Germans went from farm to farm looking for the pilot.

It was then decided that it was too dangerous to keep me on the farm so back I cycled to my teacher, slept there one night and went with him the next day to Klaas Beers, the neighbour and brother of Piet Beers. There I ate and after supper he said, "Do you want to go to your parents?"
Of course!
So we went over to Piet and I was very surprised to see my parents there. They explained that they had been there all the time although little Hetty had been farmed out to "Tante Geer and Oom Jo Boers" four or five Km. away.
From then on I had to stay inside together with my parents in a locked room.

I LIVED IN THIS ROOM FOR TWO YEARS.

A bed was made for me on the floor of the cupboard. What did I do? Peeled potatoes. Cleaned vegetables. Sorted out beans removing the bad ones. Listened to the English radio in Dutch twice a day. Played chess and read two years of De Katholieke Illustratie. I read the whole Elseviers Encyclopaedia from A to Z.

As the house was two metres from the farmhouse and connected by a passage, there was a sort of recess. There was also a door to the outside from the passage. Three metres from the door Piet made a reed wall. Here we could sit outside in the sun not seen by anybody. The only bad thing was that when Piet and Griet had visitors we were trapped and could not go back to our room. Piet had an old farmhand and we knew exactly when he would arrive so we also had to plan our visit to the toilet at the back of the farmhouse.

Slowly but surely Germany was bombarded by more and more Allied planes. We watched them from our "yard." We knew the direction, we had a map and worked out which town in Germany they had bombed. It was some fun in our misery. We checked with the radio if we were right. Sometimes we heard bombs exploding when Bergen airport was bombarded. One day an English plane was shot down and the Germans searched many farms in the vicinity. They came to our farm but only asked for eggs. However we panicked and hid in the straw. Afterwards we realised that this was not a good place to hide so we made a trapdoor in the cupboard under my mattress covered by flooring. We practised hiding, bedding and all, until we managed to do it in 60 seconds.

But even life on the farm became sticky. The rations for the farm decreased. We had our own milk, made our own butter, spun our own wool, made our own jerseys, made sugar and syrup from sugarbeet, had our own vegetables and fruit and made jam. Nevertheless for a long time we had a standard diet. One day brown beans and the next day brown bean soup. The following white beans and the day after white bean soup and then the cycle was repeated. The electricity was cut off and we ate by candlelight but worse, we could not listen to the radio. Fortunately the neighbour's son made a crystal receiver and with headphones I could hear London very faintly. It was so faint that I was the only one who could hear it.

Unfortunately the oil pumps that kept the polder dry did not work any more but they had some old coal pumps. After the battle of Arnhem we were almost completely encircled by the Allied forces and we could not get coal. The pumps stopped working. The water rose every day by about 1 cm. and started coming in under our trapdoor. With the water high, the boats which brought the goods to the market could not get underneath the bridges. That was the beginning of the starvation in the towns.

The winter 1944/45 was very bad. People were starving by the hundreds. We were baking bread and made cheese. Everyone who came to our door got two slices of bread with cheese but it was hopeless, the stream became bigger and we were forced to give one slice only. When the stream became a flood we could only give half a slice. People came to our door and offered us their winter coats for a slice of bread although it was freezing cold.

Not only were 20 000 Jews in hiding of whom 10,000 survived, but also 100 000 other Hollanders. A big task for the Underground Forces was financing them and supplying them with ration books. In the end there were ration books but no more food. One day a man was struggling to push a handcart on to the dyke. Bas helped the man. In the handcart under cover was the man's Father who had died.

On the 4th May 1945 at 18.30 the Germans signed the capitulation of Holland. I listened to my crystal radio and heard the news. I wanted to run outside but my Father said,
"We have waited so long, let's wait one more day".

After all the Germans were still here. Piet was called from the land and so were Bas and Klaas, the other neighbours. Within half an hour all the flags were out and the Germans were shooting wildly at them. All the flags went in again. The Germans left and all the flags came out again. The next day we got our bicycles from underneath the straw where they had been hidden and rode to Hetty. I was the fittest so I rode in front. Nevertheless I had a lot of pain as I was unfit. I had not seen Hetty for two years and when I saw two girls at the place where she lived I hugged the wrong girl. I had not recognised my own sister.

The next day I went by bicycle to Alkmaar to greet the liberators. The streets were full of people. The liberators did not come. The following day I went again and stood there the whole day. And there they came! I heard them from far away and I heard the shout of the crowd from far away. A colossal roar came closer and closer; and there I was at exactly the same spot and the same time as I had been five years before, Kennemerstraatweg, Alkmaar. I had waited for two days from 8 o'clock in the morning until 6 o'clock at night.

Actually I had waited for exactly five years!

Hetty came over, first for one day and later for two or three days so she could get used to her parents. She had never seen a banana or tasted a piece of chocolate.

My Mother's brother and wife and three children came back from a concentration camp. All were very sick. The youngest one, one year old, was born in the camp. His weight was the same as when he was born. I was not allowed to see him as it was too terrible to see. Aunty Julchen came back - she had been in the experimental camp and was never able to bear children. My Uncles, Han Blein and Ru Elzas had been fighting in the underground forces. Uncle Nol, Aunt Stella and Fredie never came back.

After two months we went to Bloemendaal. Annie Koedijk came back with our silver and jewellery. My Father got his property back after a legal battle.

I got a job as foreman in the port supervising 30 married men between 40 and 60 years of age, all of them Communists. I, of course was a capitalist no matter that I did not have a cent in my pocket. Thereafter I went to Apeldoorn to work for a tyre retreading firm. In November 1946 I was conscripted into the army and served for 2 years and 2 months. Afterwards I went to the Textile Technicon in Enschede and later switched to my father's business of exporting waste plastics and rubber, took a rubber technology course and finally landed in Cape Town 300 years after Jan van Riebeeck (1952). Five years later I returned to Holland, married Lenie and for a honeymoon took a boat trip to Cape Town.

It is interesting to note that our family never gave in to the demands of the Germans. We didn't give them our bicycles when these were demanded. We hid our copperware when they wanted to confiscate it. (I cannot remember if we dug it up after the war.) We didn't give them our radio. We hid our silver, money and copper when the Germans wanted them.

What was our greatest worry? It was fear. The fear of the Nazis.
The fear of being caught.
The fear of children at losing their parents and parents their children.
Fear of concentration camps.
A constant fear from morning until night.
Fear not so much of death but of a slow death.

Menno De Jong was born on 4.10.1926 in Apeldoorn, Holland, where he started school. In 1939 he moved to Rotterdam and later went into hiding on farms near Alkmaar where he remained until liberated in May 1945. After the war he was conscripted into the Dutch army, studied textiles and came to South Africa in 1952. He is married and has a son, Gerard, and a daughter, Sandra.

LENIE DE JONG - SANDERS
Enschede, Veenendaal

I wish to record these memories as a tribute to my foster parents,

TANTE JANNY AND OOM GERT VAN DIJK,

through whose kindness and bravery I survived the war unlike thousands of other children my age.

I was born Helena Mathilde Louise Sanders on 3 January 1934 but everyone calls me Lenie. My brother Johan Herman is two and a half years older than me, and Mathilde (Tilde) is nineteen months younger. My father, Comprecht Bernard Sanders, called Gerard, was the eldest of 7 children; my mother, Rosalie Mansfeld, called Ro, has a younger brother. My father was an accountant at a factory and we lived in the grounds of the factory in a small house with a tiny garden. The director of the factory was our neighbour but he lived in a mansion with a big garden.

When I was five and a half I started school, a private school half an hour's walk from home. Sunday mornings I attended a Hebrew class and I would go to shul with my father regularly on Saturday mornings. We had a kosher home and I have very happy memories of the Jewish holidays, especially Passover, which I really enjoyed. We changed everything, and I clearly remember that our matzos were round. We even had a special round stand for the 3 matzos with a curtain, which could be turned. During Succot we ate our meals in our Succah which had a roof that could be opened. My father also had a Lulav and Etrog. I also remember getting sweets in shul on Simchat Torah in a lovely fancy paper packet. My maternal grandfather was a Levite, and although he was not very religious, he had a special place in shul. I remember him wearing a long white robe and white headgear. On High Holy Days the shul committee members wore top hats and this gave a lot of decorum.

When the war broke out in May 1940 I was too young to understand what was really happening. On 2 May 1942 Jewish people had to wear the yellow star of David on their clothes so that Jews could be visible. As Tilde and I wore lots of blue dresses my mother had blue velveteen sleeveless boleros made for us on which the star was sewn which we wore on top of our dresses. I felt very proud wearing the star.

When the new school year started in September 1942 we were no longer allowed to attend our school. We had to go to a Jewish school with Jewish teachers which was much further away, approximately 45 minutes walk from our house. Our live-in servant, Ali, could not work for us any more, as we were only allowed to employ Jewish people .

People were already being picked up by the Germans and sent to concentration camps. My father served on the Enschede branch of the Jewish Board of Deputies and since 1933 had been working with the Jewish refugees who were crossing into Holland. He was also very involved in the underground movement and many meetings were held at our house. There was a lot of whispering and the atmosphere must have been tense. His group organized hiding places for the Jewish people of Enschede. They would talk about people being " b.w." or "o.w" "Boven water" (above water)" meant living normally, "onder water" meant being in hiding. One of the group members was Dominee Overduin.

On 10 April 1943 we too went "onder water". The yellow stars were removed from our coats and at dusk one evening we went to the station. We each got into a different compartment in the train. One of Dominee Overduin's sisters accompanied me and another sister went with Tilde. Johan was escorted by a gentleman.

I do not remember much about the journey, but we went to Arnhem where we stayed with a brother and sister-in-law of Dominee Overduin, also a dominee of the

Dutch Reformed Church. For the first time in our lives we ate non-kosher food.

After one day we went to Veenendaal, a village between Arnhem and Utrecht, where we lived in a very modern mansion owned by Mr. Ad van Schuppen, the director of the Ritmeester Cigar Factory, whose house was next to the factory. This house was very impressive and had two different staircases to the first floor. Mr. van Schuppen was unmarried and lived with his sister and brother- in- law, Mr and Mrs Mijnhardt, and their little daughter.

I remember that Mrs. Mijnhardt gave us a cake of soap. I had never seen such a large piece of soap before; it was pure luxury. We must have stayed here at least 3 days during which we were not allowed outside but were indoctrinated.

Tilde and I were told the following:
"Your name is not Sanders, but Visserman. You used to live in Oleander Ave in The Hague. Your mother has passed away and your father cannot look after you and that is why you have been sent to foster- parents."

As our first names were not biblical names like Miriam or Esther, we were able to keep them. I think we had to write our new name and address over and over again. My brother Johan's story was different. He was to be called "van den Berg" and was supposed to have come from Rotterdam and have no father.

One evening we went to our new foster-parents. Johan went to the Van Engelenburgs and we went to a Mr. & Mrs. van Dijk. Both foster-fathers were employees of the Ritmeester Cigar Factory.

Mr Van Dijk had wanted either to help in the underground or to take in Jewish children and had decided on the latter. They too had a cover story for our sudden appearance. This was that Mr Van Dijk had met a man in the train who had told him that his house had been bombed, his wife had been killed and he did not know how to cope with his two daughters. The underground even sent letters from The Hague to confirm the story.

"Tante Janny" and "Oom Gert" looked after Tilde and me for 2 years and 3 months. They had been married for nearly 9 years and were in their thirties. It must have been quite a change in their lives to have to look after two girls of nine and seven and a half years old, as they had no children of their own.

They were very religious and attended the Dutch Reformed Church. They bought a Children's Bible straight away and Oom Gert would read out of it every day after lunch and supper. We were also given a book of Psalms, which I still treasure. It has my name inside - "LENIE VISSERMAN".

We were enrolled at a "School with the Bible." The Headmaster knew of our origins. The classes were larger than I was used to, about 40 children compared to the previous 25. Their house was smaller than our own and had no running water, but there was a pump in the kitchen. Children adapt very easily and we took everything in our stride. We were extremely lucky as we had blond hair and blue eyes and did not look Jewish.

It was not so easy for a girl we knew from Enschede, Mirjam de Groot, who lived with foster- parents on a farm outside Veenendaal because she had dark hair and brown eyes. Mirjam had stayed with Tante Janny and Oom Gert for a little while before we arrived. She knew that Tilde and I were staying with the Van Dijk's and we knew where she lived. Her foster- parents belonged to another church and we would sometimes see her after the service on Sundays, but we were told to pretend not to know her. It was a thrill to see her all the same.

Johan attended the same school. We had strict instructions not to speak to him. Occasionally we exchanged a few words. I was petrified and I do not think I started the conversations. One evening Johan came to visit us when it was dark. This was quite dangerous as sometimes people put two and two together. Oom Gert was the oldest of 10 children and twice one of his brothers made remarks. Once he said that,
"The boy who is staying with the Van Engelenburg's is Jewish".
Another time he said,
"Tilde looks like the boy who stays with the Van Engelenburg's; she could be his sister!"
How right he was both times!!! As Johan was always a naughty and difficult child, rumours began to spread and he had to be moved to other families.

One day there was a "Razzia" to collect forced labour for Germany and all the men in our street were picked up. After some time one after another came back home. When Oom Gert did not return we were sure that the Germans had found out that we were Jewish and that our end was near. Tante Janny, Tilde and I were in tears at the thought. We were very relieved when Oom Gert arrived home and it was just chance that he had been kept a little longer.

Everything one bought in the shops was rationed. The ration coupons for Tilde and me were supplied by the underground. As our cards came late Tante Janny had to be very careful to go to the grocer after receiving our cards because it would have been suspicious if she could only produce two and not four coupons for her grocery shopping.

As we were supposed to have a father, 'he' visited us twice by arrangement. Our father was a stranger from the underground movement who brought us presents and was introduced to our friends. When he left we would walk part of the way with him in our street and kiss him goodbye publicly, so that the neighbours could see him. We put on a beautiful act and we loved to play the part. Unfortunately he was picked up and sent to a concentration camp and never returned.

Occasionally we got presents from our "father" and I think that maybe Mr. van Schuppen provided these. Mr. van Schuppen was a fantastic person who looked after 23 people both Jewish and Gentile during the war, all of whom survived. He also supplied lots of cigars to those families who were assisting with hiding people. These could be exchanged for goods.

We had to go to church twice on Sundays. Sometimes we would be let off and allowed to go on a long walk on a very hot Sunday afternoon, but these were exceptions. Some Saturdays we were taken on outings by bicycle. Tante Janny and Oom Gert never used their bikes on Sundays. We always walked to and from church.

Once we had to provide accommodation for a German soldier. He brought nice ingredients, some of which were stolen, for Tante Janny to cook for him. When he was at our house we never called our foster parents "Tante Janny" or "Oom Gert" so that he would think we were their children.

After the airborne-landings in Arnhem, in September 1944, the inhabitants of Arnhem had to be evacuated. Thousands of people came to Veenendaal. Nearly all the people in our street took in some refugees. Because we were Jewish the Van Dijks had to be very careful who they took in in case they were pro-Nazi. Some of our neighbours stopped greeting Tante Janny, because they thought we were not doing our duty, and one of our girl-friends was forbidden to play with us.

After a few days "Oom Wim", his wife and 18 year old daughter came to live with us. They knew we were Jewish girls. We only had two bedrooms so Tilde and I had to move into the attic. When the daughter came down with an infectious disease, she had to stay in isolation in the room and a big sign was put up on our house. The German soldiers avoided coming to the house.

Very often the V-1 or V-2 rocket bombs would fly over our house. They made a terrible noise and I was absolutely pertrified. There would be sirens and it was all very scary as we were not too far from the Allied lines. Many people took shelter in the basement of a nearby factory. We would take shelter in the cupboard under the staircase and the four of us would be huddled together. For years I slept with my head under the blankets, without realising why I did it.

Oom Wim's mother and aunt were also staying in Veenendaal and would sometimes visit him. As these two old ladies had lived in The Hague and heard that we also came from there, they started asking us lots of questions. Do you remember this street and that street? As we knew nothing at all about The Hague, we would answer that we could not remember. The next time the two ladies came to visit, Tante Janny ordered us to go and play outside in the street. I felt quite stupid about not knowing any streets in The Hague, as I knew plenty of streets in Enschede. One of our school teachers had also quizzed us about our "home town." (When she learnt after the war about our origins she realized why we had known so little about The Hague.) These incidents one never forgets.

The Germans surrendered on 5 May 1945, but it took a few days before we were really liberated. When we told our friends we were Jewish, they could not believe it at first. Some people who had stopped greeting my foster parents and us were very embarrassed. Towards the end of the war Mr. van Schuppen was arrested by the Germans, but he survived. When he returned after the war he asked Oom Gert one Sunday after the service if he had told us about our father. There and then Oom Gert told us that our father had been sent to a concentration camp where he had died. It was as if someone had given me a hard slap on my face. It had been kept from us that he had been betrayed as he was driving to his hiding place in Enschede. A "*friend*" had told the Nazis his plans and his motor registration number.

A few weeks after the war we were playing in the street when Mr. van Schuppen and a woman passed on bicycles, obviously going to visit the Van Dijks. We were called home.

The woman was our mother! We were reunited after more than 27 months. Tilde did not recognise her, but I did. When I became a mother it was a mystery to me how she managed not to shed a tear at that particular time. I wish I had asked her how she managed to control her emotions to such an extent. This question and many, many others were never asked as she passed away on 1 January 1969.

Johan came back to the Van Engelenburgs after the war after having been in many different foster-homes. Tilde and I were fetched to go back to Enschede on 29 June. A lorry suddenly arrived. We had not known about this as communications were poor, and we had to pack our belongings and leave.

Tante Janny's youngest sister was with us and she quickly went to the factory to call Oom Gert to come and say goodbye to us.

Before we left he threw himself on the couch and started sobbing, a sight I will never forget.

Oom Gert passed away on 18 March 1982. I am still in constant touch with Tante Janny and visit her regularly in Veenendaal. In 1987 I managed to trace our former maid Ali. When I said, "I am Lenie Sanders," she just took me in her arms and gave me a big hug.

Tilde and I were very, very fortunate to have found wonderful people prepared to take us in. Enschede had the highest percentage of Jewish survivors in Holland because of their strong underground movement and more than 500 of their 1220 Jews survived the war. I am very proud that my father had been one of the organizers. It was fantastic of Tante Janny and Oom Gert to take us under their wings. They treated us as if we were their own children. Despite all the difficulties, all the frustrations and all the lies we had to tell, these were very happy years. I still remember many Dutch Xmas carols and I often think about these times with great warmth.

This is why I would like these memories to stand as a tribute to the Van Dijks for their bravery, love and kindness.

Lenie De Jong was born on 3.1.1934 in Enschede, Holland, where she started school. She went into hiding in Veenendaal. She was liberated on 10th May 1945 and came to South Africa in 1957. She is married and has a son, Gerard, and a daughter, Sandra.

HELENE CZERNIEWICZ
Paris, Marseilles, Grenobles. Lyons

I was born in Paris in 1926, the second of three children. Olga was two years my senior and Maurice was three years my junior. My parents were born in Poland. When my father became French, he took a French surname.

I was 13 when the War broke out in 1939. There was of course, the phony war period, when no one really knew what was happening. My father was in the army. On 10 May 1940, Germany invaded France. My father had written to my mother, saying that when the Germans came she was to leave Paris. It took a while before we could get a train. Finally, we went by train to Toulouse where we stayed for 3 weeks. My father had said that we must go to Marseilles where he would try to join us. When we arrived in Marseilles and got to the hotel, we found my father already there. He had left the army. He found a place for us to stay and, as he had done in Paris, started a handbag factory where I met Max whom I was later to marry.

Now France was divided into two - Occupied France and Free France (Vichy France.) In Vichy France, Jews did not have to wear the yellow armbands. However, there was already a law that all Jews were to register at the Police as Jews. When my father went to the Police Station he was asked why he had come to register. After all, he had a French name. My father insisted on doing the legal thing. In any case, he trusted Marshal Petain's assurance that Jews who had served in the Army would be in no danger.

At the end of November 1942, Germany occupied Vichy France. We left Marseilles and went to the country into the Pyrenees. I returned to Marseilles with my father as we wanted to fetch some of the things we had left in the flat. Unbeknown to my father, I was hoping to see Max once more. The day we arrived we saw lots of French police in the streets, thousands of them and lorries and cars. I couldn't understand what

was happening. Then a woman we knew said to us,
"Why have you come back to Marseilles? Can't you see what is happening?
They're going to arrest all the Jews tonight."

I told this to my father but he said that there was nothing we could do. If anyone knocked at our door, we were to remain silent and not answer. And that night, they went to all the flats looking for Jews.

They came to our house and knocked at the door. We didn't open the door and finally they left, possibly because they saw a French name on the door. That night, after they left (and I'll never forget this) I wanted to go to my father but couldn't because I wasn't able to find the door. I felt as if I were in a box.

I still remember the feeling - that there was no door. Since that night, I have never slept without a light in the passage or somewhere. I think that that was the first terrifying thing I experienced in the war. Finally I went to my father. He sent me to Mrs. Tverdin, a friend of ours - I still correspond with her daughter in Israel - to find out who had been arrested. And that's when I found out that Mr Mindel had been arrested. *(Helene Joffe's father. See following story)*

The next day, our neighbour said that she would hide my father for a few days while I returned to my mother. I arrived at the station. This is something I'll never forget. Of course, I was carrying an Identity Card showing that I was Jewish. There were thousands of policemen at the station. I didn't know what to do. As I got on to the platform, I heard a voice,
"Your paper, Miss".

I was shaking inside. I took out my book, and I suppose it was instinctive, the instinct to survive, which made me show my book with my finger covering the top left hand corner where the word 'Juif' was written.

I got into the train and I remember bursting into sobs, crying my eyes out and people in the compartment comforting me with the words:

"Don't worry, Miss, your boyfriend will come back."

And so I came back to my mother, and then started my constant moving from one place to another, with false papers, all the time changing our identities, going to a new school. My father didn't want me to go to school as it was too risky but I wanted to. One could get arrested at school as well.

My over-riding feeling when I think about my experiences is not about hunger but about fear. I was never hungry because my father was always able to get food on the black market.

In 1943, we got to Grenobles. It was then occupied by the Italians and we knew that the Italians were not as bad as the Germans, but this was not for long. I didn't really know my mother; she wasn't a very demonstrative person but one day, I met her in the street. She was carrying a basket and she asked me to accompany her. We went to visit a family who were completely destitute; they had no money; the father had been taken by the Germans. The woman took my mother's hand and kissed her. She told me that my mother had been feeding her since her husband's arrest. This was a side of my mother I didn't know. At that time to feed a family with black market food was not exactly a safe thing to do.

Once when I was walking in the street, I saw a young man looking at me. Wherever I went, he followed. I was sure he was from the Gestapo.

My mother had always told us that if anyone of us was followed, we must not come home - otherwise the others might be arrested. We always had to carry some money and jewelry on us so that we would be able to cope if unable to return home. Go to the station, she said, take a train anywhere but don't come home.

I knew I must not go home because he would arrest, not only me, but my family as well. I went into a cafe and he followed, and came to sit at my table. Then I saw some police arrive downstairs and noticed the young boy pale and realised that he was frightened. He was obviously not from the Gestapo. I asked him whether he was Jewish and he said he was.

He had arrived at the place he was staying only to see his parents being put into a lorry. His mother had looked at him so intensely that he knew she was indicating that she wanted him to escape. He had been looking for a Jew because he had nowhere to go. He had noticed me, noticed that I looked nervous and had decided that I must be Jewish so he had followed me. I took him home. He later joined the Resistance. (On the day the Americans came, he was accidentally shot by his friend who was cleaning his gun. He had promised that he would come to see us that evening. He had been through so much.)

The Germans occupied Grenobles and the Italians left France so we decided to go to Lyons. There my father was offered a flat, in a building occupied by German officers. The man who let us have the flat was a business acquaintance who said that my mother and father were not to leave the flat by day or night. The flat was taken in the name of my sister and myself (I was then 17 and my sister 19). We told the concierge that we were from Paris and had lost our parents. Nobody knew that my mother and father were in the flat. They had to keep quiet so that no one would discover that they were there. This must have been difficult for them as they were argumentative by nature.

My sister and I both worked. When I went to be interviewed for the job, the man asked me whether I was Jewish and I told him that I was not. One day something very strange happened: About 2 weeks later while I was busy typing, I was told to go down to the archives to find a file with a certain name and number. I spent a number of hours looking for the file - it was not to be found. When I went up, I was told that the Germans had been there. The boss had deliberately sent me down to the archives - he had known that I was a Jew. I learned, after the War, that he was a member of he Resistance.

The 29 July 1944 was my sister's 19th birthday. My mother's friend needed to have an abortion and was afraid to go to the doctor on her own. My mother insisted on accompanying her. Up till then, my parents had never left the flat. My father begged her not to go. He said they were nearing the end of the war. (The Americans arrived in Lyons two weeks later.) However, my mother insisted and went off with her friend to the Jewish doctor. When they arrived, the doctor was being arrested. So my mother and her friend were arrested as well. The woman had on her the addresses of all her family so they went to fetch the father and two children as well.

It was almost the end of the War but the Germans still managed to arrange a train to transport the Jews arrested.

When the German arrived to arrest the father and two children, a girl friend of mine was there. The son of sixteen told the Gestapo that the fair haired girl was not Jewish but had only come to practise the piano. So the German asked her to play some piece of German music and let her go. He was convinced. No Jewish girl he believed could play a piece of music by a German composer. She came to tell me that my mother had been arrested. My father and we children left the flat and went to the attic. And there we sat all night, looking at one another - there was nothing we could do.

We had heard rumours about what was happening in the camps but we didn't believe them. Who could believe such stories? I remember there was a clandestine Swiss newspaper circulating in France with a picture of a gas chamber. But no one could believe this.

When the war ended, people started to come back and we went to the Red Cross to find out if my mother were alive. We had no idea where she had been taken. After Liberation my sister and I went to Fort Saint Luc where my mother had been held. We asked all those freed whether they recalled my mother. But they were all Christians and they told us that the arrested Jews had been deported. We didn't know whether my mother was alive. Then someone turned up who said he had seen our mother in Theresienstadt, but that had been some months before.

Finally, we had a telegram from her saying she was in Theresienstadt - she had been in Auschwitz and after Liberation had been sent there by the Americans. She was alive!!!

She sent a telegram saying she was coming home. She had been away for 10 months. When we saw her, we had a fright. She weighed about 45 Kilograms. She had no hair and no teeth. It took a long time for her to begin to recover.

After my mother came back after her sufferings in the camps, she was never the same. She couldn't sleep because she suffered terrible nightmares and was afraid to sleep. At that time there was no psychological help and she really needed a psychologist.

Once, when she was back, we took her out to a hotel. We sat down to dinner and the waiter came round with the soup tureen, ladling out soup for each person. When he was leaving our table, taking the tureen with him, she got so mad at him. She started to fight with him because she did not want that tureen to disappear - she couldn't bear to have food taken away. She went on hiding bread under her bed. She would wake us up at 6 a.m. and tell us to go and buy bread. We tried to assure her that there was plenty of bread but she was so scared. She came back from Auschwitz when she was in her forties but she never really recovered.

She never talked about what had happened to her in Auschwitz, except, one day when she said:

"I must tell you what happened because one day your children will never believe what happened. You must tell your children, and they must tell their children."

She told us that the Nazis woke the women up at 3:00 a.m. in the morning and made them stand naked in the snow for hours and hours, till half of the women were dead. She once saw a Nazi throw a small child in the air and then shoot him like a pigeon.

Who could believe such a story? One reads books about such things but they are impossible to believe. She once saw a dog kill a woman. Once in order to avoid standing in the snow, she hid herself in a barrel full of water. She was a strong woman.

After the War, my parents moved to Marseilles where I was reunited with Max with whom I had been corresponding. He had been born in Poland and had moved to France as a young boy. He too had gone into hiding We married in Paris in 1945 and discovered that of Max's family of fourteen married brothers and sisters, 85 individuals altogether, only one sister had survived and she died before we could bring her to Paris. We had two daughters both born in France and came to South Africa in 1951 where another daughter was born.

Life has not been a gift to me. My husband died when I was 31 and my youngest child six months old. At present my grandchild Jacques Max is bringing a lot of meaning to my life and I look forward to watching my grandchildren grow up into a better world.

Helene Czerniewicz was born in Paris in 1926 and educated at Paris, Marseilles, Grenoble and Lyon. She spent the war years in those and other small towns being liberated in August 1944 in Lyon. She lived in France until 1951 when she moved to South Africa. She married Max who died in 1958 and has three daughters, Sylvia, Solange and Laura.

HELENE JOFFE
Marseilles, Haute-Provence

I was born in Marseilles in 1934, one of 5 children of Rubin and Sima Mindel: the eldest, Leon, born 1919, the second Berthe, born 1922, then Michel, born 1924, then myself and Armand the youngest, born 1938.

Before my family was really affected by the war, I became aware of things that troubled and disturbed me. I would wake up in the mornings, and people (friends of my parents) would be sleeping all over the house, on the floors. My parents had many friends in Paris, and because Paris was already occupied by the Germans, many of these friends and friends of friends turned up, looking for shelter, for refuge. Things were abnormal at home - there was so much talk, whispering. I didn't know what it was all about and I found it frightening. Remember I was only six years old at the time ; no one told me what was happening.

In 1942 the Germans marched into the previously- unoccupied zone. We were told by these friends from Paris, who were probably trying to escape to Spain or Portugal, that we should do the same but my father believed that, as French citizens, we had nothing to fear; the Germans would not touch us.

"In France" said my father, "I sleep with my windows open."

In 1943 the Germans started to encircle certain parts of Marseilles, particularly those areas in which many Jews lived. Then my fear grew because the Germans barricaded the streets.

Every time we had to go to the shops we had to run, and I remember my fear at such times. I was never afraid of the German soldier. The German soldier was ofen very kind (He was not like the Nazis or the Gestapo), especially when he saw a blonde child _ he thought it was a German child. My father had his papers stamped as a French Jew. He was so proud of being a French Jew. Berthe who was about 21 or 22 refused to give my father her papers for stamping. She said such pride in being a French Jew was silly. There were many arguments until finally she had to give in.

Someone told my mother that she had better hide her husband because there was to be a Rafle (a gathering - in) of the Jews that night. Our apartment had two floors. Leon (24) and Michel (19) slept upstairs, whilst my parents, Berthe, Armand and I slept downstairs. That night (23 January 1943) my mother told my father to hide in his shops. We had a number of shops not far from where we lived. My father went off at about 8:30 pm but returned an hour later because he was afraid that if the Nazis came for him and did not find him, they would take the women instead. He gave his wedding ring to Leon and the boys were told not to open their bedroom doors. I remember my father's face so well. I had just turned eight. I wasn't feeling well as my tonsils had been removed about a week before.

At midnight, there was a knock at the door. A Frenchman came into the apartment; there was also a German (but he did not come inside). The Frenchman was a collaborator (a member of Milice: a French group belonging to Vichy government). My father was asked for his papers which had the stamp showing that he was a Jew. He was ordered to dress. My mother was told that she, Berthe and I did not have to go. They then went upstairs, and knocked on all the doors; my brothers did not open the doors. When they asked the other neighbours, they were told that they did not know of any other people living in the apartment. Fortunately the Frenchman and the German did not press the matter. My sister was screaming hysterically. She was told that if she did not come inside, she would be shot. When Michel heard that my father was being taken to prison, he wanted to rush after him. He is a very impulsive person but my mother held him back and hit him.

At 6 the next morning, we saw motor cars and heard loudspeakers telling us to get ready because everyone in the area was being taken away. We were to collect our things because the area was to be evacuated. We were told that the place was no longer safe, and that we were to be taken to a safer place. We were not told that the order was specifically for Jews. They said they were going to destroy the entire area.

My mother had run away from the Russian Revolution, so she was an experienced refugee. She had sewn into her corset into every seam and hem gold coins, and jewellery. We dressed in as many clothes as we could. It was bitterly cold. In the streets all the people of the area were gathered. I remember the scene; everyone in the district was marching and we gathered on the square. I remember having two dolls; one , a celluloid doll, given to me by Leon's fiancee, was my favourite. As we marched, I dropped the celluloid doll; someone tramped on it. That was my personal tragedy.

We were taken to the station where we stood until midday. We were then packed into cattle trucks, 40 - 50 crushed into each. There were buckets in the trucks. There was an Italian family who were neighbours of ours, the mother was called Assunte. I remember one of them, a girl, Yvonne, whose hair smelled of vinegar. It was so cold; there was no food, no drink. The train took us slowly to our destination, and finally we arrived in a military camp in Frejus near Hyeres, on the coast. There were Jews and non-Jews - we had not yet been asked to show our papers. There were only women, girls and little boys in Frejus. At such times, you don't break down, and despair; you simply try to survive; otherwise you die. I remember my mother putting straw on the table so that we could sleep there. We stayed in Frejus for about two weeks.

We were then told that those who had a safer place to go to could leave Frejus and go there, perhaps to the country. Otherwise we'd be taken to a "safe" place. That meant a concentration camp. The Italian family who had a little place in the country, said that we were with them. There were just women. Berthe now became the head of the family. She was a very strong woman. Before we left Frejus, we had to show our identity cards to the German. She handed all our cards to him, and, without even looking at them, he told us to go through. Fortunately, the French official was busy elsewhere. It was a German soldier who let us go through, a member of the Gestapo. I always remember that it was a Frenchman not a German, who arrested my father.

So we were saved and we went with the Italian family to their place, just outside Marseilles, today a part of the city. At this stage, we were covered with lice. My mother washed us with petrol. We arrived at the little cottage. Then Yvonne, Assunte's daughter, went to find Leon's non- Jewish fiancee in Marseilles who said that she would take charge of us, and find us a place. She took us to her aunt's chateau. As was always to be the case, we moved at night, listening for footsteps. I always felt great fear. Walking and taking trams, we finally came to the chateau, where the old aunt was sick with cancer; my mother was to look after her. So many things made me afraid in the chateau. Fear and insecurity also made me angry. I'd always loved animals but I found myself angry and cruel towards the animals. We stayed here for a while. Eventually, Berthe, having searched around made contact with the Maquis. We couldn't stay any longer in the chateau; the aunt was dying. So one night we moved again to a little village. We walked very far.

It was so cold. The Maquis had found us a place to stay - the village was occupied by German cavalry. We now acquired new papers and a new surname - Arnaud. Berthe had also heard that Leon had been sent to Germany to do forced labour, and that Michel had joined the underground as did Berthe.

We were very happy in the village. The German soldiers were nice and very helpful to us. They showed us pictures of their children. They adored my little brother Armand. He and I didn't look Jewish, only Berthe did. They thought he was a child Berthe had had by a German. They helped us build a rabbit hutch. Rabbit was very much part of French food, especially in the South because they are easy to breed, and there was no other meat.

I was already going to school. One day I met a peasant woman who asked me my name and I said "Helene Mindel." My mother gave me a hiding to remind me that I was never to forget that my name was not Mindel, but Arnaud. But, otherwise, I was happy in the village; I ran around the fields; I loved nature. I became friendly with a little girl and one day she told me that her mother's name was Rachel. She told me that her mother was Jewish, and I said "so are we". And then we had a message from the underground to say that we were in danger and would have to move. The little girl's mother had reported us.

Leon, who had returned to France and was in the underground, arrived at our village. We were told to gather our things and leave that night. I had to leave behind my little kitten. Every time we had to move on we left a piece of ourselves behind. And always we were carrying parcels. We were now taken in hand fully by the underground. They found a place in Haute Provence, in the mountains. There was a double house which belonged to an Englishman who had rented it furnished. The other half of the house belonged to the family of Alphonse Dumay, head of the underground in Mont Ventoux. We lived in a sort of hamlet where the underground, a communist one, had its headquarters. Michel was a very important man in the Maquis. Berthe was an agent. We were not always sure where she and my brothers were.

I lived very happily here; I'd grown up; I unpicked parachutes, carried messages. The British used to drop arms there for the entire Maquis. I felt I was part of it all. I lived wildly like the little girl in Jean de Florette. I used to cut wood in the forest and carry wood on my back. Once I found a wounded German soldier in one of the caves and ran to tell my brother. We belonged to the Church. We attended ser-

vices. I felt strongly Catholic; I was troubled that if I died I would go to Hell because I hadn't been baptised. I learned so much in those years. My sister-in-law to-be came to teach us. She lived with us for about a year. She was a wonderful woman. (She married Leon when Marseilles was liberated.)

When the Americans entered Marseilles there was fierce fighting with the Germans. Michel shot from the windows for three days - he was called the madman of Castellane (a square in Marseille). He was wounded. My mother was a strong woman, Our house was at the top of the hill and she would watch the fighting from a window. We used to go to the caves when fighting took place. I remember when the Americans marched into Apt seven Kilometers away from us, bringing with them sweets, and chewing gum. We lived in that hamlet till 1945 when fighting stopped. Then we packed a lorry, Berthe found an empty apartment in Marseilles, we took the law into our hands, and simply moved in.

We did not know where my father was. We had heard that he had been sent to Drancy, a transit camp, to where we had sent parcels in 1943. He died 30/3/43, shot in Auschwitz.

Helene Joffe was born in Marseilles, France on 28.10.1934. She was still a child when the Germans invaded and went into hiding in different villages in France. After the war she returned to Marseilles and came to South Africa in 1954. She is married to Louis and has three daughters, Leila Jocelyne, Heidi Sylvia and Rafaela Amanda.

EVE DAVIS
Athens, Verona, Heraclion

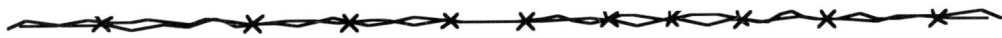

When the war reached us in 1941 the Greeks hardly inferfered with us and even when they surrendered and the Italians entered, it was not so bad except that all Jewish families had to be registered - how many people were there in each family, how many rooms in each house etc. The Italians billeted people in Jewish homes. We had to give up a room to an Italian who held a non combatant post as a censor in the post office.

Mr Salvatore was in his fifties and was very kind and friendly towards us. We eventually discovered that he was really Jewish and had only enlisted in the Italian army in order to escape from the Nazis. He wanted to marry one of my sisters but she did not want to marry an Italian. My Mother was happy to have a Jew living with us and as she was an old lady with a lot of old friends, she started telling them that Mr Salvatore was Jewish. When poor Salvatore found that the truth had got out, he left us because he felt that he was now in danger. We did not mind. We were delighted to get our room back.

While the Italians were in charge we felt safe but when the Germans took over in 1943 they started to control everything. All the Jews in Salonika were rounded up and taken to concentration camps. The Nazis promised that they would not harm the Jews in Athens and that we would be safe but we did not trust them. We felt sure that what they did to the Jews in Salonika, they would do to us. We paid for false identity documents under false names - these were easy to obtain because the police sided with the Jewish people. Instead of Eva Benmelech, I became Kula Constadino.

My father's papers stated that he was a Greek farmer. In reality my father imported silkworm cocoons from Turkey for the manufacture of silk. He came from Broussa on the Asiatic side of Turkey. During the First World War my brother enlisted in the British Navy. My parents were scared of Turkish reprisals and caught a boat to Athens where we remained. I was born in Athens - the other six children were born in Turkey. My Mother was never very fluent in Greek.

With our false papers we went into hiding. We would rent a place in the country, often paying six month's rent in advance and within a few weeks or a month, the Germans would move in to the area, would camp nearby and try to get friendly with young girls like us, so we would pack our bags and move like refugees with our little bundles to other places, losing the rent we had paid. Some people would accept us, others would not. After a while all the Jews were told that they had to register and return to their homes or would be shot immediately on discovery without explanation. So we had to come back to Athens and register and get proper identification cards.

Once a week we had to go and present ourselves at the Greek synagogue to have our identification cards stamped. Sometimes my father would take all our identity cards; other times two or three other members of the family would go. On the 24th March 1944 my father went along with my sister who was going out. I stayed at home. I heard shouting. I went out on the balcony and my sister shouted,

"COME DOWN IMMEDIATELY"

I was ironing and I said,

"Wait a minute, I'll switch off and then I'll come down."

When I went down she said,

"Leave everything and come, because the Germans are rounding up all the Jews!!"

As the following day was a Greek National Day, my mother had gone to the market to do some shopping while my father went to the shul. For the round-up the Germans had blocked off the area from one end to the other so that no Jews could escape from the shul. I left the house just as it was. We had already prepared little bags with clothing and necessities in case we had to run away. We went out of the house and waited at the corner for my mother to return from the market - we would never have been able to find her there. Eventually we got a phone call from my brother saying

"Leave the house immediately!"

but we were anxiously waiting for my mother to arrive. My other brothers and sister had already gone into hiding.

When my mother arrived with all her shopping we told her to forget all the parcels, we had to leave. She said,

"Look. I must get a few things" - money, jewellery and so she took a chance and quickly went upstairs and got these things. When my mother, my sister and I came down someone told us that they had seen my father being taken away on a lorry, so we knew that it was the end of the story for him.

We went and said goodbye to our neighbour and left. Just as we got out of the house and were at the corner, a jeep arrived with Germans and a Greek soldier and stopped in front of our house, about seven or ten metres away from us, not further than that. They were looking for us!

We ran for our lives!

We had missed them by minutes!

We were scared to walk about in the day in case some Greek would say,

"There go some Jews walking around."

We went to stay with a very good Gentile friend until it got dark when we could move to our prepared hiding place. We had arranged to leave individually so that we should not all be caught. While we were sitting and talking, we heard the sound of the boots of the Germans. My oldest brother had rented a room in this house which he had given to the Germans as his registered address although he never stayed there but lived far away. The Germans having got his address had come to look for him, had broken down the door and finding no one there had started to look for him and came to the flat where my mother, my sister and I were sitting with our friend.

When we heard the boots, we hid quickly, my mother and I under the bed and my sister under the divan. I think the knocking of our hearts was much louder than our breathing. Our friend opened the door and said,

"Who are you looking for?"

They said, "We are looking for Mr Benmelech"

So she said, "Why, what did he do? Did he do something bad?"

They said, "Yes, He did something bad and we are looking for him."

She said, "I haven't seen him for quite a long time."

As they stood talking, we lay very near to their boots, maybe three quarters of a meter away. We could see their boots clearly. Eventually they thanked my friend and left.

My friend then dropped down in a faint. We were shaking like a fish. My mother could not get her breath. We tried to revive our friend. We stayed there until nightfall when one went in one direction, the others in different ones.

My brother had organized where we were to hide. The first night I stayed with a school friend of mine and the next morning my brother came and took me to some of his friends - a very nice couple with whom I stayed. I felt very lonely as I was alone all day long while they were at work. At the same time I developed many friends in my hair - lice. I told my brother who said, "Don't worry. I have another home for you at a place called Verona outside Athens."

We walked there because we were scared to take a tram. I was very happy to find another young girl like me there. She had no mother and lived with her father. We were very happy there - my friend who was very particular was not pleased when she found that I was passing all my lice onto her, but we got paraffin and boiled all our clothing and got rid of them and took it like a joke. At night time she would take me for a walk at the foot of the mountain so that I could get some fresh air.

One afternoon we waited and waited for her father, but he did not come home from work. We waited till late but he never pitched up. Then a neighbour came and said that he had seen her father being taken by the Germans. We had heard the news that day so knew what had happened. Every time that a Greek killed a German, the Germans would take hostages. Some would be taken off buses randomly and shot in front of the public and some would be taken as hostages and sent to work in Germany. After that my friend could not afford to keep me.

By that time the family was tired of running and being apart so we rented a farm in Heraclion outside Athens and the whole family moved there. We were quite safe and happy there but within two weeks the Germans decided to camp there. One night at about two or three in the morning my sister's brother-in-law, Raphael, came in and told us,
"You had better get out immediately because they have already taken my brother and his wife and I wouldn't be surprised if they march him up here and ask where you are hiding and pick you up. I don't know where you will hide but I warn you to get out immediately!"

So we quickly picked up our bags and went into the laundry and hid there in the cold and waited for daylight. Meanwhile we could see that the German forces at the airport were being bombed. We thought it was directed at Athens but it was protected because it was such an ancient city. Instead the port of Piraeus was badly damaged. At day light we returned to Athens to look for a new place to live in. We jumped from place to place. For a while we found somewhere where we could all hide together.

One day my brother insisted on going down to Athens to a friend's shop to get some more money from his safe. We had a premonition and begged him not to go. When he did not return we knew that he had been caught. We believe that he was betrayed. He was taken to the German headquarters in Marlin Street. They hanged him up and burnt his feet to force him to reveal where we were but he never gave us away.

We ran away again because we knew that if he talked, the Germans would come to take us away. My mother, sister and I started going from place to place.

We were told of someone who could fix us up with a nice room but when we got there, the woman did not want to take us because she knew we were Jewish. It was night-time and we pleaded with her,
"What can we do now? Please, have mercy on us. Where can we go in the darkness? They will shoot us if we are out on the streets after 6p.m."

She agreed to give us her washing room, but a Greek washing room means rats and no tiles, nothing. That night we slept there and the rats were jumping all over and the next morning we got up and my mother said,
"Thank you very much but I do not think it is fair to pay money for this stink."

In the meantime the months went by and we said that if it was our luck to be caught, we would be caught. However with our false identity cards nobody knew we were Jewish. Eventually our money started to run out and we were starving. We had enough money to stay in a hotel in the heart of Athens. We were so hungry - in fact we stole to eat. One afternoon my mother sent us to buy bread on the blackmarket near the Acropolis. While we were standing bargaining, my sister pulled my sleeve and said,
"Stop talking and come with me."
She had noticed a thief stealing four loaves of bread which he put under his coat. We chased him until he could not run anymore and he said, "What do you want from me?" and we said, "Share the bread with us."
And he did, and that night we had something to eat.
During the week we would go to the Greek school and get food from a charity there which we brought to my mother who would cook it, adding a tomato or a piece of bread. From Saturday till Monday morning we would live on grapes - grapes for breakfast, lunch, tea and dinner - grapes, grapes and more grapes.

By then the Germans were getting nasty because they knew they were losing the war and they were doing a lot of bad things to the Greeks. While we were staying in this hotel which was owned by an American Greek we were very happy. Nobody knew that we were Jewish but one night about 4a.m. we heard noises, the sounds of German boots and we felt sure that it was for us.

My mother said, "Now what's going to happen?"

We heard knocking and the opening of all the doors in the hotel until our turn came. When it came to our door the owner said, "Girls, don't worry, they are looking for somebody. Don't worry but open the door."

I thought I would be clever and hid myself under the sheets thinking they could not see me. The Germans walked in and saw me, my mother, my sister and my nephew who was staying there that night. They just shook their heads, said "Danke Schon" and left. After they left some of us opened our doors and when we looked through the window we saw all the heads looking at our room and we wondered why. We went out and asked the owner and he told us that the whole hotel knew that we were Jewish but that no one was prepared to give away that information. There and then we realized what we had not previously understood - why people often sent us gifts of bread, fruit or cheese. We also learnt that the Germans had not been looking for us but for an English spy who had been hiding in the hotel in a girlfriend's room.

We stayed in this hotel until the Germans left. Sometimes I used to see my schoolfriend with whom I had stayed the first night. She would give me some food to take to my mother. She told me that her godfather was a guard at a camp outside Athens called Haidari. Formerly a Greek army base, the Germans used it as a camp for foreign Jews.

"I am sure we can find out if your brother is there."

Within a few days the answer came back.

"Yes, Vitale Benmelech is in the camp."

We were told how we could confirm that he was alive and let him know that we were too. Every Sunday people were allowed to take little parcels containing clean clothing addressed to the prisoner and receive his dirty washing. If we brought him clothes and the following week we found a packet of dirty clothing waiting for us, we would

know that he was alive. We did not want to take my mother with us because she was old and if something happened to my sister and myself so that we had to run, she would not be able to. So we went to Haidari with a parcel containing a couple of shirts and some underwear and his name and a note saying that it came from MAMA. The following week we came back and looked. There was a mountain of parcels and amongst them we found my brother's parcel. His clothing was in rags. Some had been stitched together with string. He had put his name outside so we knew he was alive.

Not long after that the Germans left. They just opened the gates and all the Jews ran for their lives. They did not know that the Germans had retreated, they just thought that some mistake had been made.

When my brother was released he took two people to a Red Cross centre in a school. They were Greek American people named Hasson who had been taken from Rhodes Island - the wife lives today in Sea Point. *(Their story is in chapter 8.)*

Then he came to the hotel. He had been given the name by the guard via my friend. We did not recognise our brother. He had a very big scar on his face. His feet were bleeding from walking without shoes. He was dressed in rags, but thank G-d he was alive. We asked him what happened to our father. He said that he had been taken to Birkenau.

All the Athenian Jews had been sent to camps. We asked my brother how he had managed to escape. Some years before we had intended to return to Turkey and had even gone to the Turkish embassy to make arrangements. The start of the war had put a stop to our plans. When my brother was arrested, he was put in a queue to be placed in the cattle trucks. He went out of the queue and told the German Kommandant, "I am not a Greek National, I am a Turk."

He was ordered back into the line and was put on the train. However, the German had second thoughts and phoned the Turkish ambassador who said, "Yes, they are Turks", and got him out of the train. He was sent instead to the Haidari camp as a foreigner, a prisoner. He used to clean out the dustbins to eat whatever the Germans had left behind to survive. That was his lucky escape. He lives in Miami today.

We were liberated by the British and within a couple of weeks we went to the police and told them that we wanted to move back into our own home. There were already committees and you could get a letter enabling you to return to your own house. So we went back but collaborators were living there. The wife said that until she found alternate accommodation she could only allow us to live in one room and share the kitchen. The rooms were bare - all our possessions had disappeared - either the Germans or the Greeks had taken them. We moved in. On a Sunday night while we were standing there, their little boy ran out blowing a shofar.

I said to my Mother, "This is OUR Shofar." So my Mother grabbed it out of his hand and said,

"This is OURS. It doesn't belong to you."

We took it and gave it to my brother who later took s'michah and became a rabbi in the Bulgarian area of Tel Aviv. He took the shofar to Israel with him. His name is on a plaque in their shul. His son, who had been in our hotel the night the Germans came, later spent some time on Cyprus as an illegal immigrant and fought in the War of Independence.

We soon got in touch with all our friends and my sister and I were invited to a birthday party. After the party we walked home, and we could not understand why the streets were so deserted. When we came home my mother told us that Civil War had been declared. The next thing half a dozen communists came into our house with their guns and knives. I said,
" Excuse me" and slipped out between them. Everyone was standing talking. I went halfway down the stairs and reminded them, "What are you doing. We have been liberated?"

I went upstairs again into the house and I realized why they had come. They had come to collect these collaborators. That night there was firing all around us and through the walls of our house. We lay on the floor terrified. Our house was blown up so although we had returned to our home we could not live in it and we had to move again after all.

My brother then got us a house with a friend of his and we stayed there until the civil war was over. Then we found another house and the whole family lived there together. Within two years my two brothers, my sister and I had married and left Greece for ever to find somewhere where we could live in safety and be proud to be Jews. And that's our story.

Eva Davis was born in Athens on 29.8.1927 and educated there at the Plaka High School. She was a scholar until the German invasion forced her into hiding in Athens where she was liberated in October 1944. In 1947 she moved to England on her marriage and came to South Africa in 1954. She is married to Gerald and has a daughter Rita.

SHMUEL KEREN(KROLL)
Pabrade, Kemelisky, Lithuanian forests.

I was born in Pabrade, a little holiday town near Vilna which had lakes and dachas. I remember at the beginning of the war we went over the border into White Russia to stay with a Polish farmer who had a very big farm in the middle of the forest. He had a large house and was building an extension to the house where we stayed. He had two sons and a daughter and my father had given them a lot of money or possessions. We lived in the new extension to the house but in an emergency we could hide away in between the straw in his barn and nobody could find us. There was my father, my mother, my six brothers and sisters, my grandmother, my mother's sister and some other members of the family who were looked after by my father - everybody relied on him. We always thought that the war would not last long and that the Russians would come back and free the Jews.

A month before all the Jewish people in my home town had been murdered. We were lucky to escape because we had left the town to stay on this farm.

For the first time ever I really came in touch with nature all around me in the forest and on the farm. We stayed there for a while and when the winter arrived with its cold frosts the farmer suddenly came to my father and said that we must move away because he was frightened to keep us any longer in case the Germans looked for us. As a little boy I remembered the wickedness of the farmer and his sons who told us to go in the cold.

We moved from here further into White Russia. where my father had a brother about ten kilometres away. We stayed next to this small town with White Russian people for a while. Thereafter we stayed in a lot of places.

I was only a young child. I do not want to describe what happened to the rest of my family, or how they were all murdered.

As I was returning to the ghetto in Kemelisky one Saturday morning after having been sent to a farm to get food, someone said to me,
"Do not go in. The Germans are busy killing the people."
I went into the forest. instead.

By 1944 the war was still going on in Germany. Eastern Poland had been liberated by the Russians although Warsaw had not yet been taken by them. For me the war was over although a lot of soldiers remained in town. Still a little boy, I returned to my town but the houses that had belonged to my family were now occupied by other people, and I could not find anywhere to stay. I moved in with some Jewish people, friends of my father, who had survived but who were very poor. They had returned to their house but there was nothing left in it.

I thought that it would be nice if I could get back some of the things that my parents had left with this farmer who after all had not kept his side of the deal. I could not go and demand anything back because I did not know any of the details of the arrangement but I certainly needed things as I did not own more than a shirt and a pair of trousers. I did not even have a pair of shoes to wear. I thought it would be nice if I could get something to dress myself in and some food.

Every Monday a market would be held in my hometown in a beautiful place next to the river. Farmers would come from all around to sell their goods and buy what they needed. I remember before the war, about 1939 - 1941, Jewish mothers would hide their children on market days because they were afraid that the Gypsies who would come to the market would steal the children. Sometimes we would hide somewhere in the house to give our mothers a big fright because when they could not find us they would panic. I did this once.

I went to the market. It was probably in September because it was beautiful summer weather. Here I met the farmer who had chased us out, with one of his sons. I spoke to them - they were quite friendly. I told them that I had nothing to wear and they invited me to their farm and the farmer's wife said that she would give me some woven material so that I could have a shirt and trousers. I remember that they used to weave it themselves on a wooden frame. I made arrangements to go there on a certain day.

It was about 20 kilometres away, a long way from my home town for me to walk so I first went to stay with another Polish farmer. He was very caring to the Jewish people especially to my family and they had spent many days with him even after the Russians came back. (I am still in contact with the children of this farmer who remember me from when we were little children. I visited them recently)

It was easier for me to sleep on his farm and get food to eat than it was with the Jewish family who did not even have food for themselves in their own home. I slept over there - it was about three kilometres away. The next day I went over the border to the other farm.

It was a big farm with a big house and the farmer, his wife, sons and daughter were waiting for me. The farmer's wife gave me something nice to eat and a parcel of material. They were very friendly. They asked about me and took an interest in what had happened to my family and what had happened to me.

I explained to them that everyone had been murdered and that I was the only one who had survived. They asked me where I came from and where I was going to go to from their farm. I told them I was going to this farm. Before we finished talking one of their sons left us and went somewhere else, I did not know where.

When I left the farm thanking them for being so kind to me the world looked bright and nice. I thought that the world was not so bad after all; people had wanted to help me and I had managed to survive for a long time by myself even though my mother and my family had all been killed.

There was only one way from their farm to the other Polish family. There was only one road in the forest to get there. On the right hand side of the road was a big beautiful forest and on the other side of the road was a swamp. I never went through the swamp. This time I walked out of the house and I felt so happy that for no reason I decided to be naughty and go through the swamp instead of on the road like everybody else. I wanted to see what the swamp looked like so I turned left next to the barn and went through the swamp. It was very difficult to go through the swamp and I came to the other farm completely wet and dirty and had to get some water from the well to clean myself with. I was glad that I had not messed the material. I slept over there for a little with their children and then returned to my home town and made myself a jacket and trousers of which I was very proud.

After the liberation I tried to get into Palestine with the Aliyah Bet. Unfortunately our ship was intercepted by the British who sent us to a concentration camp in Cyprus. I can just remember the intolerable heat.

Years later in Israel some people from my home - town arrived. It had taken them ten years to get papers to leave Poland. They told me about the war and about what had happened and they told me about my mother who had been murdered in 1944 three days before the Russians liberated us and about the place where she had been murdered. We did not know if she had been killed by the Polish partisans or by the Polish bandits, but it was definitely not by the Germans who had already left. There were lots of Polish partisans supported from London who had been hunting down Jews because they wanted a Poland without any Jews. They were quite happy when the Germans killed the Jews and hunted them down.

We were talking about all this and that and about the farmer who had given me the material. They told me that one of his sons had killed my mother most probably because they were frightened that she would claim back whatever they had taken from us when they had promised to keep us. He shot her.

I got a great shock because the memory came back to me how very politely they had asked me which way I was returning to the other farm and how one of the sons had then disappeared. He had probably been waiting for me in the forest in order to kill me too. I had the feeling that some power had pushed me away from the clean normal road which was a short cut to the other farm and had impelled me to go through the swamp instead.

I was very upset by this story and decided to take the first opportunity to make inquiries about where the family and the sons were. I was told that the son who was suspected of killing my mother had left the farm and acquired a lorry. One day somebody had stopped him while he was driving, took him out and shot him.

I could not believe it but I did have a distant relative who stayed in town, a Communist, who with another man had taken revenge on anti-Semites who had betrayed the Jews. I could not find any evidence that it was definitely him because when I went to my home-town, they had both died and nobody knew or would tell the truth and when I asked the sons of the farmer who had been good to the Jews and to my family where the other people's farm was, they would never give me a straight answer. It was as though they were hiding something from me. One day the older brother got drunk and tried to tell me something but his younger brother quickly took him away.

Recently I have visited Lithuania several times. I have arranged to have the cemetery in my village cleaned up. The majority of the grave stones had been stolen for building material although I managed to find an uncle's tombstone. I have erected a monument to my family across the border in White Russia in a small town called Kemelisky. The monument reads:

> This is a mass grave for approximately 500 Jewish people from the Kemelisky ghetto of whom about 100 are my family who were murdered on 24.10.1942 by the Nazis and their helpers - may the murderers names and the memory be cursed for ever.

Shmuel Keren was born in Pabrade, Lithuania somewhere between 1933 and 1935 and went to school there for a few months until war broke out in 1941. He spent the war years first in the ghetto and then hiding in the forests. He was liberated in June 1944. He tried to get into Palestine as an illegal immigrant and was caught by the British and interned in a concentration camp in Cyprus. After going to Israel, he came to South Africa in 1967. He is married to Elinor and has two sons, Avi Pincus and Yonatan Shai, and two daughters, Sara Rachel and Vanya Nadavia.

PESLA LIS
Slomniki, Prokocim, Niedzwiedz

On the 19th February 1939 I married my dear husband Kalman. We went to live in Slomniki near Krakow where Kalman ran a commercial flour mill with partners. We shared a house next to the mill with his partner, Shabsa Finkelstein. A few months later, the war broke out. The Polish government ordered civilians to run away East to avoid falling into the hands of the Germans. We went to Koszyce where my parents lived while my husband moved further away. The first week of the war the Germans soldiers made Jews do humiliating work like cleaning their lorries or the streets. When they knocked at the door of our house one day at 7 a.m. we were afraid to open it. My father, who was a well known and respected councillor and president of the congregation was still in his tefillin. When the two Germans saw this, they pointed their bayoneted rifles at him. I ran in front of my father and said ,

"You had better kill me! Leave my father"

This was the first time I faced death eye to eye. Somehow they apologized and left. From our house they went to the Rabbi who lived in the same street, took him out to the field where the army lorries had parked for the day, tore his beard, tortured him and left him on the field where he was later found and taken to the doctor.

A few weeks later my husband and the other men returned as the roads were filled with refugees fleeing on foot with their parcels as there was a shortage of petrol, of food and water. We decided to return to Slomniki.

One day the Germans came to the mill, hit my husband on the head twice, took away his keys and cash, and threw us out of the house leaving everything behind inside. We were luckily able to move in with my in-laws who had a two-roomed flat. After that, conditions deteriorated - every day something else happened. One day a boy we knew was taken off the streets - no one knew what happened to him; the next day acquaintances were humiliated and tortured by drunk German soldiers just for the fun of it.

Refugees from Krakow started pouring in, fleeing from the ghetto that was being built there. We found accommodation for them, started an epidemic hospital because typhus began to spread and established a soup kitchen in which I was involved. One day all the Jewish families in our block of flats had to vacate them for German officers. It was very difficult to find accommodation but somehow through my contacts with the welfare work a family invited us to share with them. The other half of their house was occupied by a VolksDeutch who ran a restaurant and bottle store for Germans, but we managed to have good relations with them, and we stayed on.

Daily life was pretty grim. We sold our possessions for food and later my husband managed to get a job in the Judenrat handling the labour contingents. One day in May 1942, the Germans came at 4 a.m. to the house where we lived with the Orbach family, ignored them but came straight to our room and gave us 5 minutes to get ready to go with them. There were Polish soldiers with them saying,

"Those are the Lis's"

They took us to the synagogue which was full of people; a third of the Jewish population in the town was there. I felt better when I realized that we were not the only people. Soon there was no more standing room. We stayed there for three days, then lorries arrived to take us away somewhere.

The Jewish community was expected to pay for the transport. Before the transport arrived, the President of the Judenrat got my husband out to help organize the collection of the money. I decided that I was not going to remain by myself. We had previously arranged a meeting place in case we had to escape. I timed my escape while the Germans and VolkDeutsches who were guarding the place were having breakfast. I got permission to go to the toilet and from there I went through the backstreets with a shawl over my head to the entrance of a bakery whose owner was a client of ours. He gave me shelter in his small pantry amongst the sacks of flour and other things. The next day after the lorries had left, I came out of hiding.

After that, we moved in with Gentile people who gave us a room. We moved in there thinking that this was the end of the story. Unfortunately on Yom Kippur there was another expulsion. People from neighbouring towns like Proszowice and Scala were collected and taken to OUR fields near the mill. There once more they waited for the unknown. I was still working in the soup kitchen, busy till curfew time carrying food, medicine, messages and other necessities to these people. On the third day they took them to the station and put them on a train to the unknown. Before leaving they gathered the old and sick and shot them, throwing the bodies in a trench.

We knew that the train was going to Krakow but we had no clue what happened after that. We wore armbands with Magen Davids; we were not allowed into post offices; there were no telephones; no communication. Only word of mouth. We were isolated from the news. We tried to find out what was happening but everything was so secretive. We tried to get information through my husband's Gentile contacts in the Grain Stock Exchange, of which he was a member and through the anti-Nazi restaurant owner who catered for Germans. A week later one of these contacts returned to tell us that he had followed their trail to Lublin. Two miles away from the camp guards would come and take over the train and bring it back empty. He said that there was no access to the camp and that nobody knew what was happening inside.

No mail service went to the camp.

Nobody escaped through the electrified fences.

Nobody came back.

Next to Lublin was Majdanek where there was an extermination camp with crematoria of which we learnt after the war but in 1942 our fantasy could never go as far as to imagine such a thing.

A few Jews were still left in town. We stayed in the same room hoping that the war would soon end. One day a neighbour, a Jewish policeman, came to warn us that there was going to be an eviction from my parent's town and he suggested that I send for them. We went to the churchyard at noon on Sunday to find one of the peasants who transported goods for my husband, called Twardowski, to ask him if he would go to fetch my parents. Then we heard that we too were going to be evicted and he promised us that he would look after us if it were necessary.

My parents, younger brother and sister were killed on the 2nd November 1942 in Majdanek, Poland having been taken away in a transport.

Early one November morning there was another round-up in our town and we were all taken so that the town would be Judenrein. Before we left, they took all the old people to the fields around our mill and killed them, and the other Jews had to dig a large ditch and throw them in. Some women went into labour there and were also killed - they were called "non-productive."

The lorries took us to a labour camp at Prokocim near Krakow, 30 Km from Slomniki near to a railway station for freight trains and near a large forest. The older ones remained on the lorries and the younger ones were ordered to get off. Before entering the barracks at Prokocim the Commander gave us a little speech ordering us to surrender all our valuables, and a big dish was passed around. Two people were taken out and searched. On one a watch was found and he was killed in front of us. This was our welcome to Prokocim.

Work did not frighten us so we did not feel so alarmed. But the conditions were unbearable. We were overcrowded and undernourished and I soon lost a lot of weight, suffered from malnutrition and some of my teeth fell out. I cleaned latrines, tended prisoners suffering from typhus in the sick bay and did heavy work in the kitchen. I was sometimes beaten. Once a guard hit me over the back because he felt that I was not sufficiently respectful and I have had problems ever since from the damage he caused to my spine and coccyx.

We realized that we would not survive there so after six months we decided to escape. Peasant women used to come to the gates to sell milk to the groups leaving to go out to work. We timed our escape for that moment. My husband looked as though he was going out with the work party and from the other side I escaped through a hole. I was thin enough to escape through any hole. We ran away to the forest and from there started to walk back to Slomniki where we hoped to find a place to stay with someone we knew - Kalman's parents and grandparents had been born there.

We slept in the forest under a very thick bush and during the day hid in the dense undergrowth. For a week we stayed with a peasant Kalman knew well, hidden under the cowshed roof adjourning the house. After four days our peasant quarreled with his girl friend who lived across the road and knew about us. She reported him to the police. In the evening two German policemen came and demanded that he show them the Jews, but he denied everything. They went up the ladder to the roof and looked around by torchlight but did not see the small hole leading to the other lower ceiling and went away with the peasant. He was released after one and a half days having convinced the police that he had never seen any Jews. We had to leave the place that night and went through the thick forest towards the village where our friend Mikolaj Twardowski lived.

There were posters all around the village warning that people found helping Jews would be shot together with their whole family and stating that any Jews found were to be caught and brought to the police station.

Mikolaj lived in a village called Niedzwiedz in a two roomed clay farm house with his wife and three children on a small farm of 4 morgen. He grew tobacco, grain and vegetables. The tobacco was grown for the Germans and all crops had to be delivered to them for payment in spirits. Mikolaj took pity on us and agreed to let us stay there temporarily in the cellar off the pantry where the produce was stored for the winter. We told him that my four brothers in Rhodesia would pay in full for our board and lodging after the war. Originally we said that we would only stay there for eight days until we could organize alternate accommodation. When he wanted us to leave it was full moon and too dangerous; when the moon was dark we used to pray and beg him to let us stay on .

Eventually we stayed with him for twenty months buried in his six foot by five and a half foot cellar which was dark, dank and infested with rats, mice, frogs, bugs and insects.

We told another couple whom we trusted where we were going. They were hidden three villages away. Neighbours became suspicious because smoke was seen coming from the chimney at night so the peasants forced them to leave. Men they knew were supposed to help them return to Prokocim camp but instead two men came who said that they were from the Polish Underground and demanded money first. The couple said that they had no money but would give them the address of people who had - and gave them our address.

One Sunday morning two chaps arrived and told Mikolaj that they knew there were two Jews there and demanded to speak to us. He wanted to know how they knew and what they were coming for - he thought we had arranged something. He was furious but eventually had to show them where we were. He opened the pantry door and showed them the cellar. They told us that they were from the underground and needed money and knew we had money - every Jew had money!

We did not have any since we had left our money and last possessions with prominent non- Jewish people in Slomniki. We told them that we had nothing on us but would send to our friends for money which we would have ready for them by the following

Sunday. On the way out they took my husband's watch which was lying on the stone where we kept our things.

They returned the following Sunday but in the meantime we had hidden in the barn. It was winter and very cold and the peasant covered us with straw and would bring us food and water. The peasant told them that we had run away into the forest and he had no idea where we had gone. They looked all over the farm, could not find us and left disappointed.

After that we managed to persuade Mikolaj to partition off the cellar which was divided into two, one for potatoes and vegetables, the other for coal and wood. We suggested that he close up the entrance to the second cellar - it was easy because the house and floor was made of clay. From the pantry, he cut out a hole and on top of this hole they put the fodder box for the cows and the pigs. We were safe and isolated there. Each cellar had a little window so that we even had a little light although it was overgrown from outside. This solved the problem.

One day two Germans came to the farm wanting to buy poultry. They noticed a patch of unharvested tobacco. It was past delivery time so this meant that it was part of a second crop which on the black market would fetch six or seven times its minimum price in cash. They gave the peasant a good thrashing and asked him to show them where he kept his undelivered tobacco. Mikolaj said that he did not have any more but they did not believe him and they came with two police dogs. We heard the commotion outside but could not get out. They searched the house even under the beds and underneath the hatching chickens and opened up the pantry where the dogs sniffed around. I could already visualize myself being marched to the police station and had buttoned my jersey in preparation. We covered our faces tightly with our eiderdowns so that the dogs would not hear us breathing and they went away.

After this incident, M Twardowski was very frightened and determined that we leave but we had no place to go to and stayed on. He had a friend who was a carpenter with a German name, Weirich. His wife sold milk outside the Prokocim camp. He himself was lazy and did not work but was capable of doing anything. He said to Mikolaj,

" You want to get rid of these people? Alright, I shall help you."

One night Weirich came over and climbed down the hole and spoke to us. We knew him vaguely and realized what would follow. He told us that Mikolaj had three small children and was a very fearful person, but that he would look after us if we went to him as he was not afraid of Germans or anyone. We should be safe at his place and he wanted us to go with him that very night as it was a dark, moonless night. He would take us immediately through the dark forest and we would soon be safe at his house. I suddenly got a terrible pain, I felt shaky and my whole body felt as though an electric wave or a heat wave had gone through it. I knew what this meant - a dark night, a dark forest and two unidentified bodies.

I told him that I knew that he was a nice man and wanted to save us and I was grateful, but look at me - I would not be able to walk, I was not well. He could not carry me on his back, nor could my husband and it was a long way. We would go to him but first I must get better. I touched his hand and he took his hand away quickly and said it was like fire.

He told Mikolaj he could not make the journey when he was sober. He needed first to drink some home made liquor which the peasants brewed and sold illegally. They sent Mikolaj's son around to get liquor even though it was past the curfew because what Weirich needed to do afterwards he could not do when sober. The son returned to say that he could not get any. He went to one place - they did not have any more; to another place - it wasn't ready; a third place was sold out. So Weirich left us saying 'Goodnight' and that we should see each other again. When he went up, I stood on my husband's shoulders and listened through the bottom of the floor to their conversation. I could hear scraps of their conversation. He said to Mikolaj,

" Look at this. Three places where liquor is sold every night and not one of them had liquor tonight. I wanted to take them away but I got limp and she was sick and had a temperature. I can't take her to my home where she will lie in bed - what would I do with her? So I shall have to do it in the forest and I can't do it when I am sober. I think they are holy people. Tomorrow you must give them a very good lunch and feed them up for a week or two so that they get healthy, then we shall talk again. You had better look after them because they are holy people." Although a would-be professional killer, I must have touched a soft spot in him.

Mikolai did have a certain feeling for us and enjoyed discussing religion while lying on the floor with his head in the hole. At the end of our conversations, he would say, "Do you believe in G- d?"
We would answer,
"Yes, of course. We will survive and you will survive and we will see that justice will be done to our oppressors and killers."

I somehow had an overpowering feeling that we would survive and I never let the thought that it might not happen come into my mind. Auto-suggestion is too mild a word, and I prayed to G-d to give us strength to survive to see the downfall of these murderers who were threatening the whole world. After the war Mikolaj called me 'PROPHET' because we did manage to survive and watched the defeat of the German army who fled in disarray in all directions.

As the front advanced, the Germans began to dig trenches near the house. We realized that they were preparing for battle and we had to do something. Mikolaj came and told us that it was no longer safe and that he was going to take his family to the forest. He felt that we could not go out because we looked like ghosts, white like sheets, and people would realize at once that we were Jews and would capture us.

We had found out that my husband's brother and two others had also run away from Prokocim and were hiding with Weirich, who agreed to take us also. We had no alternative and had to go there. I was dressed like a peasant woman and my husband was put on a cart covered with hay and straw and we were taken to the carpenter's house where the others were. There we stayed in a barn under which he dug a big hole covered by wooden planks and bundles of straw and hay. There was a concealed door which we could open. We stayed there safely until the end of the war when we were liberated by the Russians in February 1945.

A week after liberation when it was safer we returned to Slomniki. We walked for a few hours and then got a lift with a Russian soldier and reached a friend in Slomniki late afternoon. My husband and brother- in- law went to the Feld Kommandant and managed to get the keys for the mill and started to work again. It took some time to obtain papers of legal ownership. Two weeks later two men arrived with documents from the district officer appointing them as the manager to run the mill and we had to hand over the keys to them. Two month later we received the certificate of ownership and took back the running of the business.

At midnight a few weeks later, eight armed men from the Polish right wing underground arrived and removed the transmission belts threatening to kill us. Luckily, after we had pleaded with them, the leader came in saying that nobody had anything against us so they took our cash and went away. After that we moved out of the house and went to live with friends who had also returned from hiding.

The following night a Jewish man who had returned from the camps and claimed back his house was shot dead together with his cousin who was also sleeping there - the killers had not wanted to leave a witness. There and then we decided that I should go to Krakow to stay with my two aunts and cousin who had survived on Christian papers and had been given back their large pre - war flat and my husband would follow as soon as he could arrange his business affairs.

One evening after the six p.m. curfew there was a loud banging on the door and when I opened it four young masked men with revolvers in their hands pushed themselves in wanting to see my cousin who was in the bedroom with the others. I remained in the first room alone standing next to the open second floor window, realizing that they intended to kill my cousins whom they had been blackmailing afraid that now that the war had ended she would take revenge as her sister-in-law was the wife of the Minister of Culture in the Polish government who had great influence. I jumped out of the window into the courtyard screaming for help. The other tenant came out to see what was happening and the four men hearing the screams ran away as fast as they could. Luckily I only tore a ligament in my right foot and had to be in bed for a while.

We managed to get a flat sharing it with Kalman's cousin and on the 24.12. 1945 my gorgeous son was born.

One Friday in April 1946 our neighbour told us that some women at the Miadowa street market had been chasing a Jewish man accusing him of abducting the one woman's son to obtain blood for Passover. Police arrived along with her son who had gone to buy an icecream. Soon after we heard of the pogrom in Kielce where several Jews were killed because they were accused of supporting the Communists.

There was much insecurity among the remaining Jews and whoever could manage it, tried to be smuggled across the borders out of Poland. We sent letters to Rhodesia via friends who had left for England and waited patiently for the permit to arrive. By the end of 1947 it came and after much hard effort we managed to collect the necessary documents before the expiry date of 5.6.1948 and left for Brussels where we boarded the plane for Rhodesia where I had a large family waiting for me.

Weirich died after the war from a burst appendix - in the same way that he ignored morals, ethics and Nazis, he also ignored doctors and did not believe them when they said he needed an operation. Mikolaj died some time ago of cirrhosis of the liver but his wife Otylia and his children are still in contact with me and we regularly exchange letters and my children and I send them parcels of clothing and other goods. This help is much appreciated.

After living happily in Rhodesia for 28 years we moved to Sea Point in 1976 when Kalman retired. When they learnt of his death in 1993, Mrs Twardowski and her five children collected for a special commemorative gathering and said prayers for him. I sent them his clothes. Otylia is an old woman now and tells everyone that she owes her longevity to the fact that she saved two Jews during the war.

PESLA LIS was born and educated in Koszyce, near Kielce, Poland in 1915. She worked as a book keeper and secretary before being sent with her husband Kalman to the Prokocim labour camp and then going into hiding in Poland. After liberation in February 1945 in Slomniki she lived in Krakow before moving to Rhodesia in 1976. She has a son Roman and a daughter Rena.

Chapter 5

LIFE IN CAPTIVITY

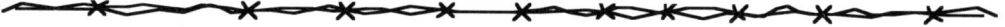

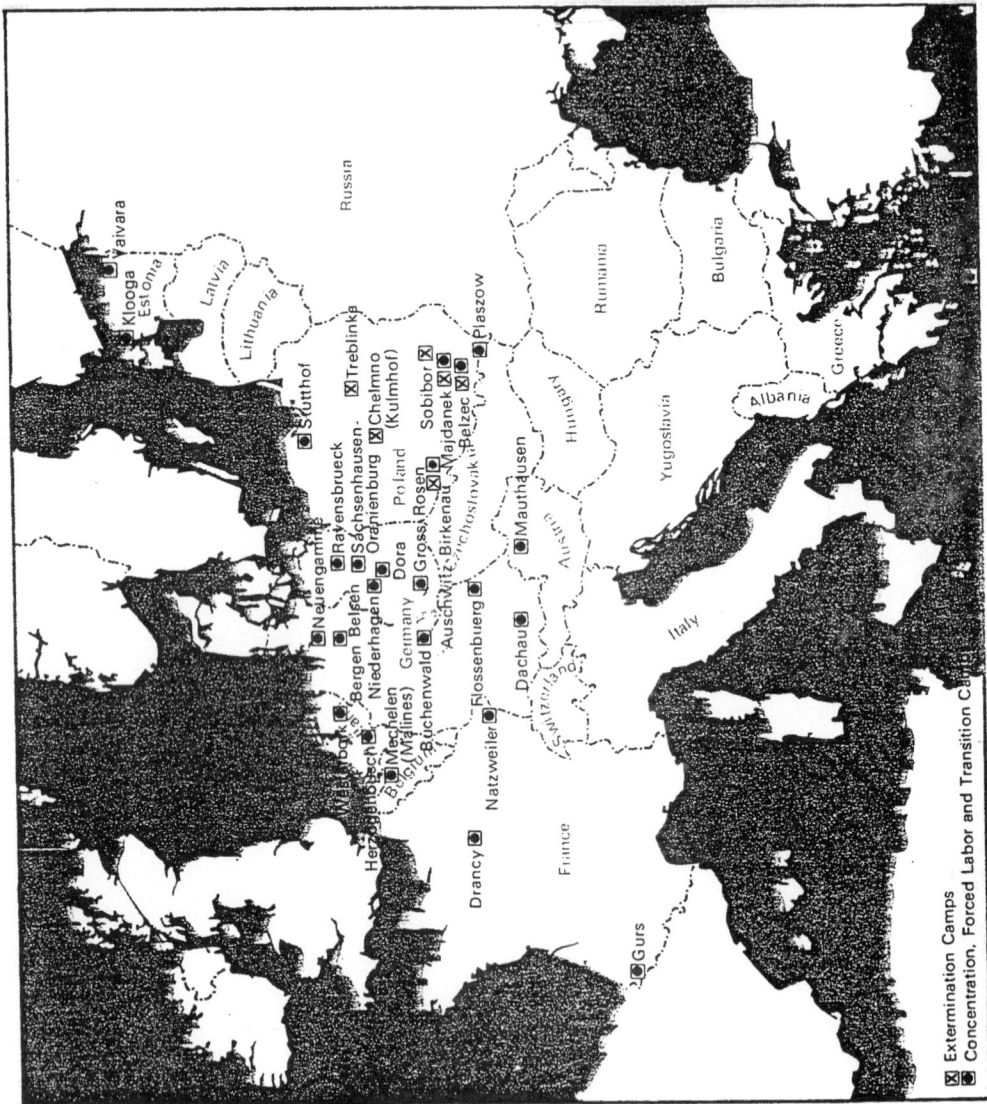

Major concentration, forced labour, transit and extermination camps in Europe, World War II
Encyclopedia Judaica

XAVIER PIAT-KA

Vilna, Lager Kunda, K.Z.Stutthoff, Lager Burgraben, Danzig

To us survivors, Holocaust Remembrance Day is not only on the officially prescribed Yom Hashoah, but every day.

The past lives with the present even more acutely with the passing of time. Memories are relived during conversation. Pictures of the past, sometimes distorted, frighten the restless nights. One is burdened by the weight of what one has experienced during the years - the unforgettable years of lost youth, and innocence; the unhappy years, of growing up with the scaffold of death over one's head. Without a family, without love but always hungry and thirsty, humiliated, beaten up and tortured, deprived of the sense of being human, yet still with hope, the unbelievable ray of forceful brightness in one's soul which made us, the survivors, endure and persevere and accumulate the power to remember and the will to outlive the tyranical era of Nazi murder and annihilation of our people.

Without memory, we would live the curse of an isolated present, a moment in time without history, and therefore without future. It would be a life without texture and meaning, without pain or pleasure, without sadnesss or joy, without ugliness or beauty, without memory or perspective. Yet memories may not be pleasant or kind. They may arrive at the worst possible time, but they give our life its special quality. I state affirmatively: I remember, therefore I am.

The Holocaust continued to pierce, to haunt, to stir up emotions not only in us, the survivors, but also in our children and their children. When the last living survivor of the Holocaust dies, the obligation to remember what happened in Europe during World War II will fall on generations who were not there. All we have now are family memories and the ceremonial commemoration on Yom Hashoah. Remembrance can be a painful burden and this Book of Memories will keep alive the flame of the survivors to be handed over from one generation to the next with the message NEVER AGAIN!

I, Xavier Piat-ka, son of Zacharyash ben Reuben Jutan and Basya (Vava) nee Goldman, testify under my solemn oath that the following episodes in my life are factually true: I have selected to document them from the many that I have lived through as a response to the neo-Nazi revisionism of history and their denial of the Holocaust.

On my desk I keep a photograph of a family gathering to celebrate my 21st birthday held in our house in Vilna. More than fifty people drank a toast to my health and success.

Within a few years they had all perished in the avalanche of Nazi persecution and murder in the ghettos and concentration camps.

The photograph reminds me of the important task we survivors have taken upon ourselves to bear witnesss to what we Jews went through during those dreadful years of systematic annihilation by the Nazis.

In the immediate after-war period it was painful to talk about one's experiences. The wounds were still bleeding, the loneliness unbearable and the urgency to come back to a normal life took priority. But very soon with the full realization of the enormity of the Holocaust, an overpowering urge forced us to speak out, to cry out our anguish, to tell all, to testify and make known the unbelievable facts of the crimes committed. I was one of the many who experienced in the ghetto the dehumanisation, the degradation, the starvation, the heavy labour inflicted upon the undernourished. I saw the "*liquidation*" of masses of ghetto inhabitants. I knew of the massacres of children and elderly, all masterminded to bring to a minimum the number of living Jews.

I was the object of inhuman treatment by the concentration camp officers and their underlings. I saw their savagery and bestiality. Till today the gas-chambers and the factories of death are the subject of my nightmares.

I still don't know why Fate chose me to stay alive. In many cases I was helped by comrades in difficult situations. And yet the inner strength and determination to outlive the oppressor helped and gave me the courage to survive. Perhaps luck was on my side too.

I remember that particular Yom Kippur night in the Vilna ghetto. Although we were accustomed to eating little, we were eagerly awaiting sundown, which heralded the end of the fast and the traditional small feast to which we were all looking forward.

The evening prayers were just about to start when the wooden gates of the ghetto suddenly opened and SS men, with death-skull insignia on their uniforms, rushed in and with the help of Lithuanian policemen started to round-up men, women and children from the streets, synagogues, yards and cellars.

Herded together, the Jews were forced to run towards a square where a company of German soldiers and Lithuanian police with machine guns already- aimed were awaiting them.

"*Raus, raus zur Arbeit!*"
These orders from the Nazi SS men were mixed with the screams of the children calling their parents, the shouts of wives for their nearest and the prayers to the Almighty recited loudly by old people.

I remember the frightening cries of the panic- stricken crowds and I can recall my feelings of doom. In the evening darkness, the strict "black out" regulations were forgotten. The streets of the ghetto for the first time sparkled strangely with the flickering lights of many candles, torches and car lights from the trucks the Germans brought in to remove the sick and the elderly from the hospital.

The pandemonium increased when the Germans started to use their rifles and bayonets to beat those who didn't or couldn't move and to kick with their boots those

who ran too slowly.

Unperturbed by the tumult and cries, the SS men dragged people from their homes and pushed them toward the ghetto gates at the end of Rudnicka Street.

With the realization that the Germans had come to take us not to work but to our death, people began frantically to look for a place to hide, to escape. Secret passages, prepared in advance, were opened and quickly closed when filled with people. I managed to escape from the street where I had been caught in a group, and ran to the block where we lived to join my father in the attic - our hideout.

Fifteen of us crammed into this small space. Not a word was spoken, not a move was made when we heard, through the thin walls, heavy steps and shouts in German. No one uttered a sound when we heard the Germans screaming at the two elderly ladies from the nearby apartment who were too ill to move by themselves. We listened to the sound of them being dragged down the stair-case. Mrs.M nearly choked her two-year old daughter keeping her hand over the child's mouth.

We were sweating profusely. My father's hand was clutching my right shoulder - was it for reassurance or from fright? After some time the mumbled cries and noises simmered down. We heard some movement from the floor below, then steps in our flats and unrecognisable talk, and a knock and then another on the wall leading to our secret place. Fear gripped my entire body. This was it! We had been been betrayed! The Germans would take us away! Nobody moved, my Father prayed silently. Immobile, with our hearts trying to jump out through our throats we waited. My father's hand was no longer on me, he had bent down, and I tried silently to help him. It was one of his cardiac attacks.

We heard a distinct shout in Yiddish: "It is over! The Germans have left the ghetto".

After a while we opened the passage and went out slowly. A neighbour, who had escaped from the slaughter, greeted us. We moved my father onto a bed and gave him his pill. I remember my aunt enquired about the meal, but we didn't feel hungry. I went down into the street; people talked about the *"actions"*. Rumours were sweeping through the ghetto. Some still believed that it was an "action" to do some work somewhere.

"You know the Nazis specially did it on a Jewish sacred day"....

At the administration centre officials were trying to register the missing, to restore some kind of order, but to no avail. That Yom Kippur night, full of turmoil and despair, seemed to be the longest night to them all. I remember not going to sleep that night and being counted wearily at dawn on my way out to work at the German barracks at the airport.

The Germans took away over five thousand people on this autumn day in 1941. They were driven to the Ponary forest, 12 kilometers away from Vilna, where they were shot and pushed into the ravines. I recall that a few days after Yom Kippur one of the survivors of the Ponary massacre of the Jews was smuggled into the ghetto. He told us about the beatings in the forest during the march to the ravines, about being subdued, half-alive and ordered on the spot to undress in groups. Then they were shot at by several machine gunners, pushed into holes in the earth. Their bodies were covered by further waves of bodies killed on the same spot. The last group of Jews left were given spades and ordered to cover the mass graves with soil before they too were shot at dawn.

Although wounded in his thigh, he had survived by faking death when SS men had inspected the results of their shooting during the day. After several dreadful hours half-covered with dead bodies and soil, he had managed to make his way out of the forest at night to a nearby Polish village where a friendly woman had given him shelter. She had treated his wound and arranged for him to reach a group of Jewish labourers on a daily assignment in the fields.

The ghetto was now in deep mourning. Nobody believed the statements of the Germans that "the ghetto is now safe and no more "Actions" will take place." The murder of innocent people was now an undeniable fact. We realised that the Germans could prepare more Yom Kippur nights for us. We were encaged in the ghetto, without any help from the outside world, surrounded by a hostile local population and an inhuman world. We were left to the mercy of Nazi murderers.

My father, Zacharyasz Jutan, and I survived these "actions" only to be evacuated in September 1943 to the concentration camps in the Baltic states. From Estonia I was sent by ship to the Stutthof Camp near the Port of Danzig where I was with him again. I last saw my father, a medical practitioner, in Autumn 1944 when he was sent to a camp near Koenigsberg, East Prussia. He did not survive.

At Stutthof I worked in the quarry breaking up and moving huge stones. I became friendly with Rachmiel Malinker, a house painter, who was tall and strong and used to help me with the large rocks. He and I became the Stutthof Latrine Painters. As the paint was stored in the kitchen, we sometimes got extra food.

As the Russians began to approach, there were rumours that the camp was to be evacuated or liquidated. There was a call for welders, so Rachmiel and I registered as welders and were sent by train to the Burgraben camp near the docks in Danzig. Our 80 year old German foreman was instructed to teach us how to weld. My welding was problematic but at least the work provided a roof over our heads from the unbearable cold, wind and snow outside. There were twelve welders in our group and each day the foreman would "throw away" some bread or an apple in the waste basket and we would take turns eating it - my turn came every twelfth day. It was his way of giving us a little nourishment.

Twice a day at Burgraben we had to stand appel. Thousands of us would stand endlessly in long rows, our tin cups dangling from string belts around our thin waists, I could feel the icy cold of the metal cup right through the paper-thin striped uniform that was our only clothing. No one was allowed to move until they had finished counting us. The fallen were accounted for and after roll call bodies were removed by those who stood nearest and dumped outside the camp into mass graves. Armed SS soldiers watched everything from their high towers ready to shoot any interruption to the appel. After morning appel we would be marched to the harbour to the welding shop.

The end of the war was approaching and our old foreman kept on muttering *"wir sind kaput" (We're finished)*. Suddenly the welding shop was closed and an SS officer told us that we were to be evacuated to Germany. We were forcibly marched northwest while the SS guards pushed us and shouted that we must move faster,

"Schnell, schnell marchieren!"

I found it difficult to march in the snow in my wooden shoes which absorbed a lot of snow, but Rachmiel supported and encouraged me. Late that evening we reached the outskirts of a village where the SS locked us into a church. They did not want the German villagers to see us. What a turnabout from the early days of occupation when they paraded us publicly to show what pathetic creatures these Jews, these pitiful, degraded, filthy walking skeletons, were. I saw an elderly woman sneak into the back entrance of the church quietly distributing food to a few lucky prisoners near the door.

We managed to sleep for a few hours, some on the cold floor, others on the pews. The three who died during the night were deposited in the field and we were marched out again into the frosty night. By morning we had reached another village where we were housed in an empty school. This time many faces stared at us through the windows. At noon some soup was distributed and marching resumed. Many of us died that night - some from exhaustion, some were shot by the SS for marching too slowly and others were shot for no reason at all. By now we were being marched very briskly, we must rush faster, faster - they were in a hurry to get us to a village by dawn, hitting those who could not keep up the tempo, using rifle butts to speed our feet along. I remember feeling that my lungs would burst, my body ached, my legs were numb but Rachmiel kept on encouraging me.

" We shall make it, do not fail me, you are doing fine."

He kept me going.

On the fourth night we reached a side road in a forest and a deserted camp near Lauenburg, in East Germany, surrounded by barbed wire where there were two empty barracks, some huts and a kitchen. In a pile of snow we found the belongings of former inmates - shoes, blankets and various kitchen utensils. We collapsed exhausted onto the bare cement floor. I found a corner near the window where I sat and watched the falling snow. Rachmiel found me and brought me some snow to drink and a piece of bread. He spoke to the guards and went with them to the nearby village . An old horse was brought back - food and soup for a few days.

The prisoners began to get sick, I too became light headed and ill. Rachmiel said that I must drink a lot of snow. He realized that I had become infected with typhus. All the POWs who had been living in this camp before had died of typhus. Knowing this, the Germans had driven us into the camp which was surrounded by barbed wire while they lived outside, and were waiting for us to contract typhus and die. In the night I staggered out half-blind over sleeping people to get outside to relieve myself; in the morning I was delirious. Rachmiel made cold compresses of snow for my head and fed me cold water. He sat beside me on the floor, his blanket under my head. I remember wanting to hit him for interfering with me.

"Let me die," I screamed, "Let me go and be finished with these awful wretched feelings in my stomach."

In the distance we could hear the rumble of many planes and bombardments. The Russians must have been very near. The SS men were preparing to leave. Rachmiel was scared that the guards might try to burn down the camp with us inside, so he secretly made an opening in the fence. In the middle of the night he covered me with a blanket and somehow managed to push me through a back window near the barbed wire fence. I weighed about 40 kg by that time and with me over his shoulder he stumbled through the forest until he came to an old farm house. He ordered the frightened old German couple to find a bed for me. They first washed me with hot water, then put me in a clean bed in a back room. Rachmiel asked for a bottle of schnapps (brandy), poured some of the alcohol into me and then used the rest to rub the lice off my body.

After a few days I awoke as though in a dream to find myself in a strange bed, three cushions under my head and a beautiful quilted duvet covering my body. Here was I in a strange house being fed good food by two German-speaking strangers! Then I saw Rachmiel Malinker. He took my weak hand in his and said;

"Glad to have you back in the land of the living, my friend!"

He told me that the day before, March 8th, 1945, the Russians had passed through the village and the Red Army soldiers had found the camp filled with nearly dead prisoners. On learning from survivors that they were Jews, the Russian officer seemed surprised that Hitler had not finished them all off. So that was the welcome from their liberators.

A few days later Rachmiel arranged for a horse and carriage to take me to Lauenburg. There we met a few other camp survivors from Vilna who had known me when I had been a Zionist youth leader and we all moved into an empty three story house. The boys helped nurse me to better health. One day they came to tell me that there were some Vilna girls in a nearby transit camp. I said that they should bring them to stay with us so that they would be safe from the rampaging Russian troops. We hid them on the second floor of our house. And that is how I met Chayela, my future wife, and her sister (who lives today in Israel). They had been miraculously saved from being disposed of via one of the barges sent out into the Baltic Sea.

We got married in Bydgoszcz and stayed in Polish-liberated Silesia, where I was treated for wartime injuries and wrote about art and theatre in the local press and my wife resumed her acting career in the touring State Jewish Theatre in Wroclaw. We went to Paris to try to find my mother, Vava, who had remained in France during the German occupation under the protection of Russian documents. I discovered that she had been caught helping Jews and sent in 1944 to Auschwitz where she was gassed upon arrival.

Photo of Xavier at his desk, Cape Town 1955

And Rachmiel Malinker? When I was stronger, he left Lauenburg for Lithuania to search for his wife and child. He was lucky enough to find them and they now live in Israel. My life and liberation I owe to him.

XAVIER PIAT-KA studied languages at the University of Vilna and Paris. Military duties found him in the Polish Army in 1939 in Vilna, where he saw the town occupied by the Soviets, the Lithuanians and then the Germans. Piat-ka was herded with the other Jews into the ghetto and then to Lager Kunda, Stutthof and Lager Danzig. With his wife, Chayela Rosenthal, (see following article) he moved to Cape Town in 1951. She died in 1979. He is a journalist and writes on a variety of subjects, of which the Holocaust was the main topic. They have two daughters Naava and Zola.

CHAYELA ROSENTHAL-PIATKA

(As told by her husband Xavier)

Kaiserwald

C hayela Rosenthal-Piatka was born in Vilna, Poland to Fruma and Nohum Rozental. Her father published the afternoon Yiddish daily. Her brother, Leib, was a Yiddish writer and poet. Chayela's own dramatic talents were recognized early and she participated in several plays at the Epstein High School and was chosen during the Soviet occupation of Lithuania to represent Vilna in the All-Soviet Festival of Songs in Moscow in July 1941.

Before she could go, her world crumbled. On June 24th the German army entered Vilna to the cheers and flowers of the Lithuanian populace. The German invasion caught Jewish Vilna unaware. Her father was taken away by soldiers and did not return. In September, Chayela, her mother, sister and brother were driven from their comfortable home to the ghetto. She had to work outside the ghetto to support her ailing mother.

When Jacob Gens, the ghetto chief, announced plans for a theatre company, many Jewish intellectuals and rabbis objected, plastering the ghetto with leaflets stating,

"YOU DON'T PERFORM THEATRE IN A GRAVEYARD."

However plans for a theatre went ahead and Chayele was asked to join the actor's group. The plays, musicals and revues soon became very popular and accepted as a necessary boost for morale and hope for survival. Nothing could keep audiences away, even the presence of German and Lithuanian officers in the audience. At the end of their first year, the group had given 111 performances selling 34, 804 tickets.

Chayele starred in many roles in these plays and revues. Her songs from *"Peshe fun Reshe"* became so popular that they were sung by the ghetto youth. With her youthful vitality and sense of humour and compassion, she soon became known as the *"Wunderkind of*

Chayela Rosenthal as she appeared in a Polish film "Children in Ghetto" in 1946

the Vilna Ghetto," At moments of crisis, Jacob Gens would order the theatre to perform in an attempt to distract and reassure the ghetto audience. Chayele became the *"Songstress of Hope"* in the midst of their suffering.

In September 1943 the Germans began to liquidate the ghetto. Rehearsals continued until the final liquidation and deportees often attended performances the night before they were led away, in fact the songs of the revue *Moyshe Halt Zich* (Moyshe Hold On), which had its premiere during the final deportations, accompanied the last of the Vilna Jews on their way to the extermination camps.

Chayele and her sister Mary were deported to labour camps in Kaiserwald, Riga. With her singing she gave the inmates a gleam of hope and the strength to survive. They loved her songs and in return shared food with her and took care of her when she was sick.

Chayela, thin and shaven-haired, was liberated in March 1945 in Lembork, where I was. We met and got married in June in Bydgoszcz. Soon she was performing in the Yiddish State Theatre in Wroclaw, Lower Silesia to the applause of a multitude of Jewish survivors of the Holocaust and refugees from Russian exile.

Once again she was bringing her audience

hope and the strength to endure. With the help of New York impresario Sol Hurok and American Jewish comedienne Molly Picon, she toured DP camps in Germany, and sang in Paris and other centres in Europe and South Africa. She then toured America starring on Broadway.

In 1951 we settled in Cape Town where she continued to delight South African audiences in plays, one woman shows and on TV. Her last starring role was that of Golde in the CAPAB presentation of 'Fiddler on the Roof' at the Nico Malan Opera House. She was terminally ill but lived fully on the stage till the last curtain, dying one week after the show ended, on 1st September 1979.

To the Cape Town survivors she was the hostess at many meetings, a source of conso-lation and tower of strength to the needy amongst us. To me, her husband, she was a joy of love, a true companion in bad and happy situations in the adventures of life and an excellent mother to our two daughters.

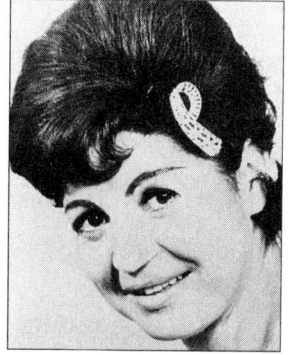

Chayela Rosenthal

As a tribute to her memory in 1987 CAPAB staged Sobol's play, "Ghetto", with Aviva Pelham, based on some factual events of Chayela's experiences in the Vilna Ghetto.

BELLA VARKEL
Vilna, Narocz forest, Italy

I lived in Vilna with my mother, two sisters and a brother. My father died when I was eighteen months old. When I passed Std 7, I went to work in a factory in Kovno with my elder sister Rita. When war broke out we ran to the station and caught a train that would take us into Russia. It was an open goods train packed full of people like sardines in a can. German planes started bombing overhead so the train stopped in Vilna. We jumped off and started walking to our home, an hour's walk away. A man called to us,

"Where are you girls going? It is dangerous to be out. We are being bombed."

We said that we were going to our mother, and took shelter behind a pillar. The streets were spattered with glass and debris from damaged buildings and there were dead people lying everywhere. Fortunately we found our mother, sister and brother safe at home.

Soon after the invasion, laws were brought in that we had to wear yellow Magen Davids and the Germans started to take the old people away for "labour". They made them send letters to their families that they were working. We did not know where they took the old people but we did not believe that Germans could possibly require old people for hard labour.

Then the Gestapo made two ghettos in Vilna into which all the Jews had to move. We stayed in an apartment block about five or eight families to a room. Every day they would take away thousands and thousands of people. We began to hear that the captives were being taken to gas chambers. Everybody in the ghetto had to go to work and you had to have permits - blue, white, green or yellow. If you did not work, you would be taken away.

We worked as slave labourers - in orchards, forests, railway stations and building sites - we would crush rocks with hammers wearing leather things on our feet. We would work at the goods stations unloading huge logs - six or eight of us girls could carry one. It was very hard labour. We would have to walk through the streets for miles from one job to the other wearing the yellow stars.

The Nazis would take away all age groups, not just the old. One day it was the turn of the fifteen and sixteen year old girls. I was fifteen, my middle sister Miriam eighteen months older. Miriam was standing in the line and I pulled her out and said that I would go in her place and she could go home, and she tried to pull me out saying that she would go instead of me. Then we both ran out of the line and escaped and managed to hide in an attic. The following day when the raid was over, we returned home.

At that time my brother Nachum, Miriam and I were working for a German company that ran a rest and recuperation centre for soldiers who had come from the battle field The centre shared a building in Stefanska Street with a girls' orphanage run by nuns . Two Feldfebles Stefan, and Walter, ran it for the Wehrmacht. We worked in the kitchen. We each had to peel three buckets of potatoes, carrots amd other vegetables, scrub the floors, clean the windows, do the washing, make the beds and clean the rooms. Some of the soldiers used to throw the dust pans in our faces and call us "You bloody Jews." They would show us pictures of Stalin and say "He is your father" and would burn Stalin's picture in front of us. The staff including the feldfebles and the kitchen staff were kind to us and fed us well but if we complained to them about the way the soldiers treated us, the chef Emil Gauss would say.

"I am sorry that we cannot help you. They would shoot us if we tried."

Once when the Germans were having an "aktion" the people working were told to sleep where they worked so that those not working could be taken away. The three of us had to sleep at the centre. It was a holiday - Easter or Christmas or something - and the six chefs had prepared a smart meal with turkeys. We were invited to sit behind the curtains of the hall stage to watch them dance. One of the soldiers invited me to dance with them but the Feldfeble told me that as much as they would like to, this was not allowed, and we had to go back behind the curtains.

When we walked back home the next day after this "aktion", we were horrified by what we saw. There were hundreds of dead bodies lying in the streets of the ghetto. We saw a man and a woman lying on a cart with their eyes and mouths open. I went up to talk to them and discovered that they had been shot. I saw a lady sitting on the corner and started to speak to her - she was dead. I did not realize that people with their eyes open could be dead.

When we reached our apartment building in Strashuna Street there were dead people everywhere. Before we left, the five or six families on our floor without work permits had hidden in a room the door to which was concealed by some cupboards pushed against it. Some bottles of wine were placed on the cupboard as a further distraction. When we moved the sideboard away we found all forty people on our floor still hiding behind it but alive, even the baby which had been almost choked to prevent it crying and giving them away.
The next day we had to go back to work.

When the Germans attacked Stalingrad the company moved closer to the front lines and the orphanage was evacuated to Germany. Emil Gauss offered to send Miriam and me to his wife in Germany to be hidden by her. We refused to go because we did not trust the orphan girls who knew we were Jewish and were afraid that if they gave us away we would be shot. He arranged for us to get jobs at the station, also kitchen work but we had to clean the trains, the compartments and lavatories as well.

One day when we returned from work the Jewish police stopped us and took our work permits away. These could be sold for a lot of money, gold or diamonds, to people trying to save their lives. We were desperate. The next day when the ghetto opened we took off our yellow stars and ran back to Stefanska Street. As we were blonde with blue eyes this was not too dangerous. The kitchen staff had gone but the guard, a tall blonde German, was still there and we told him what had happened. He went with us to the Judenrat and ordered them to return our permits to us.

That day the police stopped us again, and said that if we left the ghetto without permits once more they would put us in the ghetto gaol. I was caught smuggling a loaf of bread for my mother into the ghetto. I had hidden the bread between my legs. They took me to the police security section, where two Jewish policemen forced me onto a table, pulled down my pants, gave me nine lashes on my bare buttocks and gaoled me for a few days. I was black and blue and suffered for a long time afterwards. I felt bitter because there were no Germans around and they could have let me go.

The Germans were still taking people away from the ghetto pretending that they were being taken for purposes of labour although they were being sent to the gas chambers or to Ponary. One memory that will always haunt me was of a baby of about two months who had been hidden by its mother under her arms. When the mother did not want to part with her infant, I saw a Nazi tear the little thing away and kill it by knocking the head against the wall.

Soon afterwards they closed the ghetto gates. There were still a few Jews left in the ghetto and with backing from the Russians and smuggled arms, a resistance group was formed in the Vilna ghetto. They were determined not to let themselves be taken alive. The United Partisan Organization was committed to an armed struggle and conducted acts of sabotage in the ghetto and later on in the surrounding forests.

In June 1943 I married Moritz Lewin in the ghetto. I became involved with the resistance and my husband was also. Moritz had his own revolver which went off when he was jumping from a second floor building and shot him in the knee. I went with him to the ghetto hospital to have the bullet removed and soon after there was an SS inspection. He had his revolver with him - it was death to possess one. He hid it under the sheets and vowed that he would kill me and himself rather than be caught passively, but fortunately they did not notice.

The Lithuanian police had an agreement with the ghetto partisans and at a certain time of the night the ghetto gates would be opened briefly to enable small parties to escape and with the help of the partisans Moritz and I - and his revolver - got out and escaped into White Russia. We hid in the day, sleeping in damp ditches and walking at night and after two days reached Lake Narocz. There were sixty of us in two groups of thirty. Early in the morning we would see armed groups of Ukrainian Nazi scouts on horseback scouring the Narocz forest looking for escaped Jews to kill. They killed more than half of our band.

We built underground shelters in the forest. I would go to neighbouring farms to dig up potatoes and vegetables for the pot whilst Moritz and the others went out to disrupt the German communications. We would saw down big trees to barricade the roads. The Germans decided to get rid of the partisans so they surrounded the whole forest with tanks. Those they caught they packed together in farm houses, poured on petrol and set them alight. I saw this with my own eyes. I escaped with a few others and we went into the small deep lake with the water up to our chins and stayed sitting there for about two days and nights without food. There was a cow in the water so a butcher in our group cut up the cow and gave us bits so that we would survive.

We stayed in the forest until we heard noises on top of the surrounding hills and saw the flames of torches. One of our scouts went to investigate and reported that it was the Russian army pushing back the Germans. We joined the Russians and walked back with them to Vilna. I saw the Ponary camp nearby. We had heard from a woman who had escaped from there that a large ditch had been dug and that as the trains came in the people had to walk out one by one onto boards and were shot and would then fall into the trenches. I saw a huge big hole, like a lake. Everything had a white powder sprayed over it and it was still lined with narrow boards.

Vilna was now occupied by the Russians and I got a job in a co-operative distributing bread to the refugees. After the war the foreigners - those from Poland, Czechoslovakia and France - could leave, but not Lithuanians. My husband got papers for me saying that I was born in Lodz, which was in Poland, so that after nine months we too were able to leave Lithuania.

I did not want to live in Europe. I felt that there was no future for Jews on this blood stained soil. I wanted to go to Palestine and the best way to get there was through Italy where the Haganah organized illegal transport to Palestine. They organized guides to take us there.

Along with many other dispossessed people we travelled through Poland into Czechoslovakia, through Hungary, Rumania and Austria and finally after several months on the road, both on foot and by train we arrived in Italy. Our guides would help us across borders and get us permits to go on through the next country.

As we moved from country to country, I visited all the concentration camps and gas chambers looking for my family. My brother I learnt had been killed in a partisan group a week before the end of the war while destroying electric pylons. My mother and Miriam died in the gas chambers.

The people I saw in the camps I visited were not people - they were skeletons covered with striped clothing, barely alive. I also saw a man who had been ripped apart by two horses to which he had been tied. I saw such barbarities that for ten years after the war I had nightmares and would wake screaming. To this day I am afraid to sleep alone or be alone in a flat.

In Italy we were put into transit camps from where we could apply to emigrate. I wanted to leave Europe and go to Palestine. For two and a half years we stayed in transit camps first in Padua, then in Santa Maria de Leuca where my son Leon was born on 10th July 1946 and then in Bari. In Padua I found a friend who had a sister in Johannesburg and through her I discovered that I had a cousin in Cape Town who put me in touch with my grandfather in Johannesburg. He offered to support us in Palestine. We were going to go there by boat, but then five boats were sunk off Cyprus and I became frightened. I did not want to go through another war specially now that I had a small child to look after. My grandfather then got visas for us to come to Johannesburg and we left Italy on a converted cargo boat. Leon was then eighteen months old.

An aunt arranged for me to be taught English but I found that as a result of the sufferings I had gone through, I was unable to concentrate. The doctor advised me to give up studying as I was able to support myself without it.

That was the end of the sad story. Life has not been easy and I still bear the emotional scars of those terrible years. I suffer from severe depression and I can never forget the past trauma. I have four children and eight lovely grandchildren and I hope they will never experience such suffering. My sister Rita now lives in Florida. The world is so big that it should be able to accommodate all human beings without violence.

G-d bless the world and may we all be able to live in peace.

Bella Varkel was born in Vilna on 10.12.1926 and was educated there at the Esther Rubinstain School. She spent the war years in the Vilna Ghetto as a slave labourer, and when the ghetto was liquidated she escaped to the forests and joined the partisans. After liberation she lived in Italy, coming to South Africa on 2.2.1948. She has two sons, Leon and Frank, two daughters, Barbara and Miriam and grandchildren.

IRENE GROLL
Kusel, Camp de Gurs, Camp de Rivesaltes.

My name is Irene Groll, born Kayem, only child of Adolf and Liesel. I was born on 10 January 1933 in Kusel in the Palatinate (a West German Province of Germany) near the French border. At the end of January that year, Hitler became Chancellor of Germany. We had lived in the Kusel area for generations; my grandfather had fought in World War I and had been decorated by the Kaiser; we had not known anti-Semitism. My maternal grandmother lived in Ulmet. I was told later, by my grandmother, that Ulmet is of some archaeological interest, because it is situated on the Via Romana. She brought me to South Africa.

I led a sheltered, secure life, a beloved only child. On Kristallnacht, 10 November 1938, when I was almost 6, the Jewish males of Kusel were taken to Dachau, my father and grandfather amongst them. I remember that from that time my mother always had a suitcase packed and ready. For the first time I felt fear, not insecurity, because I had the security of my family. Whilst the men were away, my mother and I

My father and I, Germany 1936

went to Ulmet to live with my grandmother. When my father was released, he was not allowed to work; I don't know how we managed to live.

Jews were forbidden to attend the ordinary schools so for 6 months I went to a school about an hour away by train. I remember that I was the only Jewish child going to school by train because there were no other Jewish children living in the area. I can still remember the anxiety of my mother when she would see me off at the station.

Then, in October 1940, the Jews of the Palatinate and other provinces were ordered to gather in a large hall. I remember vividly needing to go to the toilet and not being allowed to do so until my mother pleaded for permission. Little things like that remain in my memory. I remember also at a later stage, not having a hankie for my nose. To me this was a terrible thing because I had been brought up as a lady and it was difficult to accustom myself to different ways.

We were taken from that hall, towards the end of October 1940 and put on a train. (About 5000 Jews were sent across France to internment camps in the French Pyrenees.) This was an ordinary train and I remember sitting on my mother's lap, watching the lights flashing by.

We were taken to Camp De Gurs in the Pyrenees Atlantique. It was cold, it was winter, everything was brown, muddy. I was hungry, ill. It was thought that I had the mumps but as I remember having my throat painted with purple stuff, it was probably diphtheria. I probably also had a stomach bug. Many of the children had this and many died.

Gurs was a concentration camp, not a labour camp or an extermination camp. Women were separated from the men by a barbed-wire fence. My mother, grandmother and I were in Ilot G Barrack 26; my father and my grandfather were in the men's camp. I remember crawling under the fence to visit them. My cousin Kurt, who later lived in America, was also in the camp. He had a baby brother. Kurt and I tried to care for the baby but he died. I remember a woman losing her mind, rushing out from our barrack into the cold, constantly looking under the barrack - for what, for whom? I was lucky to have survived this camp.

My grandparents were then sent from Gurs to Camp De Noe while my parents and I were sent to Rivesaltes in the south of France, near Perpignan. Camp de Rivesaltes was in the Pyrenees Orientales, We were in Ilot B, Barrack 20. This was about July 1941. This was also a holding camp. People with young children were sent there. I think my father worked there - perhaps he had something to do with the post. It was in Rivesaltes that I remember being taught to sing Yiddish songs. Someone must have got the children together and taught them the songs. Our family had never spoken Yiddish; our language was German. Although we were observant Jews, we were very German from a long way back.

I remember at Rivesaltes opening a suitcase and finding a nest of mice. To this day, I have a fear of mice. At Rivesaltes, I learned, for the first time, about washing my hands at the cemetery. I must have been to a burial. I remember seeing a place full of corpses. I also remember the smell of woodfire.

Then some Jewish children were released from Rivesaltes to French and Jewish authorities. My grandmother later told my aunt in Africa that after much persuasion my mother allowed me to go because she knew I stood a better chance. It was only after I held my first-born in my arms that I felt the pain my mother must have felt when she had to let me go. I remember my father and mother standing together saying goodbye to me. My father said:

"Never forget to pray; everything will be fine."

I didn't cry when I was parted from my parents - somehow, I didn't cry when I was a child. I suppose it never occured to me that I would never see them again. I still have a little cotton purse my mother made for me which she gave to me when we part-ed. I was never to see them again. I was to learn later that my parents were sent from Rivesaltes to Drancy on 11 August 1942.

I remember a girl called Margo of about 12 who became my surrogate mother. We children were taken to Palavas Les Flots near Marseilles. This was a children's rehabilitation home. I think it had something to do with OSE[1]. Here we were well fed. I remember collecting crusts of bread to send to my parents. The bread was never sent, because, before it could be sent, I had a letter from my mother saying that they were being sent to another place - destination unknown. (The destination was Auschwitz). My aunt in France was later to destroy this letter. I'll mention the reason for this later. I remember being happy at Palavas Les Flots, well fed, cared for, enjoying freedom, walking along the beach with the other children.

Then I was transferred to another children's home Le Chateau Du Masgeliers. This was also, I think, run by OSE. A Jewish doctor and nurse were in charge. I have a photo of them and of the children there. I must have had a birthday there because I remember getting a sweet as a present. I remember that there were far more children here than at the previous home. I also seem to recall that the children here were destined for Palestine. Actually I can't understand how it came about that Jewish children were released from Rivesaltes.

My aunt (my father's sister), uncle and cousins, Helene and Carola, were living close by in Brive La Gaillarde where they had sought refuge from Alsace Lorraine.

The children at Le Chateau Du Masgeliers. 1942 I am second right, 2nd row from the front

Oeuvre de Secours aux Enfants, a Jewish children's aid society which cared for several hundred refugee children.

My cousin Helene had brought food to us when we were at Camp de Gurs. The family now heard that I was in Masgeliers. Helene came to fetch me from the Home to have a holiday in Brive.

Things started getting bad for the Jews. It was then that the family approached a friend in the Prefecture who procured false documents for me. I became a French girl, no longer Jewish, named Irene Duclos. It was at this time that my aunt destroyed the letter from my mother; it was too dangerous for me to have a letter indicating that I was Jewish.

My family arranged for me to be taken into a Catholic Convent where I remained until the end of the War. I was there for about 2 years. I was brought up as a Catholic child, taught the Catechism every evening so that I should be word- perfect the next day. Of course I received proper schooling here for the first time in a long time and I became fluent in French. Truly the nuns saved my life. It was when I was at the Convent that I realised for the first time that I was alone. (By this time, I was no longer with Margo.) I felt that I was just one of many, not a special person. Nothing belonged to me. I felt like a leaf floating in the wind, blown hither and thither.

After the War, when I left the convent and moved in with my family, I used to go to the station to meet the train in the hope that my parents would return. My family returned to their home in Alsace Lorraine. Then my uncle who, with his wife, had come out to Cape Town in 1936, discovered that three members of the family were alive - my grandparents and I. (There was another uncle who had arrived in Cape Town in 1938). My cousin Helene, now married, felt, together with the rest of the family, that it would be better for us to go to South Africa where a better future awaited us with Uncle Albert and Aunt Leni Mayer who had two children of their own, Lucille and Ralph.

I was re-united with my grandparents in Romans, where they were living in an old aged home. My grandfather was not well. It was so sad that he died six weeks before we left for South Africa. After surviving so much! Oma and I went to Paris to get our papers. My Uncle Albert organised and paid for everything. It took until 11 April 1945 before our visas were granted. There was I, a girl of twelve, dealing with officials. I could speak French; my Oma could only speak German.

Oma and I eventually travelled by train to Lisbon. We were supposed to be met at the station, but no one was there to see to the next stage of our journey. There we were, at night, with nowhere to go. A man approached us, offered to take us to a pension. We had no alternative but to follow him. He was good to us.

When I think of the past, I remember that through all the bad times there was always a thread of kindness. We spent about six weeks in Lisbon waiting for a boat. We arrived in Cape Town on the 27th August 1946 and were met by my two uncles. Imagine the responsibility my Uncle and Aunt Mayer had undertaken! An old woman and a teenager had arrived - they had experienced so much; my Oma had suffered so much.

I was one of the fortunate few children to survive - fortunate to be taken in by a caring, loving family, to live in a sunny beautiful land, to put down roots. My husband George and I have been married for 40 years. We have four children and four grandchildren. I have thwarted Hitler's Final Solution.

IRENE GROLL nee Kayem was born in Kusel, Germany in 1933. The war years were spent in camps in Gurs and Rivesaltes in France and then in hiding in Brive where she was liberated. She came to South Africa in 1946, is married to George and her children are Lynn, Allan, Leslie and Gillian.

DAVID KORZUCH
Markstadt, Finf Taichen, Gross-Rosen, Buchenwald

I was born in Shemyeshitce Poland, near the German border. I was the youngest of nine. In 1941 a ghetto was built in our town and we were moved into it. Nazi guards and kapos kept us imprisoned inside the wire fence. My three sisters refused to move into the ghetto and went to another town: we never heard from them again.

My school days came to an end - I had been in the third class. No longer attending school, I would climb through the fence and go into town and return with food for my family, two nuns often helped us. I was fearless.

Then my brother Alteshima was caught in one of the selections and sent to the Markstadt labour camp. We used to send him parcels of food and old clothes.

My barmitzvah was celebrated in the ghetto with my parents, grandparents and two brothers. Soon after my barmitzvah the ghetto was liquidated. People were herded into the centre of the ghetto where they were separated. The old people and children were put on one side, the young people and adults were put on another. I was placed with the chidren but as my family were all with the adults I slipped out when no one was looking and went to join their group.

However my grandparents and father were taken from us and my mother was sent to a camp.

I never saw any of them again.

There I was, a boy of thirteen, all alone in the group of adults selected by the Nazis to work.

After four days in the central hall with very little food my group was sent to the city by train and from there to the labour camp at Markstadt where I found Alteshima. He was in a different section but we could see each other. We were moved together all the time until Buchenwald.

In Markstadt I worked very hard for a building construction firm carrying bricks and bags of cement, catching and throwing bricks until my hands were raw. We were like human robots, slave labourers for a German firm called PAUL KLUM who got building contracts from the German Government.

These years felt like twenty years - if you survived one day it was as though you survived a year. We got up 5 a.m., got ready, got a piece of bread, were counted and marched with our German boss to the place where we were working outside the camp. The work was backbreaking torture, the weather conditions appalling. The freezing cold was soul destroying but there was no respite. We had no camp clothes and we were "lucky" to be able to shower and change our clothes once a month. Some people treated us nicely, some treated us badly and some were only too happy to be bad. I would wash the cups for my boss, a master builder. Sometimes he would give me a piece of bread. I was a child.

Paul Klum had the contract to build a concentration camp at Finf Taichen about 30 miles outside Breslau and this is what we were building. When it was built we were transferred there. Outsiders were brought in to run the camp and for the first time I began to understand the meaning of horror. Cruelty, instant obedience and harsh discipline. We were given striped clothes and had all our hair shaved. The food was even worse than before.

We still continued to build for Paul Klum. One morning when we were being counted on appel I was standing in front and a man pulled me out and said that he had another job for me. I was to be a "runner" for the SS - to make coffee, to clean shoes, open and close gates etc. This was a lucky break for me, a privilege. We did not have to work outside in the cold all day and got more food. I shared the little extra bread with Alteshima.

One day I was sent to fetch a plumber. I misunderstood and brought an electrician or vice versa. You did not make mistakes in the camp and I was beaten, lost my job and was sent back to build. After a few months I feigned sickness and was sent to the infirmary. The respite did me good. I got to know some of the Kapos and managed to get a job in the laundry. There were thirty barracks in the camp. Once a month we got clean clothes; our dirty clothes were boiled in cauldrons to kill the lice and were hung outside to dry.

For survival I always formed a gang with friends - we supported and protected each other, and shared food. No longer a child, I was now always very wary, alert and watchful. This partnership might have been one of the reasons for my successful survival. I would choose people who had their wits about them. We would live from day to day.

I remained there until the end of 1944 when Finf Taichen was closed. The war was ending and the Germans did not want the Russians to liberate us so they moved us into Germany. We walked 8 days in the snow to Gross-Rosen.

It was one of the worst experiences of the whole horrendous period. They pushed us into barns at night and the next morning there were twenty or thirty people who had died from being crushed to death, stampeded by the people pushed in on top of them. I used to climb a pole and sleep on the roof beams. I would sleep while my friend would watch over me so that I would not fall to my death, then I would take a turn.

Each night of the march they gave us a piece of bread for the next day's meal. You had two choices - either you ate it right away and went hungry the next day, or kept it for the next day and risked being killed in the middle of the night for the food. We stayed in the camp for ten days in the snow. There were no roofs. The barracks were open. The snow was pouring down. We stood in the mud.

We stayed in Gross-Rosen for about 5 days, then we were put into cattle trucks and travelled for 5 days to Buchenwald. We were each given a piece of bread. We thought it was our daily ration but it was meant to last us for the whole five days. It was a nightmare.

Alteshima became ill on the journey with a lung complaint and was put in hopital in Buchenwald. I would visit him every day. He was very weak. One day I came there

and he was not in the hospital any longer. I realized that he must have passed away during the night.

It was very difficult in Buchenwald. We did not work there, but just sat around doing nothing. When we worked outside the camp we could sometimes organize a little extra food but in Buchenwald this was not possible because there was no connection with the outside world. Buchenwald was divided into six or seven areas. I used to move between the areas.

I was like a delinquent, a desperate person who would look for anyway to get some food, even stealing a piece of potato skin from a pig's trough on the marches in order to eat.

In the other camps there were bad times and not so bad times, but in Buchenwald it was just the end of everything; there was nothing else but bad.

By the end of March there were more than half a milllion people in Buchenwald; Russians, Norwegians, Danes, homosexual Germans, German "spies", political prisoners. While I was at Buchenwald, my brothers Max and Israel arrived. They had been in other camps. It was wonderful to be reunited. Unfortunately Israel died of dysentery shortly before the end of the war.

The Germans used to gather people ostensibly for transports to another camp. They promised the prisoners food if they went but I did not trust the Germans. I was sure that the end of the war was approaching and I wanted to survive. I always went to the back so that I would not get caught. Max would also hide. They would round up people and put them in a hall from which they could take out 5000 or 3000 people a day. I was correct because those unfortunate captives were taken outside, made to dig ditches and shot.

The Germans had wired the perimeter of the camp and intended to blow it up when the Americans arrived but fortunately they were caught unawares. We were liberated by the Americans on the 11th April 1945.

Barely 5 000 remained alive out of the 600 000. Max came to find me in my block, number 66. We were the sole remnants of our family which before the war had consisted of parents, grandparents and nine children. The Americans put us into the houses where the SS used to stay.

I ran to the village to organize food. We were not used to eating and my brother became ill from eating too much. I was very careful to eat only a little. After six weeks the Red Cross arranged for the Ort Oze[2] to care for us. Four hundred of us were sent to Ecoui in France. Max was put in a sanatorium where he remained a long time.

I was sixteen years old and behaved like a wild animal - undisciplined, uneducated, aggressive, resentful, unmethodical. I was ready to prove that no one could push me around. I would fight anybody at the drop of a hat. I was put into an OSE orphanage which took in 250 orphaned survivors. There were nurses, teachers and psychologists. We were placed in different houses and were divided into groups to be trained in the areas we chose. They taught us sport and languages, and tried to instill discipline and normality in us but I did not like discipline - discipline was something I associated with the camp and now that I was free I wanted none of it. I wanted to be a dental mechanic so I was sent to a Progressive School - I did not have sufficient schooling to go to a government school. I progressed well and started to adapt to a normal world. We were also helped by a landsleit society[3]

Max and I decided to go to Argentine where we had an uncle but they would not allow Jews to get in so we applied for Paraguay and crossed the border illegally into Argentine. I met my South African wife there while she was on holiday. It took three years to get permission to join her because the South African Government thought that if I were born in Poland I must be a Communist. Max remained in Buenos Aires and recently moved to Israel where his son lives.

In 1958 I went to South Africa and we got married. I have a lovely wife and children and despite missing out on my childhood and adolescence in the ghetto and camps, I have made a success of my life although I have always been hampered by my lack of formal education.

I have become a normal human being but I retain strong hatred towards the Germans and the Poles. Our blood drips from their hands.

Those in charge of the camps had to perform their jobs but did they have to be so murderous?

Did they have to kick you in the shins whenever they passed you?

Did the Poles have to assist the Germans with such enthusiasm, and continue with the slaughter of the Jews even when the war was over and a handful of survivors tried to return to their homes?

I refuse to speak Polish. Sometimes in nightmares I return to my village and walk the streets and go to my school but I would never, <u>never</u>, go back to my village. I would not give the Poles the satisfaction of humiliating me because I came out alive. I cannot understand how Jewish people can return today to visit the ovens of Auschwitz and look for their "roots" under the trees in the bloodsoaked forest of Poland.

I hope that my children and one day my grandchildren will read my story. None of us dare forget...

DAVID KORZUCH was born in Shemyeshitce, Poland in 1930 and while still young was sent to labour camps. He was liberated in Buchenwald in 1945 and after moving to Paris and Argentina he arrived in South Africa in 1958. He is married to Ettie and has two daughters, Barbara and Beverley.

---

2 A Jewish organization for vocational training founded in Russia in 1880, After the war schools were also formed in displaced persons camps in Germany and Eastern Europe.
3 A society to assist people from the same town or area.

MARTHA MANNSBACH
Beverungen, Theresienstadt.

M y husband was the Parnass, the headman, of Beverungen in Germany. We had to stay until the last of the community had gone. People with little children went first, then middle aged people, working people and at the end it was the old people and the Parnass because if a message came that people had to go to the transport the message came to us. They all went to different camps, we did not know where. We were the last Jews to leave the town. I shall never forget.

We were sent to Theresienstadt. People who weren't there say that Theresienstadt was mild compared to the others. It must be the truth, I do not know, I was not at the others, but it was not so mild, I am telling you.

Theresienstadt was a military city before the war and there were a few beautiful houses where the officers had lived. We were told that these were children's homes. The children were taken away from their parents with nurses and doctors and after a time they were told that the children were going to go to Switzerland in a transport. They left. They never arrived.

The women had to make deep holes for water pipes under the streets. However there was no running water - my father had to go to the pump for water. People from different areas were kept in different parts of Theresienstadt. For example, I was from Westphalia, my father from the Rhineland so we stayed in different sections and would see each other now and again fetching food or something. At first the men and women were all together, but later the men were placed by themselves. We stayed in a large room like a kazerne, a warehouse, a whole lot of people together in the same room. We slept on planks, a bridge with a lappie over it.

Leo Baeck was in Theresienstadt with us in the section with the Berliners. He was like the prince. He gave lectures although he was not allowed to and someone

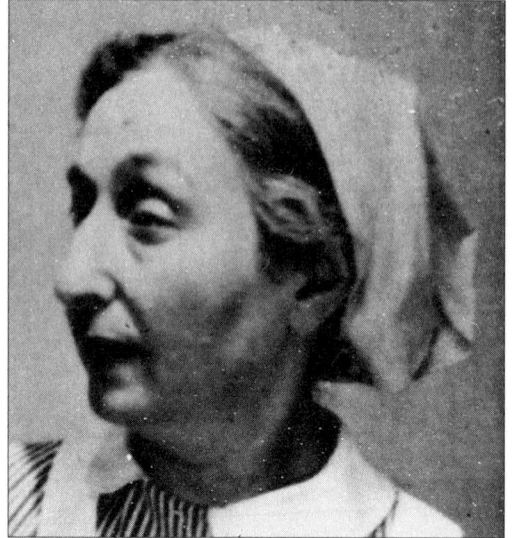

When the nurse died, I was given her uniform - and I was the nurse!

was always watching out at the door.

Many people became ill with dysentery. There were many old people and only a few my age. I used to clean the floors and then I started helping to wash the sick people. One day I was appointed a nurse. I do not know how it happened - I was given a paper on my head and a stripe of white material. When a real nurse died, I was given her uniform, that of a Berlin nurse with the stripes. I put it on - and I was the nurse!

My husband could not work because he was sickly. He was a diabetic and had a heart complaint. I used to give him insulin injections. When we went to Theresienstadt they took my handbag, emptied it and took everything out, including the insulin. I said, "Oh, No! That's for my husband!" but they took everything away and a woman tried to help me. My husband's diabetes went away on the inadequate camp diet. When the camp doctors, also prisoners, were able to get a pill for my husband, they gave it to me.

We were in Theresienstadt for three years and my husband became very weak and had another heart attack. The doctor said to me, "He will not make it any longer."

There were no cushions and he lay on the floor in the large room while I sat against him for support. Then I had to go on duty. Luckily I had a friend Margaret, a wonderful woman from Vienna, whose old mother of over 80, like a doll, had been in my ward while my father had been in hers; both died in the camp.

She said to me,

"You must go and fetch your food, you must have something to eat."

I said, "I can not move out from under him, he is in a coma."

She said, "You go out and I shall support him. Go and eat and I will look after your husband."

She took over from me and got in and held his hand like I had been doing. His mind was clear even though he had his eyes closed and when I came back he said,

"I pretended that you were lying there and that I was lying on your shoulder" and he added,

" With whom will you do this tomorrow night?"

We were freed by the Russians. We heard them "cnattering" with the motor cars and then the Germans were on the run, shooting and Russian wounded were brought into our sick rooms. They could not speak German and we could not speak Russian, but we had to help them. We could only talk to them with signs. They were so tall and I was only a little one but we got on well; they did not like the war either. We got out of our room and only the sick people lay there.

It took a long time before German cities started to send big omnibuses to bring home their citizens. They had a list of those who had been deported and those who were still there. My husband was lying there very sick.

He said, "I hear people were fetched from that city and this city. Everyone is being fetched except us!"

I said, "Those are the big places. We are not from a big city. Soon the buses will be from Bielefeld and then from Bielefeld district where we lived."

I told him that to keep him quiet but he had an understanding till the last minute, so we waited and waited and one day on my return my husband said,

"I hear that a transport from Bielefeld district has come."

I asked, "How do you know?"

He said, "I may be lying here but I know more than you."

I already knew about it but I had not wanted to tell him because how could I manage to transport him - and I did not want to disappoint him if it were not true. Later on I had to tell him that there was an omnibus for the district in which we lived. It was as though a light came on him. He was so weak and he was lying there and I put on the suit that he still had - we could not even fasten his trousers as he had lost so much weight. I got him ready and offered him a drink.

He said, "I don't want anything here any more. I want to eat and drink when we go home."

I took his cloth and washed his face and he died!

I called and called him.

My friend was with me and she said,

"Martha, you have seen death so often. Can't you see that he is dead?"

So that was the end.

The bus was standing there and the people inside were waiting for it to leave. We had a friend from a mixed marriage who was already inside holding our rucksacks on his lap because he knew how weak my husband was. He had missed the opportunity to leave on an earlier transport because he had wanted to help us. Margaret told him that my husband had just died. He wanted to get out but the busdriver said,

"Whoever gets out now, stays here. We are leaving in 5 minutes."

Margaret said, "Mr Myers stay in the bus, your wife is waiting for you and we shall look after Mrs Mannsbach."

So the transport went and I stayed behind. I can't tell you what I went through. Margaret was still with me. She was a trained nurse, a very capable woman and she helped me. When we had to carry corpses she would say to me, "Martha, you take the light side, I'll carry the heavy side."

So she helped me and waited with me till they took him away and she went with me to the end of the camp site where we could not go any further, then I broke down, and they brought me to my bed.

I had been part of the working system but

as I was supposed to have left on the transport, I was no longer entitled to rations. I could not get any food. Margaret said to me, "Don't worry. I 'll share my food with you."

I did not want to eat but she brought her soup and insisted that I ate some to keep alive. I did not have any bread, nothing - I did not exist for the camp and there was no officer you could go to so for one week I lay there alone after three years of living with my husband in Theresienstadt.

I said, "This is the end!"

"No!" said Margaret, "We are carrying on!"

"Margaret," I said, "I cannot stand the fact that you have to work and share your food with me. You will break down. Can you find out if I can also get work somewhere?"

She said, "I shall only find work for you because you want it, and do not want to take my food any more. I must keep you alive. I shall ask one of the doctors to help you."

(The doctors were also prisoners.)

Through her I got a job in the sickbay, again as a nurse, not that a nurse was paid any better than the other prisoners. We just got rations - our bread and food, no money. It was better food than before, but we were all hungry.

One day this poem was stuck under my door as a gift for me. I do not know who left it for me.

> Always if you think that you can not carry on any more
> A little light comes from somewhere
> Which forces you to think again
> about sunshine and happiness
> And the heavy daily work is carried out more easily
> And once more with strength, courage and belief.
> These words are meant for you also..

A few weeks later Margaret got a transport home to Vienna. I corresponded with her until a few years ago when she died. She was a wonderful person. She was strong and I was so small. I shall never forget that friendship.

I had another friend there. Gertrude was from a mixed marriage and had been brought up as a Gentile but when persecu-

tion started she said,

"I am born from a Jewish father."

She would distribute the food - later I also had to do it if she were not there and she would say,

" Martha, there is a bite over, you can have it."

If I asked whose it was she would say,

"We need people like you here. If I give it to you, you must eat it."

A year before the end a transport went to Switzerland which had an arrangement with Germany to exchange German prisoners in Allied hands for people from the concentration camp. They came to Theresienstadt looking for single persons. I did not qualify nor did Margaret because her family were big business people in Vienna. Wealthy people were not allowed out. Gertrude went to Switzerland, with a blanket over her arm, and a suitcase, not a rucksack, so that the Swiss people could see how well we were looked after.

Another friend, Elsa Salomon, worked with me. She came with her little boy and her husband, a fine old man, who had lost one arm in the First World War. At first the Nazis said they would not take those sort of people. They celebrated their son's barmitzvah there. He said the prayers, that was all. She got some white scraps of cloth torn from the shirts of people who had died and with these she made a new shirt for her son.

It was my fiftieth birthday in the camp and she made a poem for me as a present, written on a scrap of paper with a pen borrowed from the office. It is still a treasured possession.

They disappeared, like all the rest.

The mother, the father and the little boy.

I lost three sisters, my brothers-in-law, nephews, nieces and their children, all in different camps, none of us knew about the others and I did not know where they were.

This is what I should like to tell you. When the Germans had realized that their enemies were coming, they took all the corpses not yet destroyed and made everyone stand in a line in the street and pass the corpses from one person to the other up to the river Ohre. Many thousands of corpses were thrown in.

Some doctors from Vienna went to the commission after the war and got permission to go to the river Ohre which sur-

> In our small rooms every day brings
> A lot of trouble and a lot of work
> and a lot of people who are very sad.
> But today throw sadness overboard
> And put all the worries away.
> Because today is your Birthday
> And everyone wants to wish you.
> Carry on being brave as you are now
> And do not worry any more.
> It will be as it has to be.
> Life brings a lot of rainy showers
> But know that after all this trouble
> G-d makes happiness for every human being
> And we wish that for you and your dear ones
> There will still be many happy hours together.
> This we wish you for today and for ever
> From all your friends,
> Elsa Salomon, Theresienstadt.

My 50th birthday present

rounded the camp to say Kaddish.

Today there is a memorial plaque which reads:

25 000 paper urns containing ashes were thrown into the river Ohre

Amongst them, in the water, is my father and my dear husband.

> Martha Mannsbach was born on 28.10.1893 in Huls, Germany where she was educated. When she married she went to live in Beverungen. She was transported to Theresienstadt where her husband died. After liberation she went to Canada and then joined her brother in Northern Rhodesia. She moved to South Africa in 1963.

JUDITH DIAMANT
Theresienstadt

The Holocaust began almost as soon as the Germans occupied Czechoslovakia in March 1939. Very soon afterwards Jewish children were expelled from Government schools. For the two years that remained for the community all children had to attend the only Jewish school in my home town - Ostrave, in North Eastern Moravia. It was situated in the old quarter of the town, close to the river, which formed the eventual border between the Protectorate of Bohemia and Moravia and Poland. The daily trek of a group of us to school right across town was always fraught with fear. Passing the German school we were attacked, often beaten, bombarded with chestnuts or snowballs with stones included. The yellow star set us up as targets. Many times we would run back home to fetch an adult to walk with us.

Then came the rounding up of the Jewish community. My beloved grandmother, aunt, the rest of the family and all friends were taken away. Because my mother had married a non- Jew at the beginning of the war, both she and I remained behind under his protection. My mother died in 1943 of TB. No one would treat her as it was dangerous to be in contact with a Jew, medical ethics notwithstanding. My step- father was very good to me, sent me into hiding together with the children of my mother's best friends who were only half- Jewish. Six months later a Gestapo man arrived at my stepfather's business, advised him to bring me back and threatened that if this were not done the other children would be brought back with me. So that was how I came to be put on the train with others destined for Theresienstadt.

Alone at eleven, very scared, I must have had some food with me, and my stepfather must have arranged for some adult to watch over me, but I don't recall any of this. After 24 hours of shunting from line to line, air raid warnings etc. we arrived in Theresienstadt in the middle of the night.

We walked with our baggage through the fortification of the garrison of old. We were met by a group of paramedics, our identity and bags checked. Then we were told we had to shower. I screamed and refused to undress. We had by then heard of the gas chambers and the so-called showers and so had the paramedics.

One lovely young woman, whom I never saw again, undressed and entered the shower with me, holding me tight all the way. A wonderful humane gesture.

All the necessary documentation over, I was sent to a children's dormitory. It was a terrible shock to see the three tiered bunks with 32 children in a small room. My own bedding was the only comfort, no longer smelling of home, after it had passed through fumigation, but mine nevertheless.

I was so lucky to be taken under the wing of an elderly lady, who had come from Denmark. She took care of us, taught us under clandestine circumstances, a child always standing guard. She supplemented our almost starvation rations with some of the goodies she was allowed to receive from Denmark through the courtesy of the King. Then came the day, in April 1945, when our beloved Bertha Wolf left to join the White Buses to return home via Sweden. We were heartbroken and so afraid that it was another ploy to get rid of some more Jews. However, she did arrive safely. I met her after the war in London. It was a memorable reunion, all the bad experiences forgotten!

The morning after I arrived, my mother's great friend, Auntie Milena, a nursing sister, heard that some children had arrived on the latest transport. She searched the homes, fearing that her own daughters might be there, and found me! I brought the latest news of the family, which reassured her and her sisters. They took me over, the only child, some link with a better life! I was so fortunate. A few weeks later I became ill with pneumonia, and had to be taken to hospital. Before much could be done for me, my aunt was warned that there was to be a *"selection"*, it meant *"an injection and the crematorium"* So she spirited me away, hid me in the woman's quarters where a roster of aunties took care of me until I could go back to the children's home.

Early in 1945 the death marchers began to arrive. As the Russians pushed the Germans west, the death camps were cleared. Those who did not perish on the way arrived in the already overcrowded ghetto. I roamed the streets looking into old houses where every space housed a bedridden individual. I was trying to find my young aunt, who had been shipped with my granny to Birkenau- Auschwitz. When I saw someone who could be her, I would drag Aunt Milena to come and identify her. But it was never her!

In April or May America persuaded the International Red Cross under the Chairmanship of Count Bernadotte to negotiate with the Germans to take over the Ghetto. Shortly afterwards the Russian and American troops thrust the German army out of the occupied territories, and on the 9th of May the gates were opened but we could still not leave.

There was an epidemic of typhus and one needed a health certificate to leave. I still have the voucher which allowed me to board a train, with my wonderful aunts. We passed through Russian and American lines, from one known address to another, always wondering if the families had survived. And so home, as Pepys might have said, only to spend the time in a sanatorium, for a cure for TB and a session of drastic delousing, leaving long blisters along my hairline. The vermin were more resilient than we humans were.

The burdens of those bad years carry on consciously and sub-consciously. The excessive fear for my children - the great effort not to cling, trying to minimise the damage from which so many children of survivors suffer .

One would wish to forget, but one must mourn those who have gone and be ever vigilant against these terrible outbreaks of hatred which decimated not only 6 million Jews, but also another million Gypsies and many millions of others for no other reason than being who they were.

Judy Diamant nee Riff was born in Ostrava, Czech Republic on 21.7.1932. She went to school there until the Germans closed Jewish schools. She was sent as a child to Theresienstadt where she remained until liberated in May 1945. After living in Kenya, England and Italy, she came to South Africa in 1965. She has two daughters, Sarah and Naomi.

ALIDA COHEN
Amsterdam, Westerbork, Bergen-Belsen

My name is Alida (Lientje) Cohen (born Borstrock). I was born in The Hague, Holland in 1933. My mother was born in Holland, my father in England where his father was a Rabbi of a London East End Congregation. The family returned to Holland before World War I broke out.

I was one of three children - I was the eldest, my sister Mimi is 14 months younger, and my brother Leo was 6 years younger than I. We were a very religious family. My father was in the printing business and also taught Hebrew.

My family in happier days

After the Germans occupied Holland, we had to move from our house to a sort of ghetto. I could no longer attend my school and had to wear the yellow star. My father, deprived of his living, had to find other ways of earning money for his family. When he left in the morning, we worried that he would not return. For a while, I was sent off to a school some distance away. I recall my mother seeing us off at the tram every day - how she must have worried about out safe return!

In September 1942, my parents, Mimi, Leo, my paternal grandparents and I were arrested; my grandparents were sent immediately to Auschwitz and we were released for some reason. During December my father was arrested during the day and that same night the Gestapo came to our home and took us away. We were transported to a camp called Westerbork, a transit camp in Holland near the German border. From there, people were sent to Buchenwald, Theresienstadt or Auschwitz. We, however, remained there for several months as my father was a British subject. But soon the time arrived when "foreigners" were also called up for transport, and ours was one of those families.

My father took ill that day, and a doctor arranged for him to have an operation immediately and, as at that stage, they only transported the complete family, the four of us waited for my father to get better.

Once again we were called up but this time my brother (who was about 3 years old at the time) had to have an operation on his leg. Again we stayed at Westerbork until papers finally came through that we were to be sent on to Bergen-Belsen.

There we starved. My parents worked all day, and we three children remained in the camp, dirty and full of lice. I looked after my sister and brother. What an experience that was! To tell everything would take me a couple of days. We remained in Bergen Belsen until the end of March 1945, shortly before the British entered the camp on 15 April 1945.

We had to walk to the station. My mother was ill and so very thin that my father had to carry her there. It was very hard for him because he, too, had become so thin. The Germans ordered him to leave my Mother on the roadside. He refused and was very lucky not to have been beaten up this time.

Then we got into cattle trucks. We did not know our destination. The train stopped frequently because there was heavy fighting going on - the Americans were advancing. On one of the occasions that the train stopped my father and us children carried my mother off the train and laid her down on the grass verge, in the hope that some kind person would find her in time to save her life.

When we were liberated the Americans took us to a village called Hilleslaben where we were given accommodation. My father stole a bicycle and went to look for my mother. She had been liberated by the Russians and put into a hospital. He made arrangements to have her transferred to the village hospital in Hilleslaben. He was admitted there himself the next day. So there I was, aged eleven, having to fend for my younger sister and brother in a strange village in Germany with my parents in hospital and I myself ill.

When my father was discharged some weeks latger he was on sticks because he was still too weak to walk but at least we were together again. We could not return to Holland immediately because it had not yet been liberated. But at last we travelled, by train, boat, and road until we had returned.

My mother was very ill, my brother was ill and I had TB. I was sent to a convalescent home in Switzerland and arrived in the clothes I had been wearing all the time although my father had managed to buy me a night dress. There I was well cared for. For a while I worried about my mother because when I left Holland I had not said goodbye to her - I didn't know where she was. At last, I got a letter from her in Switzerland.

Finally when I returned to Holland, we began to make plans to leave as a family and we decided to go to South Africa where we arrived in Johannesburg in 1947. My father, Michael, never recovered and died in Johannesburg at the age of 48. My mother, Engelina was killed in a motor accident and Leo passed away in Cape Town aged 45.

Although I have suffered such a lot in my lifetime and am still plagued with dreadful nightmares, I am blessed with a wonderful daughter and son-in-law and two lovely grandchildren and they give me much pleasure.

ALIDA COHEN was born in The Hague, Holland in 1933 and educated in Amsterdam until the War when she was sent to Westerbork, then to Bergen-Belsen and was liberated on 13.4.1945 on a train in Hilleslaben near Magdenburg en route to Auschwitz. Her family came to South Africa in 1947. She is a widow and has a married daughter, Michelle, and two grandchildren.

ISRAEL AND RAY KETELLAPPER
Westerbork. Bergen Belsen

(continued from Chapter four)
Mr KETELLAPPER
One afternoon we went to visit a friend of my wife whose husband had been picked up so she was all by herself. We had tea. All of a sudden there was a knock on the door and there were the Gruene Polizei. "Pass bitte." We showed it to the policeman who said, "You - you are also Jews - also away." So we were all arrested.

We were taken in a truck to the station and when we arrived, there was Hauptscharfuhrer Austerfunke. I went up to him and said, "My wife has a British Passport. We have a special stamp that we are going to be exchanged for German soldiers captured by England and we are going to Palestine."

As I said this, he took his hand and gave me a klap. I walked back because I knew if you stayed there they would finish you off. We went by train to Westerbork where we met up with my parents-in-law and her brother who had already been there for a few months and I had to work there.

Mrs KETELLAPPER
I went to work in the laundry which was very nice because it was clean and gave me something to do. We stayed there a few weeks and then gradually more Jews came into the camp so more Jews had to get out. There were transports every week and they loaded up a few thousand Jews and carted them off and eventually our turn came to be carted off. We went in a normal train through Germany up to Celle, a small place near Hanover.

Mr KETELLAPPER
All of a sudden the train stopped and there were the SS with the dogs. We had to go out of the train and they were around us. They told us to go forwards and we had to walk to the camp, not knowing that it was Bergen Belsen. As we arrived at the camp we had to go in and stand in a big square.

Mrs KETELLAPPER
I met up with my parents and my brother who had come there from Westerbork.

Mr KETELLAPPER
They asked us,
Who can work? The Jews are just swindlers and don't want to work. Those who can work, come forward."
So I thought to myself, "Let me step forward because maybe I shall have a chance". So I stepped forward and the Scharfuhrer came to me and said to me,
"What can you do?"
I said,
"I can paint barracks or whatever must be done."
He took me out and I remained there. He gave me a number and we had to go back to the barracks and the next morning he told me on the square that I was going to be the Commander of the Mahlers (painters.)

We stayed in Bergen Belsen for about two and a half years from 1942. I worked every day. I met a very nice Scharfuhrer in the store where they had all the food available for the camp, for the SS and the soldiers. It seems funny to say a "nice" Scharfuhrer but actually with the SS, there were people who had some heart because they had not chosen those jobs. Every morning that man placed a tin with dry porridge and sugar on a shelf for me plus a closed tin of meat. I put these in my bucket under the paint.

Each morning I had to go through the gates and say,
" Mahler Commander that and that number with twenty Jews."
I was in charge of them. At night I had to do the same. There was a band that played music as you went out to work. Our first stop was at the store before they took us into the SS camps where we had to work and paint the barracks inside and outside. In the meantime in my bucket was that meat tin underneath the paint. I never used the paint because I just had to see that those

people were working. Every morning I used to eat the porridge but all the food and all the bread I gave to the family.

Mrs KETELLAPPER
This really did not help very much because I gave the food to my brother who gave the food to my father who gave it to my mother so subsequently there was not much but it kept me going. It didn't help my parents because they got sick and died within three months of each other.

The most tragic thing in the camp was when they separated children from their parents - they might never see their parents again. We had no children so it was easier for us but you became very selfish. You had to look after yourselves - it was self preservation. My husband used to say,
"If you don't want to live anymore, put your head under the cushion" but I used to think to myself, somewhere at the end of the tunnel, there must be some light.

I met up with a lot of interesting people in the camp - French girls in the same predicament. I had a wonderful friend called Yvonne who had two little boys and one day she offered to give me her diamond bracelet in exchange for my 3 inch square piece of bread to feed to her children. I had never seen anything like it in my life but I said to Yvonne,
"I cannot eat diamonds, I need the bread."
Material things in the end do not mean anything to you if you want to live.

In the camp I have never seen so much suffering, so many people dying. One morning the first contingent of Black Jews arrived from North Africa. I had never seen Black people in those days and I had not known that there were Black Jews. They had a lot of kids. The climate was freezing cold and snowy and they did not last long.

There was an old man who stole a pair of socks and we all had to go into this big square and stand on one foot to find out who was wearing the sock. We stood for hours it seemed while the Germans came along all nicely and warmly dressed in their winter coats with fur collars and gloves. It is a funny thing that these things can just happen and you think to yourself - what is it all about? It was not only Jews - we had gypsies, we had priests, all sorts of people.

Mr KETELLAPPER
While I was in the SS barracks Commander Joseph Kramer and Ilse Koch called me in to decorate their place. I had been a display manager for a big company in Holland. I had to hang up lamps which were made of human skins and curtains. The Commander was very sadistic and all of a sudden when I was up on the ladder he put his foot against the stepladder and knocked it over. I fell on the floor bruising three or four ribs, but I got up because if you did not get up straight away, they would kill you. They took me to hospital. The SS were so sadistic - they first hurt you, then fixed you up but one way or another they wanted to kill you.

Once when it was Yom Kippur, they gave the whole camp goulash full of fat - we never got any meat - and thousands died. The rabbis never touched that food nor did my wife's brother who was 19 when he died, just a piece of bread. There was nothing else but pork - they did not want to give you anything else. Sadists.

There was a Stube Commando. Every day they used to take twenty Jews outside the camp to take tree stumps out of the ground. They used to take with them food for the guards - goulash and noodles and ein-topgericht or whatever and they would put them in a circle and the Jews would have to take the stumps out of the ground which is the worst part of cutting down a tree. Every day they would come back with fifteen Jews, so five Jews were either killed or shot. In the morning the poor people who were in that group had to go without knowing if they would return to camp.

Ilse Koch always kept a whip in her boots and when she passed she used to use it. I was whipped. It was nothing but sadism. If you have not been in these situations you cannot visualise that people can do these things to you just because you happen to be Jewish. I only hope to goodness that it will never happen again,

Mrs KETELLAPPER
I was working with the dirty German uniforms that were sent from the front. We had to take them apart and clean the pockets and it was a real messy dirty business. I became sick with typhus plus diphtheria. I could not work any more and I went into hospital - they had a little hospital. There

was no food, no treatment, there was nothing, no milk, no nothing.

There was a young German doctor who looked after me. I could not eat of course. This young doctor always managed to get me a little milk and he was in his own way not a very bad guy, as Germans go. He had a little bit of a heart and he looked after me. One morning he came up to me and he told me that he had a job for me. I asked him what kind of a job and he said that they had an officer's mess around the corner and that if I wanted to work for them, it would be nice to have me and all that.

I said, "What's 'all that'?"

I did not fancy 'all that.' Not that I thought I was brave to refuse the offer to go into the brothel. I saw many young women with children doing that job there, only because they could get some food for the kids. They did manage to get more food than the normal person but they still could not get very much themselves. It was not that I was brave just that I could not do it. He then let me go back when I refused. I went out from the hospital if you could call it a hospital. I could never work again because I was too weak and sick and I just could not do anything.

When the end came, and Germany was collapsing, we had to leave the concentration camp. We do not know how many corpses were lying there when we left the camp, stacked up like piles of logs. They burnt the whole ruddy lot, which was maybe a good thing. The Allies were coming and they wanted to fix it up and cover things before they came .

We were carted off to the station and the doctor came with a whopping black Mercedes - that is why to this day I hate Mercedes - and he said to me and my husband,

"Come into the car and I'll drive you to the station." He had a bottle of milk and he said that he did not know how long we would have to be in the train and he did not know where we were going but that he really did admire me for refusing his offer. He gave me the milk and then he said to me,

"Now I am giving you the milk and then I am going to shoot myself," and I said,

"If that is how you feel, that is what you must do "

He took out his gun and shot himself when we were in the train. I don't think his corpse meant anything to me by that stage because we saw so many corpses lying around and being burnt including my parent's corpses.

Mr KETELLAPPER

We were in the train for FIFTEEN days not knowing that we would be there so long and there was NO FOOD OR DRINK. Nothing at all - fifteen days without water or food or sanitation. A terrible mess.

On the train were approximately 3000 of whom 1500 survived. The first day they took us on the line from Celle near Hanover to Hamburg because they wanted us to get to Poland to be gassed. They had never had a chance to swop us for Germans from England to go to Palestine. One contingent of 400 people did go out from camp - for so many Jews, so many prisoners who had been captured came back. But when we were in the second contingent the Red Cross came from Switzerland and told us that the British government had decided that they would not send any more German prisoners to exchange for Jews to go to Palestine, so that hope was finished and their promise was actually broken.

England knew what was going on in Germany and if they wanted to they could have bombed the railway lines to the camps. They flew over the camps and bombed outside, but never the railways.

They took us over a bridge to Hamburg and when the last compartment of our train went over the bridge, the bridge was blown up by the Germans. The idea had been to get rid of us, the evidence.

They then took us back on a side line to Berlin. On the other side of the train was another train of military soldiers who were coming back from the front who were being pushed by the British. We had been allowed to keep the clothes we wore and were not put in uniform because we were supposed to be going to Palestine. I saw a German with a large loaf of army bread so I gave him my gold watch for it. We went through Berlin which was being bombarded and through the night it was like daylight because everything was burning.

By the 12th day my wife could not walk

any more, she was just sitting there. The ones that died they just pulled out and put on the station. They did not know what to do with the bodies any more

Mrs KETELLAPPER

The last day of this awful train, it was quiet. It was horribly quiet. There were no sounds and a door opened and a big Russian soldier came in and he said in Russian to us,

"YOU ARE FREE!"

and we just looked at him. We didn't understand what he was saying to us, we only understood that we were free. But what to do with all the people who couldn't walk?

So they got all the men who could walk and who were mobile to find some means of transport - a wheelbarrow, a bicycle, a horse and cart - to take us to a little place called Trobitz. There was not a German in the village and it was a very small village. John got a wheelbarrow and I sat in the wheelbarrow and we came to a house there which was open. All the Germans had run away.

I had always promised myself that if I saw a picture of Hitler I would cut it up and flush it down the toilet. It seems very childish, but I came into this house and there was an enormous picture of Hitler hanging on the wall. I could barely move, but I took it off the wall and I tore it into little pieces and I flushed it down the toilet and I felt much better.

Then my husband got sick and had to go to hospital with typhus and there was no place for me in the hospital, so I had to stay in this enormous house by myself. We shared it with another young Jewish couple who had a baby and we had a Russian woman doctor who was absolutely tremendous. She had to shave us because the typhus lice lived in the hair and I said, "Please don't shave off my hair."

It is funny how you think of things like that at times like that, and she did not. They took the young couple out because they also got sick, but they could not take me out because I could not walk. The Russian doctor brought me food every day, things that I could digest. You have to eat carefully after such starvation. I saw many people in that village die from eating. All the shops were open because the German owners had fled. The survivors took whatever they wanted until the Russians started to distribute it in the normal way so that everyone got a share.

I was in this house for two weeks until my husband came from hospital, and after six weeks they told us that all those who had already had typhus could return to their place of origin, because they were scared the disease would spread.

The Russians took us in a very big lorry. I could not get into it so a very nice Russian put me inside on those wooden planks. The Americans came and took us to a place smack in the middle of Germany called Luneberger Heide where all the Allies had met. It was quite interesting because there were photos of Churchill and Roosevelt and Stalin and we were handed over to the Americans. That was like one big party - you could never imagine how they could have won a war because they had kitchens with icecream makers and pancake makers and coffee makers and I thought to myself - That is the way they won the war?

The Americans emptied out their living quarters for us, which had actually been where the Germans had stayed before them. They had beautiful blue blankets and blue sheets. To lie at last between two clean sheets and a blanket was something that stands out in my mind.

Then the Americans took us in big bombers to Holland where I landed up in hospital in Eindhoven. For eight weeks I stayed in the Catholic Hospital there while John went through to Amsterdam through the Red Cross. His aunt had discovered that he was still alive and took him under her wing, and then a Red Cross ambulance took me to another hospital in Amsterdam.

While I was in this hospital there was a young girl of about four or five next to me, really sick. The nurse told me that her parents had left her as a little baby on the doorstep hoping that someone would find her. Some gentiles did, and had brought her up. They were going to adopt her and some lawyers from a large organisation came to find out how this Jewish child could be adopted by gentile parents. As they were about to sign the papers, the door opened and in came a Jewish couple who were looking for a little girl and they recognised the child through a mole on her bottom.

Had they come 5 minutes later, the child would have gone and they would never have known what had happened to her. It was a terrible thing for the gentile couple to have to give her up, but they did.

A lot of Jewish children went into convents with the nuns and they became Catholics. They never saw their families again and they became integrated into their Catholic families, which might have been a good thing as it had saved their lives.

Then we went to the large house of a Baron in the country who had opened his house for people to come to recuperate. It was lovely there and peaceful. Afterwards we came back to Amsterdam where we acquired a house from the church and John worked until after a while he decided that he wanted to go to South Africa where he had lived as a little boy.

ISRAEL KETELLAPPER was born in Holland in 1917 where he married Ray (Dolly). After hiding in Amsterdam they were caught and transported to Bergen-Belsen and were liberated in Trobitz in May 1945. They moved to South Africa in 1952 where his wife died in 1993. They have two daughters Bettina and Patricia.

MIRIAM (MARYSIA) LICHTERMAN
Warsaw, Maidenek, Auschwitz-Birkenau, Ravensbruck, Malhof.

T he following short description of my life during the Holocaust 1939-1945 I wish to dedicate to the memory of my dear, unforgettable parents, **JACOB JOEL** and **PEARL TEITELBAUM**, and my wonderful brother **ISRAEL**, who perished at the hands of the Nazis. My parents were taken from the Warsaw ghetto on a transport to Treblinka in 1942 on the eve of Yom Kippur; my brother died in the Warsaw Ghetto uprising in April 1943.

My older sister, Henia, went on Aliyah to Palestine before the war with her husband Alter and little son Moshe. Many years were to pass before I met them again.

We came from Warsaw in Poland, where we were part of a very warm, happy, middle class Orthodox family. This home environment which my parents created, the high moral standards and values with which I was brought up and which I was also taught at school, and my family background stood me in good stead in the terrible years that followed and helped me remain a mensch, a human being with dignity even in the inhuman conditions in which I found myself later. In looking back I know that those formative years at home made me the person I am today.

Since May 1945 I have divided my life into 3 parts, "**before the War**", "**during the War and the Holocaust**" and "**the years after the War.**" The first part is represented by my carefree childhood and teenage years, surrounded by loving parents, sister and brother, aunts, uncles, cousins, friends, schoolteachers, holy days, celebrations, happiness and tears. This changed abruptly in September 1939 when my world turned upside down and eventually became a horror I would much rather not think about. The years after the war became the third part. In the early post-war years I seldom spoke openly about my experiences. I did not really want to relive the nightmare and the trauma of what I went through. Also, I was so busy rebuilding a new life together

with my late husband, Cantor Jacob Lichterman, whom I married in 1945 after the War, that we simply did not think about it although we certainly did not forget.

In 1983 I attended the World Gathering of Holocaust Survivors in Jerusalem. At the various functions and commemorations which took place we were addressed by speakers who included Prime Minister Menachem Begin and famous writers, also survivors Simon Wiesenthal, Samuel Pisar and Madame Simone Weill. All emphasized how vital it is for us, the last witnesses, who are getting older and dying out, to record our experiences, to tell the world what happened. There has been a frightening rise in Neo-Nazism and Holocaust denial. I was astonished to hear a professor from the Hebrew University in Jerusalem say that he did not have sufficient material about the Holocaust to teach his students adequately. It made me realize how important it is for us to talk about it, and that our talks have to be recorded for posterity,

I was a young schoolgirl in Warsaw when war broke out on the 1st of September 1939. **This certainly was the last day of my youth.** Warsaw was bombed incessantly. Immediately after its occupation by the German armies, the Nazis started a programme of brutal persecution of the Jews who were concentrated into ghettos. At that time Warsaw had a population of about two million, 350 000 of whom were Jewish. As various decrees and instructions were issued we had to move into temporary homes inside smaller and smaller areas, taking only what we could carry in our hands. The most valuable possessions were left behind to be looted by the Nazi Commanders. This taught us how unimportant possessions were when life was at stake.

Despite the hunger, cold and deprivation we tried to keep some semblance of normal life going in the ghetto. We would get together to study, play chess or cards or comfort one another. I remember going with Israel to hear Rimsky-Korsakoff's Peer Gynt played by top out-of-work Jewish musicians. My mother, the eternal optimist, would say that as long as Jews could make music, nothing could destroy us. My father of course was more realistic. To this day, when I hear Peer Gynt I do not really hear the beautiful music, but see my brother and parents in that ghetto environment.

Transports would leave from the ghettos to so-called "labour camps". In the beginning when the first transports went to Treblinka, two men in our neighbourhood managed to escape from there. They had been selected to remove the white bands with a blue Magen David from the sleeves of clothing and to load these clothes onto waggons going to Germany. Under cover of darkness they hid themselves among the clothes and escaped in the waggons. They made their way on foot back to the ghetto and told us what was happening in Treblinka. We did not believe them. We thought they were exaggerating because the mind could not fathom the fact that humans could behave like this to humans. Or even to animals.

We soon learnt that they did not exaggerate at all.

There were two ghettos. Israel was in the large ghetto while we were in the small one. Before the complete closure of the ghettos Israel had managed to get through to see me and had said that they were planning an uprising and that he would rather die resisting the Nazis than in a gas chamber. It was the last time that I was to see him. The uprising took place in the bigger ghetto in April 1943. That ghetto was completely destroyed during the uprising; we only saw the sky lit up by the fires.

In the small ghetto 10 000 Jews worked as slave labour for an SS firm, Toebens, in a building which had housed the commercial faculty of the Warsaw University. Jews cost nothing, just a portion of bread and hot watery soup. My parents paid a lot of money to get working cards. They were not really working but in 1941 one could still make a plan to remain in the ghetto by working. I learnt to sew on the machine and make belts for dresses, which, we were told, were sent to Italy.

At Toebens we worked from 7 p.m. to 7 a.m. When we finished the night shift early one morning in September 1942 on the eve of Yom Kippur, the doors were locked and we were not allowed out. We realized that this meant that a selection was taking place in the neighbourhood and that they did not want to get us mixed up with those being taken away.

When I got home, I found that my parents had been taken away. Every one had been taken, and I was alone.

Some time later I found myself in one of the transports in a cattle train. There was a junction a few miles away from Warsaw. If the train went left, it went to Treblinka; right led to Lublin. Trains to Maidenek had to travel via Lublin. If you went to Maidenek, you still had a chance, but if you went to Treblinka this led straight to destruction. I remember tall girls trying to get to the little barred windows to see which direction the train was going. When we found that we were not going to Treblinka, we knew that we would land in Maidenek.

On arrival there was a selection on the spot - one either went left or right. Some people went direct to the gas chambers, others went into the camp. Maidenek was a transit camp for me. I stayed there for six or eight weeks during which time I worked in the fields. It was not constructive work. We just went outside the camp into the fields and dragged stones from one place to another. It was terrible. All we got at the time was some hot water with weeds floating in it and a portion of bread. Nobody remained a long time in Maidenek and I was transferred to Auschwitz- Birkenau.

What struck me on arrival was the fact that we were tattooed with numbers on our arms. Our individuality was lost completely and we became numbers. I remained in Birkenau from July 1943 until the end of 1944.

I remember a particular day in 1944 when the daily transports of Hungarian Jews came. It was a Sunday and we did not go out to work nor did we stand appel at the crack of dawn like on other days. It was a very warm day and I was outside in front of the block trying to wash my wooden clogs, to tidy myself up. I watched on the horizon this magnificent ball of the sun shining. In the background the chimneys were smoking. On the other side of the block I heard some Ukrainian girls, not Jewish, singing. I thought to myself, **"This is macabre - the sun is shining; I hear singing; and on the other side I see black smoke belching from the chimney where people are being gassed and burned."** I thought I must have died and was probably in hell because it was too macabre that the same sun could be shining here over this scene while not far away in the village of Auschwitz it was also shining for normal people over a normal world.

When we went out of camp, we were always told to sing so that when trains arrived on the tracks the occupants would hear singing. One day when we were asked to sing, we saw cattle waggons lined up on the tracks. There were little faces peeping through the barred windows of the cattle waggons. We knew they were our Jewish children. We felt utter helplessness and despair. We could do nothing, we could only murmur to ourselves and hang our heads in shame that there was a world outside this camp that knew about this and allowed it to happen. There was no help coming from anywhere. I shall never forget this sight.

Another unforgettable event was a selection when I had just recovered from typhus. I was very thin and looked very bad. My number was written down during the selection for the gas chambers. After the selection we all went back to our blocks and the following day when the blockalteste - the woman responsible for the block - came to call those girls whose numbers had been written down in the selection, the girl who was lying next to me on the bunk had her number called out as well as a few other girls, but mine was not called out. It was a selection at which many thousands of numbers were written down. One of the girls in the schreibstube - the administrative office - knew me, recognized my number and removed it. She was my guardian angel throughout my stay in Auschwitz-Birkenau. She was responsible for my staying alive.

Meeting her in the camp was nothing short of a miracle. I attribute my survival to the intervention of a Divine hand in the person of this Czechoslovakian girl. Let me describe how I met her.

In my transport to Birkenau there were about 500 girls in one group. We were in one barrack. Next to me in the bunk lay a girl from a small town near Warsaw, who had a brother a few years older than herself. In 1939 he was a student at the Warsaw university and during the summer vacation he went across the mountains into Czechoslovakia on an excursion with Jewish students and became friendly with a Czechoslovakian girl student. He arrived in Auschwitz - Birkenau in the same transport as his sister. This young man saw this Czech student taking the register of the people who were arriving. The Czech girls came a year before us. Most died out in epidemics and those who survived were the leaders in the camp. He managed to convey to her that his sister had also arrived.

After appel when the day was finished, she came to the block of the new arrivals looking for his sister, who happened to be the girl next to me. She spoke German and Czech and this new girl did not quite understand either language. I became the translator as I had done German in school, I had relatives in Germany and my German was fairly good. We became friendly. (This Czech girl arranged with our blocalteste that the sister should not go out to the field but remain as the block cleaner. Six cleaners were responsible for washing the mud off the floor, fetching the bread and cutting it up into portions.)

We used to chat whenever she came to see me. She arranged for me to help her in her work. I could not stay in her block but I would return at night with a little extra bread or something she could share as she had certain privileges being in the schreibstube. When I became ill with typhus she hid me in the daytime in a little cubicle beyond the section where she was working and where I would work with her. I could get hot water which I would not have been able to get had I been in my block. Also I would not have been well enough to go out to work, and would have been sent to the "revier". This was a sort of hospital where one did not survive longer than a week or two. Then the whole hospital was emptied out and the inmates sent to the gas chambers.

After the selection in which she had removed my number she realized that I had to be taken away from the main camp because all those who looked like I did were sent to the gas chambers. We were all thin but I looked as if I would die the following day. It would have aroused suspicion had I still been around. She managed to get me into a group of women and girls who were going to the Muster "show" camp. From there I was eventually evacuated and lost contact with her. I still wonder what happened to her. The Almighty must have sent her to watch over me.

The "Musterlager" was a very small camp in Auschwitz itself prepared as a show camp for Red Cross representatives who were supposed to visit. I found myself in this camp sometime at the end of 1944. It was actually much worse than the rest of the camp because at the time there was no food at all. The only improvement was that we had eiderdowns instead of blankets and we were two per bunk instead of five. I worked at night in the "nehstube", the sewing room, where we repaired the uniforms which all inmates wore. There was no food and no sleep. It was terrible - the beginning of the end in Auschwitz.

I should like to describe another memorable incident. One day in Autumn 1943 soon after our group arrived in Birkenau we were detailed to work outside building a road by putting down large stones, then little stones on top and then sand which would be pressed down. One morning we were weeding a field not far from the camp, near a road used by the SS. There must have been about 100 women working in that field, divided into groups. In my group there were 6 girls. A group nearby noticed a miserable apple tree with a few green apples growing on it. When the aufseherin had walked away from us and was out of sight, they shook the tree, picked up the apples and ate them. Just then a high ranking SS officer drove past on his motor cycle, saw what was happening, and dismounted. In a barking tone he asked where our aufseherin was. We were terrified. The girls nudged me,

"He will kill us! You can speak German. Speak to him!"

I answered in German that the aufseherin had gone to the toilet. He wrote down the numbers of the girls he saw picking the apples and although I was not part of that group he wrote down my number also because I had stepped forward and opened my mouth. That evening when we returned to the camp and were standing appel, the lauferine arrived, spoke to the blocalteste who read out the numbers of eight girls who had to go to the bunker for the night for picking apples. I was included.

The lauferine was the contact between the administration, the SS running the camp and the camp. She was a girl originally from Belgium, from a very old transport, even earlier than the Polish transports who had survived. She spoke perfect German, French and Polish. She had emigrated from Poland to Belgium when she was a young girl with her parents. She was the one who had control over the bunker. We were two groups who got four nights bunker - we were locked up after a day's work in a sort of a bunker where four girls could barely stand together. She was supposed to lock us up for the night and get us out in the morning. She took it on herself that we only spent two nights bunker. She was a wonderful person, full of compassion. She once achieved the impossible - an escape from Auschwitz together with a male inmate but was recaptured after three days.

One late afternoon as we were marching through the main gates we saw her. She had been put on show and was barely able to stand there. The sight of her swaying and standing there will be with me the rest of my life. Eventually she was executed.

The Russian army was coming nearer from the East and the Allies were approaching from the West. On the 10th or 11th of January 1944 Auschwitz was evacuated by the hundreds of thousands. We were dragged deeper into Germany - the snow was on the ground, it was bitterly cold. We were given a portion of bread and a blanket, and we were marched towards Germany. We did not walk along the main roads, we walked by day and stopped at night. We sat and lay in the snow; we were falling by the thousands by the wayside, and those who fell or could not walk any further were shot on the spot by the guards, who walked with dogs. This was the infamous *totenmarch* - the death march. Eventually we crossed into Germany where we boarded trucks in a group. It was the same group with which I had left Auschwitz, but it was a much, much depleted one. I still do not know how I managed to survive.

We were taken into Ravensbruck. If

Birkenau and Auschwitz were hell, then Ravensbruck at that time was the worst hell of the lot. If there can be a distinction between hell or hell, then Ravensbruck was really the pits. From all over they gathered people - other camps were also evacuated - and everybody was pulled deeper into Germany. We just used to lie in the barracks on the ground and 12 o clock at night some containers with hot watery soup came. This was our only sustenance. Had our group not been transferred with our aufseherin we would not have survived that hell.

We were transported further north to Malhof, a very small working camp. The men who had been in that camp before us had been tailors who had been evacuated deeper into Germany. We were there a few weeks until the beginning of May. The Kommandant went about 50 km away to fetch the Red Cross parcels available to us and every camp inmate was supposed to get one of these parcels. He managed to go with a truck and load on a certain amount of parcels - every two girls got a parcel. These parcels sustained us until we were liberated - without them we would have been finished. They contained condensed milk, cheese, rusks, sugar and coffee, but we did not have hot water to make the coffee. The Camp Kommandant was supposed to return for more parcels but he could not get through. We knew this was the end. The end of the war. We were between two advancing armies - the Russians approaching from the East and the Allies from the West.

Soon after that the Camp Kommandant must have run away without any one knowing it. We stood outside the camp gates on the road in a column ready to be transferred to another camp, waiting and waiting for the command to start marching. We could not understand why there was nobody around and why we were not being ordered to march.

Those at the head of the column then realized that actually there were no guards. There was nobody guarding us! We were in the middle of the road. FREE!!
Alive, but not really free.
Yet free, because nobody killed us.

The guards had run away before we had even started marching. They were anxious to get to the Allies. Anxious to get away from the Russian front. They knew that if they were caught by the Russians they would be finished, but if they got to the Allies they might stand a chance of surviving. So now the boot was on the other foot!

We started walking by ourselves knowing that we could not remain in the middle of the road. We did not know where we were going but we thought we might reach the Allied front ourselves. We broke up into small groups. All we had were the leftovers from the Red Cross parcels. Eventually we were overtaken by a Russian advance guard of high ranking officers on motor cycles who saw who we were. The army did not go through the area where we were but side stepped us in order to meet with the Allies.

I found myself free, in a group of people, survivors of various camps, in the beginning of May, in the middle of ruins somewhere in the middle of Germany. With my own eyes I saw on the road the remnants of the once powerful German army, only they no longer wore shining boots and they did not click them anymore. There were no shouts of "*sieg heil.*" Their uniforms were torn and they were trying with their last breath to run, to get away from the advancing Russian army. We saw prisoners hanging in the forests. That was the day of my liberation.

I remember thinking of the day in Autumn 1939 when the mighty German army had entered Warsaw and our lives had changed overnight never to be the same again. It did not seem to have been five and a half years ago but a hundred years ago in another lifetime.

We remained in an evacuated camp, where the Russian authorities had instructed us to stay. Then a command came to begin to disperse. We were a mixture of people from all over Europe. A friend with whom I had been since Auschwitz went towards the Allies in order to return to Belgium where non-Jewish friends had been looking after her daughter. She was hoping that the child was still alive. She doubted whether her husband was. I joined a group of 18 people who were going towards Poland. We walked for a few weeks.

We walked in the day-time and hid at night in abandoned buildings. There were also many German refugees on the roads, mostly elderly people who would hide in churches. Our group included three Hungarian sisters, the daughters of a rabbi, who planned to walk with us to the Polish border and then make their way home. I became friendly with a woman who knew how I dreaded returning to Warsaw. She persuaded me to go with her first to Cracow which had escaped the bombing. She had been told that her husband had been seen a few months before in a camp.

When we reached Cracow in July 1945, we went to the Polish woman who had been their maid and with whom they had left some valuables. She told my friend that her mother had come back from Auschwitz. She had not gone on the death march but had hidden in the camp with two other women. When the Russians arrived she came out of hiding and had managed to return to Cracow in January. She was working and had a room of her own. It was an unforgettable reunion. A week later her husband arrived. I decided it was no use postponing my return to Warsaw. I must go home and make myself known in Warsaw at the Jewish Committee and the Red Cross where one registered and where records were kept of who returned and who survived.

Two weeks passed before I reached Warsaw again but it was a very different Warsaw. It was not the Warsaw of my dreams and it was not the Warsaw of my childhood and it was not the Warsaw of my memories.

When I arrived at the station and looked around me, I just wanted to run away - I did not know where I was. I did not recognize it. There were only ruins in the streets, ruins of the bombings, ruins of the ghetto uprising and ruins of the Polish uprising in 1944. There were also ruins in my heart.

I knew that my parents were gone, my brother was gone with the fires of the ghetto uprising. He was one of those who had planned it. He had wanted to die resisting.

So I was back in Warsaw but it was not back home. I never got home. There was no more home. I never returned to what I lost.

Everything was gone with the ashes. Everyone I loved was gone with the ashes, and so was everybody else.

But I had this vision of a better world to come after the hatred, the destruction, the Holocaust. I thought there would be no more wars, no more violence, a good world where humans would behave like humans. I soon learned better.

I made my way to the Central Committee of Polish Jews and registered. I was given a place to stay with three other girls, and coupons for food. I sent a cable to my sister in Israel to let her know that I was alive.

In Warsaw I met Cantor Jacob Lichterman of the well known Nozyk Synagogue where as a young girl, before the war, I had watched my cousins and others getting married in the beautiful ceremonies, and where at the beginning of every academic year in September I used to attend special services together with delegates from other schools. Now it seemed as though 100 years had passed, in another lifetime, when I was still young. He was soon to become my husband; together we left Warsaw to build a home away from the ruins and ashes of Poland and start a new chapter in our lives.

MIRIAM (MARYSIA)LICHTERMAN was born in Warsaw, Poland where she went to school until the outbreak of war in September 1939. During the war she was moved to the Warsaw Ghetto and from there to various concentration camps, Majdanek, Birkenau, Auschwitz, Ravensbruck, and Malhof where she was liberated in May 1945. After moving to Brussels and London she arrived in South Africa in 1948. She was married to Cantor Jacob Lichterman, who died in Cape Town in 1986. They have two sons, Joel and Ivor.

JACOB LICHTERMAN

(As told by his wife, Miriam)

Warsaw ghetto, Maidenek, Auschwitz-Birkenau, Buna-Auschwitz.

Cantor Jacob Lichterman was born into a large strictly Orthodox middle class family in Warsaw. Every brother and sister had the gift of a fine voice as did his father, Itzchack Meyer Halevi, who died before the war. Young Lichterman attended the Krinski gymnasium and Institute of Higher Jewish Studies in Warsaw. Since childhood blessed with a beautiful lyrical voice and having a great love of Jewish liturgical music, he studied music at the Warsaw Conservatorium as well as Jewish liturgical music and composition with various composers and cantors. As a young soprano he used to sing in the choir of the prestigious Nozyk Synagogue where, at the age of 19, he became the Cantor, a position he held until 1941 when formal worship was forbidden and the synagogue closed. Thus he became the last cantor of his synagogue and the last cantor in Warsaw.

In 1942 there was still a tram with a star of David instead of a number on it which ran from the small ghetto to the large ghetto and back through non-ghetto territory. Poles were not allowed to travel on it.

When the President of the Jewish Community, Engineer Cherniakov, was asked to sign the order for the deportations from the Warsaw Ghetto and the final liquidation he committed suicide rather than do so. The SS went into the ghetto to arrest fifty hostages, mostly leaders of the community. They rounded up forty eight and stopped the Jewish tram for the additional two. Jacob Lichterman happened to be travelling on it. He thus became the forty ninth hostage. They were taken to the infamous Paviak prison and went through a terrible time of daily beatings, hunger and torture. He was released into the ghetto six weeks later to find desolation, the streets littered with Jewish belongings and dead bodies. The SS had already started liquidating the ghetto and transporting people to Treblinka - ostensibly to labour camps in the East but by then everyone knew that this was not so.

He managed to avoid deportation by having a working card from the SS firm Werterfassung where he was supposed to be restoring musical instruments and works of art which the SS had looted from Jewish homes after their inhabitants had been deported. One day a high ranking Nazi officer, apparently Himmler himself, visited the workshop and ordered it to be destroyed. The Nazis had no more use for Jews in the ghetto which was to be completely liquidated.

Cantor Lichterman fought in the Uprising, was wounded in the leg, and had what was then considered to be the luck of being transported to Maidanek instead of Treblinka. It was the end of April 1943, the end of the uprising, the end of the Warsaw Ghetto. From there he was transported to Birkenau-Auschwitz in the Buna-Monowitz complex.

During his incarceration in the various concentration camps which were all part of the Auschwitz complex he experienced a few close brushes with death. But every time divine intervention saved him miraculously.

Once he was in a workshop with a few inmates and the foreman, an SS man, who thought it would be fun to hang him. As he was preparing the rope, a high-ranking official happened to walk into the hut and unintentionally diverted the foreman. Later the foreman pretended that it was all a joke but had the official not walked in at that moment and stayed there until the end of the work shift, the joke would have turned to reality and Jacob would have been hanged.

On another occasion in Auschwitz his number was written down for the gas chambers because he had an inflammation in his leg which had been wounded during the Ghetto uprising. He managed to send a message to a friend, Berel Regutgowitz, who was a Belgian Jew who also loved chazanut and had been a chazan and the gabbai of the synagogue in Brussels. Before the war Berel had owned a shoe factory. Now he ran the shoe repair workshop for the SS

Berel bribed an SS man with a pair of new boots and saved his friend Lichterman from the gas chambers. Berel survived and we visited him in Brussels and later in Netanya, Israel, where he settled.

In January 1945 when Auschwitz was being evacuated in the wake of the advance of the Russian army, they were each given a portion of bread and a blanket and started on the totenmarch, the death march, the evacuation of Auschwitz.

One evening while they were walking on a road near a forest that was still in Polish territory near the German - Russian border a courageous man abandoned the marching column and ran into the forest. The guards opened fire, but could not chase him. As the guards were shooting, more men broke away from the column to run into the forest under a hail of bullets and Jacob was one of them. Some were shot by the guards but a few managed to reach the density of the forest.

The prisoners ran further and further, deeper and deeper into the woods, until the shooting stopped and they knew that the column must have moved on. They dared not leave the forest because it was all German-occupied territory.

There were about ten men in the group and they stayed in the forest all night in the cold and the snow not daring to look outside. The following night they decided that if someone did not go to look for food, they would starve and freeze to death. They knew that there would be villages in the area although they did not know exactly where these were. That night Jacob and two other men were chosen to venture out. When they saw a light from afar, they went up to it and knocked on the window of a peasant's hut. No one answered; the occupants were too frightened to open. They had to return empty handed.

The following night they tried again and this time the peasant gave Jacob a bottle of black coffee, three pieces of bread and a box of matches and told him not to come back as Germans were still in the area. On returning to their group in the forest they were in such haste to pass the flask to each other that they dropped it, spilt the coffee and had to watch the precious liquid seep into the snow.

They stayed in the forest for ten nights after which they split up into smaller groups. Jacob returned on the eleventh night to that peasant, a VolksDeutch (a Pole of German origin) who told them that the Russians were very near and hid them for four days in the hay in his barn. At night he would bring them hot water, black coffee and bread. During the day the barn was locked. One morning the peasant opened the barn and said,

"You may come out. The Russians are here."

This was sometime near the end of January 1945, before the war had actually ended. He made his way to Warsaw. It was many weeks before he reached there through a country devastated by the retreating army and the advancing Russians. On arrival in Warsaw, he discovered that he was the only member of his family to have survived.

He became a member of the Executive of the Central Committee for Polish Jews, the Cantor and Chaplain to the returning Jews. Together with Rabbi Dr Kahane he officiated as the chaplain to the forces mainly at funerals, reburials, marriages and holiday services.

I met him in Warsaw in July 1945 after my return there. The Central Committee for Polish Jews had offices with empty rooms used for returning people. Although the top few storeys were burned out - a skeleton remained - the rest was still solid. In the late afternoon people would congregate in the courtyard. One could meet returning people and ask about relatives, about friends. The questions always were:
"Did you see my mother, I know she was in this camp?"
"Where were you? In which camp?"
"Where did you come from?"
"Do you know what happened to this one?"
"Do you know what happened to that one?"

Every face was eagerly awaited because a new face, a new person, meant more news, more information, about what had happened, who was likely to come back and who would never return. Jacob Lichterman spotted me - my face must have been familiar to him and came up to me. I recognized him because in the good times we used to attend weddings and other services at the Nozyk synagogue. Eventually we got married.

But we could not build a new life on ruins and graves. It was a long road to South Africa via Brussels and London where he officiated in various synagogues. The late Rabbi Dr Schonfeld in the uniform of a high ranking English officer came to Warsaw to rescue the Jewish children hidden with nuns and Gentile families. Cantor Lichterman helped in this task. He had access to lists with names of these children. Three transports of Jewish children left for London and eventually arrived in Israel. Rabbi Schonfeld offered my husband the position of cantor to his United Synagogues in London. Thus we were able to get out of Poland and come to South Africa.

Soon after arrival here Cantor Lichterman was approached by various Jewish newspapers - Dorom Afrika, Barkai and others - to write about his experiences. In one article he described how one morning while they were standing appel in Birkenau to be counted, some prisoners supported a man in an upright position who had died a few minutes before in order to receive his portion of bread. After this appeared in the press we received a phone call from a Jewish man in Doornfontein who expressed disbelief at anybody being so hungry as to do such a thing.

In April 1983 there was a gathering in Warsaw for the 40th anniversary of the Warsaw Ghetto Uprising and the rededication by the Polish Government to the Jewish people of the Nozyk Synagogue. This was the only synagogue in Warsaw to survive the destruction and had been used as a stable during the war.

The Polish government invited my husband to conduct the services at the Monument for the Fallen during the Warsaw Ghetto Uprising and the rededication of the synagogue. It was a heartbreaking return, this last service in the beautiful shul where over the years he had stood in prayer and song in front of a large congregation, now no more. While there he was interviewed by the press from all over the world, the radio, the BBC, the Dutch radio, etc. He also gave talks here nd a report to the Board of Deputies. As the Argus foreign correspondent reported,

"For Cantor Lichterman small in stature but magnificent in voice, it was a last sad look."

From the heartbreaking visit to Warsaw, Cantor Lichterman travelled on to the United States where he attended the Brit Milah of his grandson, Mayron. It was a journey from heartbreak to celebration, from sadness to rejoicing, from destruction to a new life and the continuation of the Lichtermans and the Jewish people.

LEON BORSTROCK
Westerbork, Auschwitz, Birkenau, Gross-Rosen,
Buchenwald, Theresienstadt, Mauthausen, Dachau.

I was born in London and moved to Holland with my parents. I went to school in Amsterdam and was studying to be an architect when war broke out. From Westerbork I was sent by cattle train to Auschwitz-Birkenau in the winter of

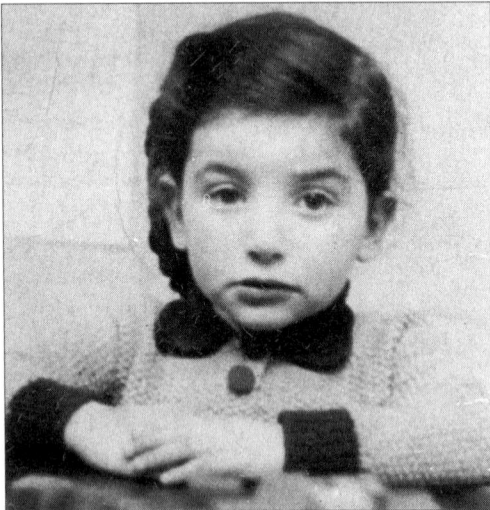

My daughter Frederika

1942. When we got off the train there was a selection and I never saw my family again, not my wife Roosjie, not my five year old daughter, Frederika, nor my six month old son Jacques. They were all gassed.

When we arrived, an SS officer impassively announced that there was no hope for us and that those who did not go through the chimney would be accommodated in the camp even if there were a million of us.

I was placed in a wooden quarantine block with eight men. Our heads were shaved, we were undressed in the snow and taken to a sauna where we remained for two hours. The doors were then flung open and guards on both sides of the building let loose wild

alsatian dogs. Sweating from the sauna, we fled naked into the snow. We were then given ragged jackets, trousers, berets and wooden shoes. Each day we got a bowl of nettle soup, peppermint tea and 225 grams of bread, two thirds of which was made of sawdust.

Eighty per cent of the 1 700 who had arrived together in our transport were dead within six weeks.

At first I was employed building a crematorium until I was reassigned as a signwriter. My father had taught me this skill and I had also studied at the Royal Academy for Art in The Hague. I was the only one in Auschwitz qualified to do this and I was transferred to a work commando in the Waffenmeisterie - the munitions workshop - where I had to spray paint cars and motor cycles and write on them in Gothic lettering. Later I was sent to the camp headquarters where I would inscribe the names and functions of all the SS officers in the camp into a register. These records were sent each month to the SS headquarters at Sachsenhausen near Berlin. As a result of this I was not treated as badly as the other prisoners and I was sometimes able to help them.

After the attempted assassination of Hitler in 1944 all German mail had to be written in German, and as some of the SS officers came from countries like Poland or Hungary, France or Holland, they could not write in German, so they would get me to write letters to their families for them and would pay me with bread, potatoes or occasionally salami which I shared with the others.

I wrote for eighteen hours a day while the SS officers dictated to me. Frequently they would say,
"Jew, make one mistake, and we'll put you in the chambers with your brothers!"

Twice I was lined up with other prisoners to be transported out - once to clean out the Warsaw Ghetto after the uprising, and the other time to work in the Myszlowits coal mine in Poland. Both times I was instructed to remain behind as a sign writer.

The kapo (commander foreman) who pulled me out of line each time was Josef Anders, a Communist. He was a forthright and well liked man, who had noticed my skill at sign writing and seemed to have taken a liking to me. He told me that I should always look forwards, not back because old iron could not beat glittering gold. By this he meant that the Germans with all their iron did not have a chance against the Allies with their financial resources. He looked after me until he was sent with the Volksturmer to the front. Because of the protection he offered me, I escaped the worst of the ill-treatment that the other inmates got.

Then I was sent to the gas chamber. We were in the barracks with seven men per bunk and one morning an SS doctor walked in and began selecting prisoners too ill to work. I was strongly built and was ordered to carry one of the condemned men to the gas chamber - a wooden building with a low roof and a sign on the door saying ENT-LAUSUNGSKAMMER. (Delousing room.)

By now we were completely desensitized. We were so bombarded by the horror and butchery that our minds stopped functioning normally. Nothing shocked us anymore, even though some days the air was so thick with the stench of burning bodies that we could not breathe. I just accepted the fact that I would never see life again and marched to the gas chambers with the fellow prisoner on my shoulders.

When I arrived, there were hundreds of naked prisoners standing outside, helpless, waiting. Many were afraid. Many were terrified. Many were not.

It was forbidden to pray in Auschwitz but I could hear men mumbling Kaddish.

Where was the Almighty NOW, I wanted to know.

If you commit a crime, you must pay the penalty.

But to be Jewish is not a crime.

By the grace of G-d, when I reached the entrance I was ordered back. An officer decided I was strong enough to work. Not so that poor unfortunate.

This incident was repeated twice more. On the third time I was sent into the gas chamber itself. With the building rapidly filling up with condemned men the SS Obersturmfuehrer poked his baton at me. If I was fit enough to carry someone on my shoulders, I was fit enough to work, he ruled.

Back I went to work, to Block 15, a barracks housing four hundred men of the Sicherheidsdienst (SD or Security Services.) These were engineers, toolmakers and artisans whose skills were essential to the functioning of the camp.

One night we returned from work to find a naked body, full of bullet holes, strung up at the entrance. A note was attached to it warning that this was the penalty for escaping.

One afternoon during a workbreak we played a short game of soccer and I suddenly felt a vicious spasm of pain in my groin. I shuffled back to the office and asked for a letter of admission to the infirmary. The drunk officer told me to write it myself. I limped to the hospital where the doctor examined me, diagnosed a hernia and told me that I needed an operation. I climbed onto the operating table and waited. The doctor, Dr Mengele, asked me what sort of anaesthetic I preferred. I chose local, because I was scared what he might do to me if I were unconscious.

I stayed in the hospital for 22 days. Dr Mengele had left a swab inside the wound and it was festering. One of the Jewish male nurses warned me that Dr Mengele was going to do one of his selection rounds next morning and that any patient not getting better would be sent to the gas chamber. That night the nurse washed my wound in an effort to close it. At 6 a.m. Dr Mengele in his white coat began his rounds pronouncing death to some. When he got to my bed I waited very tensely. I was ordered to go back to work. The wound however was still far from healed.

On my way back to the barracks the wound burst open and I collapsed. I could not return to Dr Mengele because that would have meant the gas chambers. I made it back to my block and crawled to my bunk. There was a Dr Valentine in the camp, a Jewish prisoner, who refused to work in the infirmary but went from block to block assisting the prisoners. Someone summoned him and he covered my wound with a black ointment and a piece of plaster. I returned to work and the swab came out within 48 hours, stuck to the plaster.

In May 1944 a guard found an oil rag burning in the coal stove in my block. He lined up 13 men, twelve of whom were Poles and ordered the guilty man to step forward. No one moved. The guard decided that as I was the only Jew in the commando, it must have been me. That night at roll call my number was called and I had to step forward. I had to take down my trousers and before everyone I had to bend over a table and count out loud as two SS men gave me twenty five lashes with elephant hide batons.

The next morning the guard asked me if I would admit having thrown the rag into the fire. I insisted that I had not done it and he immediately ordered our work commando to line up again. If no one else confessed then I was to get another twenty five lashes. Josef Anders stepped forward and courageously informed the officer that he refused to permit an innocent man to be punished a second time and assured him that he would find the culprit himself. He cross questioned each man in Polish and soon discovered the identity of the guilty man. For four days he was kept folded in a box, one cubic metre large, with only water to sustain him.

After that the officer treated me far more humanely.

As the German armies crumbled and the Allies advanced, plans were made to evacuate the concentration camps, in order to exterminate the remaining Jews before the fast approaching Russians could save them.

On January 18, 1945 11 000 men left Auschwitz for the long march to the West.

On 29th April this column reached Dachau a distance of more than one thousand kilometres. Only 156 remained alive.

We slept on farms during the day and marched by night. We ate grass and bones from dead animals found along the route. I learnt that there were two types of grass. The soft kind was edible; the hard grass cut one's intestines. We had procured scraps of clothing from every conceivable source in a vain attempt to defy the sub-zero German winter. Those who collapsed of exhaustion were shot in the neck and left on the road.

The only strength we had was our own will. Such was the determination of the SS to kill us, that even when Russian cannons were within earshot they still rounded up Jews along the way and forced them to march.

From Auschwitz the column was marched to Gross-Rosen and then to Gorlitz and then to Buchenwald where the Royal Air Force started to bomb us, mistaking us for German soldiers. We took off our striped jackets and laid them out on the road to identify ourselves as prisoners and only then did the bombing stop.

At the Buchenwald concentration camp our guards were Norwegian prisoners of war. The Americans were 20km away and most of the Germans, particularly the SS, had left us.

There were many Dutch prisoners there. One was a Roman Catholic priest who had been arrested for hiding two Jewish families in the cellar of his church in Holland. He approached me, threw his bible at me and disappeared. I looked for him the next day and tried to return it to him. He said that he would only take it back if I accepted his food in return. He felt that I was a Jew who was a witness to what had happened and he was prepared to die in order that I could live. I was not prepared to accept his offer. He died in the camp.

Before leaving Buchenwald we recognized among the prisoners a Czech who had been a foreman to the Jewish women in Auschwitz. He made sexual demands of them and if they refused, he handed them over to the SS. The women were powerless to do anything about him in Auschwitz. Here it was different. We murdered him and threw his body in a canal.

From Buchenwald the handful of survivors were marched to Dresden, and then to Pilsen, and then to Mauthausen and then to Dachau where we were liberated by the American Army.

When I was liberated I weighed 37 kg. I made enquiries, through the Red Cross, about the rest of my family and discovered that my younger brother Jules aged 21 had been shot at Mauthausen ten days after being sent there.

My brother Harry aged 17 had been shot at Birkenau because he had refused to work for the Germans.

My brother Michel survived Bergen-Belsen

but died after the war.

I also made enquiries about Josef Anders and was told that he had died in a Brussels prisoner of war camp. I sent his widow some food parcels. She sent me a picture of her husband.

When I returned to Amsterdam, thin, ill and shaven headed, a neighbour recognized me. He returned to me some of my clothes that he had managed to rescue from my apartment when I was taken away.

In the pocket of a jacket I found a photograph of my daughter Frederika.

All that remained of a life that had gone up into smoke.

Why am I recalling these events? I believe that I owe it to posterity and particularly to the memory of my relatives and fellow prisoners who never survived to ensure that this horror is never forgotten.

Leon Borstrock was born in London in 1913 and moved to Holland with his family. He was educated in Middelberg and Amsterdam and was training to be an architect when war broke out. He was taken to Westerbork and from there to Auschwitz, then Gross-Rosen, Buchenwald, Theresienstadt, Mauthausen and Dachau where he was liberated in 1945. He married Lily in London in 1946 and came to South Africa in 1948. He died in 1988. He has two sons, Jeffrey and Milton, and three grandsons.

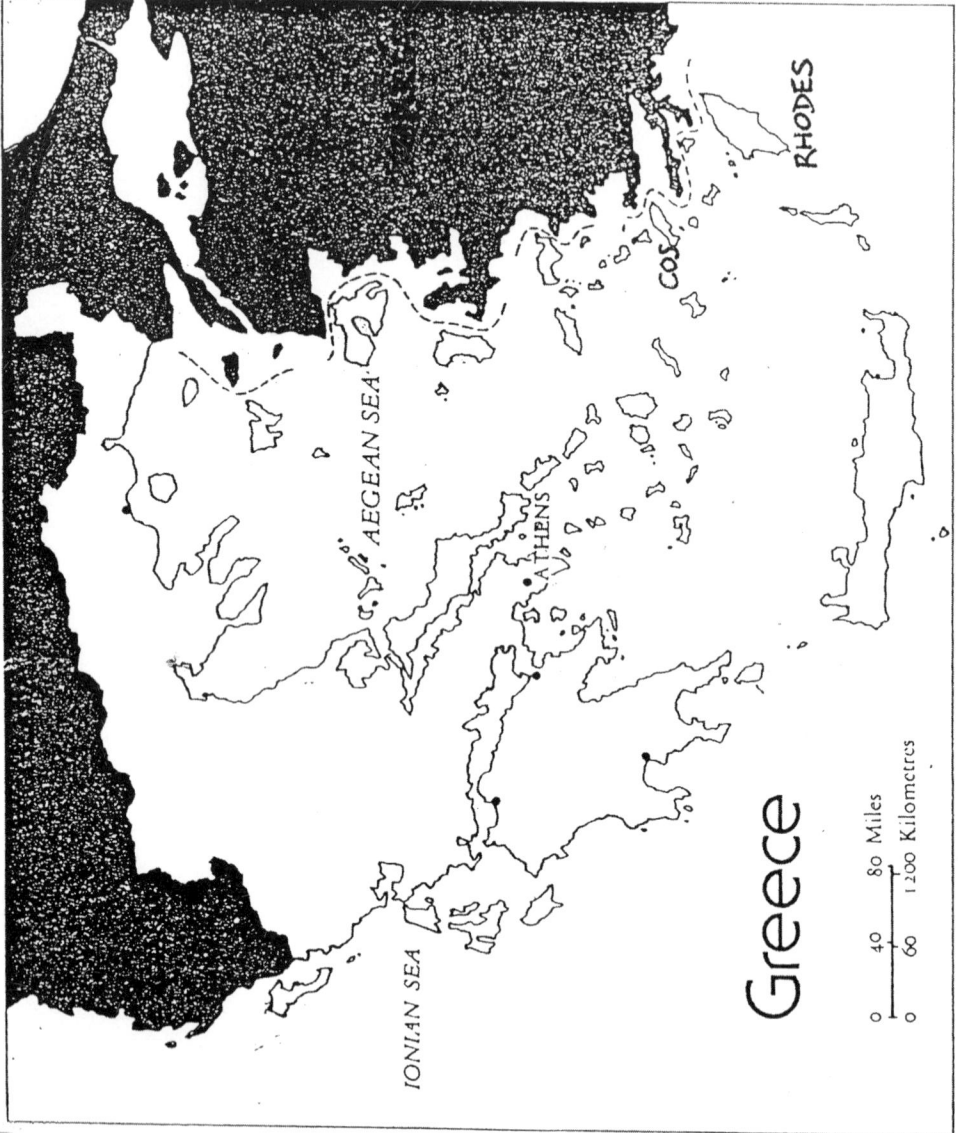

Rhodes Island

Chapter 6

FROM RHODES ISLAND TO AUSCHWITZ

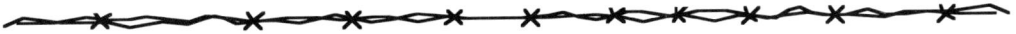

CLARA SORIANO
From Rhodes Island To Auschwitz

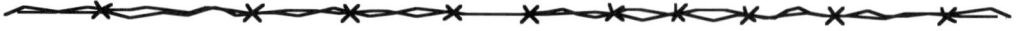

THE MARTYRS OF
RHODES AND COS

For fifty years
you have slept
While we with desperate
shrieking screams
Have shed the
most bitter tears
At your lack of
proper burial.
While you rest in
eternal dreams,
We live in eternal hell,
Since you suffered such
an Unjust and
atrocious death.
By this sadness we
are afflicted.
By this memory we
are haunted.
Half a century has
already gone

Since that past so
cruel and dark
Our pain so alive
and enduring.
You who hear us from
the hereafter,
You who share with us
our anguish,
Is it not enough
That you were sacrificed?
You became the holocaust
For the glory of our faith?
Forgive us
for lamenting,
And disturbing your
tranquility.
There is no limit
to our suffering
We pray that for eternity
You will rest in peace.

Clara Soriano was born in Rhodes
Island. She was in Auschwitz,
Theresienstadt and Dessau.
After liberation, she went to the
Congo and came to South Africa
in 1974 with her husband. She has
a son and two daughters.

VOYAGE TO AUSCHWITZ

It was a summer's day
Enriched with the sun's rays
Shining and full of life.
A people's hearts were being broken.
Born on the island of Rhodes
Higgledy- piggledy they
all were mixed,
Pressed and compressed
into human lines,
Their eyes protruding in horror,
Prepared for the cruel fury.

You were the front of the lines,
You, the younger and stronger,
To keep up the pace - forward ,
Forward, march....
March to the death.

You the older and the aged -
For you there is no mercy -
Hasten your tired steps.
Their cruel rules you must accept.
There is no choice.
March, push
To the doors which mark your death.

What can we say to our children
Their eyes distended by fear
In hunger and tears
Pressed and compressed
in the cattle wagons?
No water, no bread.
The pangs of starvation,
The anger, frustration.
Shed your tears beloved ones.
The memories of your grannies
May your spirits calm.

The savages have decided
To ensure your end.
No mercy touches their hearts.
The stories of your grannnies
Make no mark on them.
It's the children we must tell
About our faith,
The belief in only one G-d.

No! We have not been abandoned.
We wish to believe
In the pages of history -
Those inglorious pages,
Those black, black pages
Written about us -
Where we shall see the final defeat
Of the Teutonic barbarity.

Innocent are the poor infants,
Innocent our beloved cherubs,
Rocked tenderly with love
in the arms of their mothers.
The halos of these martyrs, "these mothers,"
Crown them perfectly.
. They loved these innocents so tenderly,
These children, their children, who cries
Are the whimpering of violins
Unable yet to articulate
The sweet name "Mama."

Immaculate and pure
Are these souls of these innocents
But nothing will ever touch these monsters
Even at death's doors
And the children must also
continue to march

Guards and torturers
They too are born in the womb
These German Ostragoths.
All of us, they want,
All till the very last.
March, march, shove continuously
Under threats of violence.
A defenseless flock.
At the crematorium doors
You shall find your rest.

A dense black cloud
Exudes from the chimney.
Suffocated and gassed
Is to be their end.
Turned into dust
For the wind to blow away.

VIOLETTE FINTZ
Rhodes Island, Auschwitz, Dachau, Bergen Belsen.

My name is Violette Fintz (nee Maio). I was born September 1911 on the Island of Rhodes. On 19 July 1944 when I was 33 years old, I was arrested on the Island of Rhodes, together with my Mother and Father, two sisters (Sara 25 and Miriam 21) and a brother. I was the eldest of the children. (One sister was already living in the Belgian Congo). Nearly 1800 Jews were arrested that day.

On July 17, the President of the Jewish Community, Mr. Jacob Franco, received a letter from Athens from a group of three Germans known as the Rosenberg Commission. Mr Franco was told that he had to order all the Jews to gather together the next day (18 July) at the aeronautic command at Tchemenlik. They were to bring with them jewellery and all their valuables. We knew nothing about what was happening in Europe because our radios had been sealed and we were completely cut off from all the news.

As soon as we entered the aeronautic building, two German officials together with an interpreter, Costa, began with great brutality, to take our identity cards and Work Permits. What a terrible sadness it was for all of us there. We didn't know what was to happen to us. On 19 July, the Turkish Consul managed to liberate 39 Rhodes Jews because they had Turkish passports. Another 10 were similarly liberated on the Island of Cos. It is impossible to describe the sorrow and desperation of the next three days. The three people (two Germans and Costa) started collecting gold, jewellery and money with great cruelty, without any consideration for the old, the sick , the very young. The results of this collection were 4 bags of money, title deeds to property, gold, and jewels.

After 4 days in this building without food we were given soup and the order to leave. We had to carry our own luggage. It was terrible to go from this building to the port. The old, the sick, those who couldn't walk properly, the little children, were beaten, lashed, as they struggled to the port. We embarked in three small tankers that left Rhodes the next day (21 July). We had no bread or water. The Captain of the tanker that we were on was an Austrian. He called me to his cabin and asked me for details of the tortures we had been subjected to by the Germans while in the aeronautic building. When we arrived at the Island of Leros, the captain refused to sail further until we had been given bread and water. It was thanks to him, to this wonderful man, that we were given water and some food on the journey to Piraeus, which took 10 days. We arrived at Piraeus on 31 July. Conditions on the journey were very bad - shocking sanitary arrangements and very rough seas.

We disembarked and this was terrible. The old and the very young were flung into small lorries. We travelled to the concentration camp at Haidari near Athens Conditions there were shocking; remember it was August and very hot; we had nothing to eat or drink; people were dying of thirst. We spent four days in Haidari under these conditions; only on the fourth day were we given something to eat - a plate of soup - and straight away we were marched to the station where we were put into cattle trucks.

Written on the outside of the compartments were the words: 8 Horses and 80 people. We were pushed into the train, with lashes, 70-80 people into each compartment. In the centre of the compartment was a barrel for toilet purposes; in one corner was a little stack of bread, and in the other corner a little stack of dry onions and a little barrel of water (imagine, giving onions to make us thirstier!). The journey from Athens to Auschwitz lasted 14 days .

The compartment had one little window with bars; we suffocated. Men, women and children were nearly naked because of the great heat. The toilet barrel was overloaded and, by the time the train stopped and we were told to empty the barrel, we were covered with the contents. Next to me, there was a mother with one child of a year old, who were related to us. The child was so thirsty that she cried continually and, like a little dog, she licked the sweat from her mother's face. This scene has never left my mind. Whenever I see a crying child, this little child comes to my mind.

We arrived in Auschwitz on 16 August. We had been on the move for a month, having left Rhodes on 21 July, ten days having been spent on the boat.

When the train started to slow down we saw from afar through the window thin people without hair, and I remember saying to the people: I think we have been brought to a madhouse. Finally, the train stopped and straight away the Germans started their ferocity, and lashed everyone who couldn't move quickly enough. We heard an Italian voice saying,

"The children to the old".

In the camp, we came to realise what these words meant: every young mother who carried a child in her arms was sent to the left. To the crematorium. A few mothers were saved when they gave their children to the older women to carry. Thus were the children and the old people sent to their deaths. Some young girls lost their lives through trying to help their married sisters carry their children.

I came down from the train holding my mother with one arm and my sister Miriam with the other. An SS grabbed my mother by her hair and took her away from me. I turned back and said,

"Ciao, Mama,"

and an SS man gave me a lashing on the head for doing this. Crying, I continued walking with Miriam. We were taken to a place underground and given the order to remove our clothes. They started to shave us, our head, under our arms, our pubic hair. It was already dark when they gave us the order to enter the bathing area. For one month our bodies had never had a bit of water. We were looking forward to this.

We were given soap; the soap was black, and only afterwards did we hear that the soap had been made from the dead. After the bath, we came out of another door, naked and wet; it was very cold.

They brought us a stack of clothing and everyone was given one item. It didn't matter what it was - two left shoes, a bathing costume, something too small or too big. It was already evening when we were ordered to walk and, after two hours, we entered the gates to Auschwitz. Then it was that we saw the name for the first time.

I was with my two sisters - Sara and Miriam. The women had been separated from the men. We had not seen my father or my brother since the train had stopped and I had taken my mother's arm. We were taken to Barrack number 20. It was already full and with great difficulty, we managed to find a little place to sleep, after a month of continued torture.

Life in the Barrack was appalling. There were three bunks, one on top of the other. There were fifteen bunks in each row - five people to each wooden bunk. One blanket for five and because the bunks were one on top of the other, the wooden bunks would sometimes collapse and people and bunks would fall onto those below, and we used to hear screams. In the very early mornings, we were called to Appel, a call-up. We stood in lines of five, at a distance of half a metre from each other, so that we shouldn't be able to warm one another. If, by chance, we approached closer, we were lashed. If you tried to help someone who fell, you could get the death penalty. We would wait in line for hours. The Lager Kapo (a beautiful Jewish woman, dressed like a queen) used to count us.

I was "matriculated", i.e. tattooed, by a Jewish girl. My number was 24425. Menstruation stopped because of hunger. We had to wash a little bit in the toilets, in front of the men who tried to clean the toilets (a job often done by Rabbis). We tried to wash with a cloth and a little bit of water. We had very little food - one litre of soup for three - and one slice of bread a day. In the morning, as soon as we were up, we went outside the barrack where there was a barrel of green water. We were "lucky" if we were able to get a little of this water. The consequences of drinking this water were serious: it caused inflammation of the tongue and blisters all over the mouth. It was a bromide, a tranquilliser (worse than a tranquilliser) to keep us totally passive. After the Appel, we used to have to work - moving heavy stones from one place to another for no purpose whatsoever.

During those first days that we were in Auschwitz, we had no idea of what happened to people whom we no longer saw. One day, when taking the stones from one place to another, the SS woman ordered: "Italian women, sing."

We started to sing the beautiful song, "Mama" in the hope that our parents might hear us and then know that we were alive. Then the Polish girls laughed and asked whether we wanted the Mamas to come out of the chimneys from which we saw the smoke. And that was the first time we realised what was happening to people whom we no longer saw.

Relationships with other people in the camp were impossible for us Italians. We spoke Italian - we couldn't speak Yiddish, German, or Hungarian. We Italians were so illtreated; because we couldn't understand, we were often slow in following orders and therefore we were beaten. We heard the guards shout,
"ITALIANS. DIE."

Many terrible things happened to us in Auschwitz but I must mention one that happened at Yom Kippur. Some of the men who were working in the toilets told us that the next day was Yom Kippur (1944). The Polish girls, the Kapos, who distributed the soup asked us on the morning of Yom Kippur whether we wanted the soup then or in the evening after the fast. We girls from Rhodes didn't understand what was happening and because we were very religious, we said we would have the soup after the fast. To punish us, we were given nothing to eat for 48 hours. Our soup was eaten by the others during Yom Kippur. 48 hours without food is a very serious matter. It was a madness to try to fast in Auschwitz .

The Kapo of my barrack was Rahela, the Jewish girl, beautiful but so cruel. There was no need for such cruelty. No German was watching us in the Barrack. I believe she was punished after the War. We saw the Germans only when we went out of the barrack to carry the stones. I never saw a German in my barrack.

So much happened in Auschwitz and even if everything didn't happen to me, I need to bear testimony to what happened to others. For example, one day the Kapo asked whether there was a pregnant girl in the barrack, in which case she would be given a double ration. Very kind! One girl from Rhodes was taken away. When she came back, thin, a black shawl over her head, she told me what had happened: she had been operated on, without an anaesthetic, the foetus had been removed and put into a bottle and shown to her. She had not been closed up, so after a short while, she died from infection. Such things happened in Auschwitz.

A girl from Rhodes had, as her duty, to light heaters with petrol. She forgot to light one. The German came and asked who had been responsible and she was given 25 lashes on her shoulder. I saw her in Brussels in 1984. I hadn't seen her since Auschwitz. She told me that when she screamed from the pain of the lashes, the German saw her gold teeth and took something from his pocket and pulled out the teeth. When she cried out again, in pain, the German stamped on her feet with his heavy boots. This girl today lives in Toulouse.

Another girl, Mathilde, was one of twenty girls sent to a little river to do certain work. One girl ran away, was missing. Five girls had to be shot the following morning because the one girl was missing. Mathilde was one of the five. She told me her story in Brussels. Imagine how you feel when you know that you are going to be shot the next morning. You're crying. In the morning the girls were lined up to be shot, the Germans were ready with their guns and suddenly the missing girl was found.

I was in Auschwitz from 16 August 1944 till after Yom Kippur. On my last day in Auschwitz, we heard there would be a transport. My sisters Sara, Miriam and I were naked and had to pass in line before Mengele. I passed, my sister Sara passed and then I turned my head and saw that Miriam had been made to stand in a line behind Dr. Mengele. Sara and I started to cry because we knew that a selection was being made. We continued to walk. We were in the street of Auschwitz, Lagerstrasse (in the camp but outside the barrack). We heard a voice from the men's side asking in Greek,

"Where are they taking you girls?"
We told them, "To the transport."
And the answer came back, "Poor girls!"

They knew we were being taken to the crematorium. We arrrived at a big block (Birkenau). We were about 1 500 girls and we were given the order to undress completely. It was already late at night. One after the other we entered the barrack and there we were, awaiting the order to enter the gas chamber although we didn't know this at the time. Hours passed and about dawn we heard a voice, "**Raus**"' and we dressed and we went out. We saw a train outside with dead bodies inside and we were put into the train with them. The train left Auschwitz. Afterwards we heard that we were the first people to come out of Auschwitz alive.

After two days and three nights, we arrived at Dachau. There were 84 girls from Rhodes and all were very sick. The German woman in charge asked me to take care of these girls. (I was not as sick as they were.) They led us to a sort of cellar (no windows with two benches on either side) and I managed to accommodate the girls like sardines. The place was filthy and we had nothing with which to clean it. With my hands I managed to clean it up as best I could. There was very little water, but the soup was a little better than the soup in Auschwitz. We had a slice of bread and a little bit of margarine. The German girl used to come every day and shout that if we didn't go to work we would have to go to the crematorium. How it was possible for such sick and weak girls to go to work, I don't know.

While we were at Dachau twenty of us were sent to clean the German barracks.

The snow was deep and we had a long journey. I took a blanket and put it on my shoulders. I had two left shoes. It was a calvary to walk. We arrived at a little hill and on this hill there were barracks. I heard an Italian voice saying,
"Here's an Italian girl."

These were Italian prisoners of war! They got permission for me to stay there. They dried my dress, gave me another blanket and something to eat and told me to have patience because the War would soon be ending. When I left, they gave me a packet of bread. I'll never forget these brave young men.

I had last seen my brother Leon on the train that took us to Auschwitz. He was 24. I found him at Dachau. I could hardly recognise him. He was very thin and sick. One day the girls told me that my brother was in a line moving out of the camp. I had the courage to jump through the wire and put my arms around him. He said "Look at my leg." It was gangrenous. He had spilled a barrel of soup over it. I told him to have courage because the War was coming to an end but he said that he had no more strength and had bad diarrhoea. Later some girls told me that they saw his body lying in a camp near to Dachau (about a month later). He was my only brother. He was 24.

I can't remember exactly when we were taken by train to Bergen Belsen - probably about January 1945. Sara and I found Miriam there. She was already in a line going on a transport. When she saw me, she put her arms around me, and said that she would not leave me. I asked a girl to take her place. That girl survived; Miriam was o die at Bergen Belsen. That is what is called luck. Miriam was not well and was very thin.

All the German camps were terrible - they were Hell, they were Purgatory but for people to survive Bergen Belsen is a miracle. For me, Bergen Belsen was the worst camp. As the Germans realised that they were losing the war, they began to send Jews from all over to Bergen Belsen, hoping that they'd manage to get rid of all of them that way. Everyone in this camp was sick with typhoid or cholera. Every day, they died in their hundreds. We were covered with lice. Miriam had a very high temperature. She needed water, I took a tin to find water. What I saw as I walked to get the water, was unbelievably horrible. Corpses were piled up. I managed to get some water. Miriam washed her face, drank a little and kept the rest.

Before we went to Bergen Belsen, we were put into bunks. I had the sickness of the Lager - I couldn't swallow. This was because there was no saliva. And on the third day, a Hungarian girl was eating an onion. Sara put a little bit of onion into the bread and at last I managed to swallow and so my life was saved. At Bergen Belsen there was no work - we lay there, sick, eaten by the lice. As Liberation was approaching (beginning of April 1945), they gave us no food for 15 days. No food, nothing to drink. The block was full of girls dying. From these girls we heard the sound of dying. There was so much diarrhoea.

About 10 April 1945 we began to hear the sound of gun fire. The Kapos told us that within a few days the Red Cross would be arriving, that no one was to leave the barracks because if we did so we'd be killed, so everything was done in the barracks. On 15 April the first English tanks entered the camp. The soldiers had to wear masks because of the disease. For two weeks after the Liberation we remained in the same situation for the English gave us nothing. They said that those who could walk should walk to the Barracks. The sick would be taken by ambulance. I could walk, and I left behind Sara and Miriam, believing the promise that had been given about the ambulance. A month later, my sisters had not yet arrived. Then Sara arrived with a bicycle and told me that Miriam had died. She had been given a bath in cold water and she had died from pulmonary pneumonia. I found it impossible to console myself. A girl of 21 who had witnessed the Liberation and yet died so soon afterwards!

For five months we were in Germany without any change in our circumstances. The British did not help us. In one of the camps (after Liberation) prisoners of war arrived. I met an Italian prisoner of war who took care or me - Enrico Marino. I always hoped to find him later but failed. Had it not been for Enrico, I would not be alive today. He wanted to marry me but he wasn't Jewish. I went, as his wife (as many girls did) to Rome. Of the 84 Rhodes Islanders who were in Dachau, only nine were left. Three of them were sent to Sweden by the Red Cross, two died there. With the help of Enrico, my sister and I arrived in Rome on 8 September 1945. We were put up at the home of a woman from Rhodes who lived in Rome.

In November, Sara and I returned to Rhodes because I hoped to get my job back with the Singer Sewing Machine Company. After a year I couldn't stay in Rhodes because of my health. We returned to Rome and from there we went to the Congo where we had a married sister who had been there since 1938. Sara took the plane to the Congo. I wanted to go by boat from Marseilles but I became so ill that I spent 2 years in hospital in Lyons. Only in 1949 did I get to the Congo. I worked for Singers. Then I went to Rhodesia because the climate in the Congo and the dust from the mines affected my breathing very badly. In Rhodesia I married. My husband was also from Rhodes but he'd come to Rhodesia in 1926. I married in 1951. I have a son. After 23 years of marriage, my husband died and because my son had come to South Africa, I came here in 1974.

I have been so disillusioned by life and people. I expected things to be better after the War but they have not been. I thought that, coming out of Hell, things would be better but look at the world today. There is no peace, there is always fear of the future. I can't sleep in peace because of nightmares. I remain very sensitive. I was not like this before the camps. I cannot bear it when I hear people say that the Holocaust never existed.

I often speak to people about my experiences. Some cry with me, some don't want to hear. If G-d made a miracle which enabled me to survive then I must give testimony. I must never forget and I can never forgive.

POST SCRIPT

In October 1994 I was invited to return to Rhodes Island to tell my story in a film commemorating the Fiftieth Anniversary of the deportation of the Rhodes Island Jews being made by a Belgian film company, Les Filmes De La Memoires. It was an emotional experience revisiting my old home, the palace where we had been imprisoned and the harbour where cargo boats identical to those we had been transported on were moored. Rhodes was like a lost planet. The Jewish community have all gone, there are no familiar faces in the streets, the buildings in the Judairia are delapidated, the great synagogue damaged and barred. At times I was surprised that I had had the heart to relive my past for the camera. I am happy I had the opportunity to participate in recording our experiences for future generations to see but it was hard.

Violette Fintz nee Maio was born in Rhodes on 15.9.1911 and educated at the Alliance Israelite Universelle Rhodes. She was a manager at the Singer Sewing Company until being transported from Rhodes by the Nazis. She was liberated in Bergen-Belsen on 15.4.1945. She subsequently spent two and a half years in the Congo, 23 years in Rhodesia and has been in South Africa since 1975. She is widowed and has a son Nissim Isaac.

LUCIA AMATO

Rhodes Island, Auschwitz, Willemstad, Theresienstadt

I guess I must start with the terrible journey to Auschwitz. The train wagons were packed over capacity. We could hardly sit on the floor, and could not stretch our legs. In one of the corners, there was a small barrel - that was our toilet. In order to maintain some sort of privacy, we would use clothing as a curtain. At the stations when the train stopped, the guards would open the door and shout and scream, **"Raus! Raus!"**

Many of the older people could not get up and walk because their knees and legs were so stiff from being bent for so long. A guard would climb into the wagon to empty the toilet, and I remember that one just kicked it onto the floor so that the contents spilt all over the floor, and onto us.

Later when we were transported to Athens, we were guarded only by five German soldiers. There were hundreds of us. I often wonder why we never thought of killing them and escaping. There were some strong men among us; but I suppose we were not brought up to kill, and of course, we never realized what was going to happen to us.

Auschwitz was the most terrible period of my life. The day after our arrival, we were told by the inmates who worked in the crematorium that our parents had all been killed the previous day and that the smoke we saw was the burning of our parents. They also told us that it was no use crying for them,

"You must be brave and save your own lives or the same thing will happen to you".

But we could not, we cried and cried for a long time.

Every morning at 3 o'clock there was the call-up. We would have to stand outside in the freezing cold weather for a long time. We never had any underwear. I remember trying to warm up my sister by hugging her, and the `Kapo' would hit us and separate us. We had only one meal each day - usually a small bowl of soup made out of potato peels which we had to share among five or six of us.

I was there with two of my sisters. The younger one died very soon as she could not handle the hunger, the conditions and the bad treatment.

One day, one of the prisoners was found missing during the morning call-up. The guard told us that unless we told them where she had gone, they would shoot 10 of us randomly. We were very scared that they would kill us all. The next day she was found and brought to our block.

We could hardly recognise her. She had been so badly beaten that her body had huge bumps all over, especially on her head. The Germans then gave us batons and forced us to beat her. That was absolutely awful! We were crying while we pretended to do so. Finally she became unconscious and we were convinced that she was about to die. The Germans threw a bucket of iced water over her to revive her, and she did not die. That was enough to put any one off trying to escape from the camp.

From Auschwitz we were transfered to Willemstad, where we worked in an ammunition factory. Every morning, we had to go to work on an empty stomach and it was only when we returned that we were given this watery soup and a piece of bread. I would always give my elder sister some of my portion.

One night, I remember that I was so hungry that I began to lick the sides of the cauldron; the "Obersiering" caught me and hit me with a baton and then kicked me all over my body. Then she stuck me in the corner of the room and two other "Obersierings" came towards me, one of them holding a pair of scissors. I thought this was the end of me, and that she was going to cut my throat with the scissors.

Instead they cut off the little hair that had just begun growing again and I was thrown into the snow and left there for two hours or more. As further punishment, I was moved to the night shift at the factory. That was very difficult because one needed to sleep during the day and that meant one would miss lunch, the only meal.

We were moved from that camp to Theresienstadt by train, during the Allied bombardment where we were liberated by Russian soldiers. I remember that they brought us a lot of chocolate. They caught some of the guards and told us to stone them, but we could not do that.

LUCIA AMATO was born in Rhodes Island in 1921 and attended the Scuola Isralite. She survived Auschwitz, Willemstad and Theresienstadt
from where she was liberated on 8.5.1945. From Rome she went to Rhodesia in 1947 and moved to South Africa in 1978. She married Moise Amato in Gatooma, Rhodesia and has a son Alby and a daughter Janette

R.A.

Rhodes Island, Auschwitz, Bergen Belsen, Dassau, Theresienstadt.

I did not tell my children about my experiences for a long time because I did not want them to grow up with hatred. I cannot help but hate the Nazis with all my heart for what they did. It took many years for those feelings to lessen. My children often asked why I had a number on my arm, printed all skew because the woman who stamped it on was nasty and rough. I would tell them that it was a telephone number. My daughter once came to me with a rag and soapy water. I thought it was to wash her doll, but instead she told me that she wanted to wash my arm because it was "dirty". The number on my arm was a constant reminder to me and a constant mystery to my children. I thought about having it surgically removed but to me that would have been a betrayal of my parents and their memory. I would not have been able to live with the guilt of having been disloyal to my parents.

In Auschwitz we communicated with the Yiddish speaking inmates, it was from them that we learned about the gas chambers and the crematoria. The decision of who would live and who would die was left up to Mengele. Ironically, he was called "the angel of Death" and not the Devil.

In the camp we did everything in fives; five in the bunks, and five queuing at a time. The work that we were forced to do served one and only one purpose - to destroy us through suffering. The only way to survive was to erase the thoughts of losing one's family. Because of our hunger and deprivation, there was no room for sadness, a state of mind that renders one very weak.

The hardest thing to comprehend was that these animals had murdered my parents. The physical struggle was painful, but the moral pain was continuous and never subsided; the thought of having lost my loved ones made my heart bleed. My family of eight was no longer together as in the happy times we shared in the past. I had always been surrounded by relatives - now, I was alone for the first time ever!

After one of the selections, one of my sisters was sent to a military camp. My younger sister, aged 22/23 was one of the people kept in a sealed block separated from the others. They chose the youngest and most beautiful. From there they were taken to the crematorium. But before this happened I had the opportunity to visit her one last time. She knew the end was near and insisted that I take her jacket that she had bought in exchange for some bread, as she knew she would no longer be needing it.

Two days later we left Auschwitz for Bergen Belsen. After having been there for a few days the Germans came to ask us who would like a bath. We were apprehensive as we thought this might be a trrap. By this stage I had given up hope and had nothing to lose so I got up as the first volunteer. From there many followed me.

When we arrived at Bergen Belsen some Hungarian women recognised some of our group. They said that we looked terrible. We had not realised how we had changed because we saw each other every day.

The saddest day I ever remember was Christman Eve. The Blokova came to give us our daily ration of bread. As it was already dark, she switched on the light but got caught by the guards as this was not permitted. The following day, Christmas 1944, we were punished and had to stand deep in the snow without any warm clothes or food. Our days continued full of humiliating tasks to get our morale down.

In February 1945 we arrived in Dassau, where I went to work in the aeroplane factory. It was a long walk each day with mismatched shoes. There we were given striped prisoner uniforms and a new number. I worked shifts which alternated weekly, day then night. I never got much sleep because the food was served at lunch time and thus I could not rest during the day for fear of missing out. The day that we left for Theresienstadt, I actually had not slept for eight consecutive days. It's absolutely incredible how one can go without sleep, drink, food, warmth and hygiene when one has to.

April 12th 1945 we were deported to Theresienstadt. The Nazi officers wanted us to continue walking. There was one kind old captain who put his foot down and refused to allow it. He ordered trains to be sent to fetch us and if that were not possible he intended to leave us in the camp for the Americans to liberate us. Luckily for us the trains did arrive and we were transported in cattle truck with a ration of one loaf of bread to last for the journey of eight days. Naturally many, many more people died on the way.

On 20th April 1945 I arrived at Theresienstadt, weak from our long trip and very sick.

The 8th May 1945 marked our liberation by the Russians.

The very first time that I had sugar was in Theresienstadt. They gave me sugar in the coffee. It was absolute ecstacy! The Jew in charge even gave me an extra piece when he saw the way I reacted.

The very first time that I actually saw myself is a moment I shall never forget. This was after liberation and I got such a fright when I saw myself in a mirror that I screamed; I looked like a monster. My facial features were dented, my body was hollow, my hands were only covered with veins and skin.

After we had been liberated we were allowed to live in the deserted homes, and we had to go to a particular place to get our daily food. The Russians who liberated us gave us soup in the morning, and tobacco at lunch which we would exchange for bread.

Seven of us lived together in one room, and we were all from different countries.

One day I was so hungry that I stole some apricots from a tree growing on someone's property. The owner ran out and wanted to kill us but we escaped.

There was a very special person whom I met in Bergen Belsen, **Anna Cassuto**. She was a woman of 34 who had four children in Italy. Her husband was a Rabbi in Florence who was tortured by the Nazis because he would not divulge information about how many Jews there were in Florence as many of them were in hiding. For this he was deported to Germany. He never returned. She gave me moral support in the camps. At night, she would say, "A day has passed, one less day of suffering". One day when we were outside, she showed me how to dig and encouraged me all the time. She had a strong will to survive and she was like a rock to me. I was with her until my arrival in Italy on the 5th August 1945.

After spending a year in Bologna, Italy, I went to the Congo to find my brothers.

I tried to forget the nightmares but forgetting is treason, treason to our parents and family who perished. I think that survivors of the Holocaust who did not lose family members are more able to distance themselves from the memories of the Holocaust. I simply cannot do so. All along I think that the children knew that I was hiding something from them by my silence. They also knew I was different from the other mothers. For example I would never let them see me sad about anything. I wanted to teach them to love life. I think I did the right thing because they grew up without hate.

R.A. was born in Rhodes Island. She was in Auschwitz, Theresienstadt and Dachau. After liberation, she went to the Congo and came to South Africa in 1974. She has one son and two daughters.

GIUSEPPE CONE
Rhodes Island, Auschwitz - Birkenau, Rizertau Charlotte Gruppe.

We were all very happy in Rhodes until the racial laws. The foreign Jews had to leave the island and many went to Turkey. One day in 1939, my brother and I went to the Mandraki, the harbour, to look for a boat so that we could escape to Turkey. But I just could not go through with it, I had a wife and three children as well as my own family.

When the Germans arrived, they went to the police and obtained the names of all the Jews on the island. These were all rounded up including my mother, my two brothers, my wife, my children and myself. I shaved my hair so the authorities would think that I was Turkish and as a result I was able to go in and out of the camp until three large freight ships arrived and we were all pushed inside amongst the cows and sheep to be taken to Athens where we remained for days waiting for the trains to take us to G-d knows where.

When the wagons finally arrived, we were loaded, about one hundred people per wagon. There were no toilet facilities, only a few buckets which were emptied at some of the stations where we stopped. How I remember the embarrassment and shame I felt for my own children who toppled into these buckets causing everyone to be covered in their excrements. The smell in those wagons was absolutely unbearable. They gave us only rancid bread and a few watermelons from time to time. The journey took about fourteen days.

When we finally arrived at Auschwitz, we still did not have any idea what was going to happen to us. We were ordered to leave the few possessions we had taken from Rhodes in the train. We thought that we would now be fed but instead the Germans began to shout to us to get off the train, fast! fast!

The men, the women, the aged, the children, the sick, the babies were lined up for selection. When it was my turn, I was asked how old I was. I said I was thirty five. I had to turn around for them to see from my buttocks if this was true and since these were still firm, I was told *"Arbeit!"*, which meant work.

The old, the women and the children were all sent in the other direction to the gas chambers which were working day and night. A Salonikan Jewish prisoner confirmed that all those people were killed. Only about one hundred of us Rhodeslis escaped death, young men and single girls. Our heads were shaved and we were given black and white pyjamas and clogs, then sent to quarantine for forty days and forty nights. I remember Bochor Alhadeff, Leon Maio and Israel Levy had to stay behind in the infirmary.

(Leon Maio was the brother of Violette Fintz whose experiences appear at the beginning of this section.) Our arms were tattooed. My number is B-7251. We were rollcalled by our number and I had to reply *swaing zipsin ain an fiftzin*

We were then taken to another camp, Rizertau Charlotte Gruppe, a coal mine which apparently used to belong to a Jew. Many died there of hunger, cold and beatings. Here I worked with civilian technicians. I was selected with other prisoners to place the mine explosives. For the explosions they needed big stones to use as supports to release the jacks which supported the walls and roofs of the gallery through which the coal trucks were wheeled. We dug the tunnels and removed the stones by hand.

I suffered a terrible injury while working in these coal- mines. From the strain of carrying these heavy rocks, I developed a huge bulge on the top of my leg. The pain was unbelievable but the hospital would only accept you if you had a fever. Eventually, I had a fever and could then be taken to a doctor, a strong Polish Jewish doctor prisoner who anaesthetized me with chloroform only, cut up the bulge and withdrew the infection with a long stick and gauze and as soon as I woke up, with the cut still bleeding and covered with toiletpaper, I was sent back to work. Luckily, my body was still strong and I recovered.

We moved to another camp whose name I don't remember where we had to load the wagons with bricks to be used to build a new kitchen for the prisoners. Many more prisoners died there. I remember, one day, looking at my hands which were covered in blood from handling these bricks.

I spotted a barrack and decided to hide in it. One of the SS officers saw me and chased after me. He chased me from room to room until we got to a room with no exit. He hit me on my head with his baton so powerfully that I collapsed. I never understood why he did not kill me. I was sent to the doctor who bandaged my head so that it looked as if I wore a turban. Of course, I was immediately sent back to work. The next day when I saw the SS officer he asked me what had happened to me, as if he did not know; I knew I had to say,

"I don't know".

Another time Eli Hugnou wanted me to escape with him through the toilets. I could not go. He went alone and hid there. The Germans realised where he was hiding and set the whole toilet on fire and there he died.

As the Americans and Russians were approaching the area where we were, we were sent to Mauthausen, further south in Austria where my brother died. We were transported in open wagons with no food or drink, and were covered in snow, protected only by the flimsy layer of our pyjamas. The majority of the prisoners froze to death, only the very strong survived this journey. When we finally arrived, the camp was full so we had to spend the night sleeping outside, on the road in the cold, one next to the other. More died during the night.

The next morning, we were told that we were to go somewhere else. This time we went on foot, in the snow without boots. It was unbearably cold but we had to walk regardless. I remember walking with a few of my friends from Rhodes, Josepu Hasson, Ner Alhadeff and Joseph Menashe. All of a sudden Joseph started slowing down. Although a very brave man, he could no longer go on. We urged him not to give up and offered to carry him. The Germans saw that he was slowing down and took him to the side, shot him and left him to die alone in the snow. We went on until we reached a camp in Ebenzen. The Germans treated us worse than slaves, worse than anything imaginable.

In that camp, I suffered a terrible attack of dysentery. One of my friends advised me to stop eating the little bread that they gave us. So I hid it under my mattress. When after a few days, I began to recover I realised that someone had stolen all my bread. How hungry I was!

Here again we worked in the mines. Once when we were outside near the wagons, supervised by the SS and their German shepherd, the dog was served a bowl of food with bones and meat and hearty soup. I could not control myself and as soon as the SS left I threw stones at the dog which ran away. I quickly grabbed his bowl and gobbled up its contents. I ate so fast that my stomach bulged out. I could not believe that all we would get would be a slice of bread for lunch and a bowl of soup for supper while this animal was so well fed.

There was another time when I was so hungry that while walking, I would pick up old dried animal bones and chew them with my teeth or even pick up asphalt from the road and chew on it like gum to keep going until the next "meal". The hunger was terrible.

One day, there were screams and shouts - the Americans had finally arrived to liberate us. Many Germans managed to escape and others were made prisoners. I heard that there was a German officer who even tried to poison all the inmates when he heard that the Americans were coming.

It was horrible to see how many inmates died after liberation because when offered food (biscuits), they ate too much and their bodies, unaccustomed to food, could not cope. I also remember that a cousin of mine was given a thermometer by one of the Americans which he mistook for food and was so hungry that he ate it and died of mercury poisoning. What a pity after having surived all the atrocities.

We were sent to a Weimar hospital where we remained for about a month. My legs were terribly swollen and remained like that for a very long time. I remember how for many days, whenever I was given food, I would save it and hide it under the pillow or the mattress from fear that the next day we would face starvation again. This habit lasted for a long time.

Those few who did survive were generally young and fearless, 15 to 16 year olds like Jaquitou Hasson, Samikou Modiano, David and Joseph Castavel. I think I survived because I had been an athlete in Rhodes and had thus developed a strong body, but more important a strength of mind and will-power. I cycled, swam, did trapeze work, boxed, played football, walked, ran and I often had to push myself. Perhaps another explanation can be the fact that I gave a lot to charity in Rhodes even in the time when we had nothing. I remember that the poor would say "G-d will grant you a long life!", maybe... Of course, luck was also very important, often more than physical or mental strength.

My brother only survived until Mauthausen, where he was taken ill and I never saw him again. My sister managed to escape to Palestine. My other brother had gone to the Congo in 1936.
The rest - all dead!

When I recovered we went to Rome where we were cared for by a group of women. The first night of Pesach, we were invited to the home of one of these women.
We would often go there to have things mended and to tell our stories. Later I married her

POSTSCRIPT BY MRS CONE
In the begining my husband had a lot of nightmares every night. The good thing was that the survivors would often get together and reminisce about their experiences and sometimes even laugh about them. A laughter of sadness! Sometimes he talks about things and I let him because I know that it is good for him to get it out. It is not that it is difficult for me, it is only that it is sad. The amazing thing about this man is that he is always optimistic about everything and does not worry or complain about silly things. Worse could happen! Worse had happened before. First the Holocaust, then some very difficult years in the Congo. Then we decided to come and live here and even then he would say that if things did not work out, we could still go to Italy or Israel. But things did work out and we have found happiness here.

GIUSEPPE CONE was born in Rhodes Island in 1910. He was a gymnast. He survived slave labour in Auschwitz-Birkenau, Rizertau Charlotte Gruppe, Mauthausen, and Ebenzen and was liberated on 5.5.1945 when he went to Italy and Zaire arriving in South Africa in 1967. He is married to Miriam and has two daughters Rebecca and Sara, and a son Matteo.

SARAH JERUSALMI
Rhodes Island, Auschwitz, Lagers V11, X11, and V, Dachau

I grew up in the Jewish quarter of Rhodes Island, a very nice clean place surrounded by a citadel with several synagogues. We were like one big family. My own family was large; I had five brothers of whom four left Rhodes before the War. My father's uncles had banks. They built a school, the Joseph Notrica, which is still in existence. On the whole there was little anti-Semitism before the Nazis came although I remember that the Greeks would sometimes throw stones at us when we went for a walk outside the citadel on a Saturday.

Anti-Semitism came in 1939 one year before the war and we were no longer allowed to attend government schools. We decided to join my brothers in the Congo but it was too late and there were no ships. I had to start work because my brothers could no longer send us money. My father's business suffered because he was unable to import goods and he was not in good health.

We suffered a lot of hunger which is something in my life I cannot forget. When we had bread my mother would give more to my brother Salvotera than to me because I was a girl. We had a difficult time but we still kept kosher. I remember at Pesach my father went to the village to make the flour and my mother prepared the matzos with it.

Then there was the BLACK PESACH. There was a very big bombardment on Pesach as the people were returning from shul. Ten people were killed and we ran away from the citadel so when they caught us we were not even in our house.

The first time I began to see Nazis in Rhodes was before I was deported, in 1943 and we were very scared of them. The Italians had said that they would protect us but when the Germans took over power in Rhodes in July 1944 we knew it was the end of us because there was no possibility of running away from the island.

One day all the men had to bring their papers and the Nazis kept them. When my mother went to ask why they kept the men there - my brother was only 16 - she was told that if she wished to be with them she should go home and come back with her things.

So we took all our jewellery, some food and clothes and we went to join them. It was only when we were there inside that we realized it was the end of us because they took all the jewellery from us and started to hit the people because those inside wanted to communicate with those outside. We were so afraid.

It was like a nightmare. We were not even allowed to go to the windows to see what was happening outside. We were not allowed to do anything. It was terrible. They did not give us anything, just water and coffee. We stayed there about two weeks. In the meantime the Turkish consul came to take out all the Turkish subjects.

They put us in a small open boat without cabins with two or three Germans and took us to Piraeus in Greece. The Germans took away my glasses. A blind man was behind us and he started to call for his daughter Joanna and a Nazi came and killed him. When we arrived in Piraeus they kept us in a block in miserable conditions and gave us only soup without any bread. Many people in our group died.

One of the things which I will always remember is this journey from Athens to Auschwitz, in those cattle wagons where we were treated like animals, with no water or food. The things that took place in those wagons were below any level of human dignity. We could already feel that we were going towards death.

It was the most terrible thing in my life. We could not breathe because we had only one small window. We had to lie down one on top of another, the children crying and there were old women. So many of us died in those wagons and were thrown out at the stations by the German officers as if they were rubbish bags. The officers had absolutely no feeling of compassion. At the stations the wagon doors were opened slightly to let in a little fresh air, and we received a little water from time to time, of course insufficient for the number of people in the wagons. Sometimes the people drank their urine. The little food we took with us from Rhodes was used up mainly in the journey to Athens and in Athens itself where we waited nearly two weeks for the train to arrive. I remember chewing on a few raw chick-peas. Some days we would get a stale bread to share among all the prisoners (about a hundred per wagon).

When we finally arrived at Auschwitz late one day nearly a month later, they put us in a queue, separating the men from the women, the children with the mothers. The scene of the selection, the separation of parents and children with the crying, the screaming, the beatings of the old, the young, the ruthlessness......That I could never forget for as long as I live.

Those who were selected for work were taken to the disinfection room and showers and we never again saw our mothers or our fathers. They gave us a soap to wash with and shaved our hair off and took all our clothes and threw us old clothes and clogs, whatever size. They could not care! I got a short jacket, another was short and was given long trousers.

To think that when we arrived, we thought, due to the smell of barbecue, that we were going to be fed a decent meal; we had no idea that this was the smell of burning flesh, as the SS later told us laughing: "the smell of your parents and children".
This was the hardest shock, the hardest thing to understand, the hardest thing to believe; it numbed us totally.

Without being given food, we were shown to our block where other inmates were sleeping squashed like sardines, but worse. We were shocked that the Germans had the audacity to put us together with men because all we saw were shaven heads. Then we realised that this was a block of

women and without our hair, we too looked like men. We went into these blocks crying because we had been the whole day without eating or drinking. We thought that at last we could lie down and get some rest but we were thrown all together five on a bunk with one blanket to share between us. At 2.00 a.m., we finally put our heads down, only to be woken up at 4.00 a.m. for roll call outside the block. Still without food, we were sent straight to work. All the time we could smell that smell of burning meat, but we were still unaware of its significance, unaware of the fate of our relatives and friends. When we asked the German woman officer if we were going to be fed we were told that the only meat available was that of our parents.

This was such a blow to me. It totally broke my heart. I understood from that moment that these people were out to end our lives and the lives of our people. This is when I told myself,
"Sarah, do not let them destroy you, you must fight and stay alive to tell the world what you saw."
And I did. I did everything that was humanly possible to stay alive, whether it was stealing from the kitchen or singing for the officers for an extra bread portion.... The things I did not do to survive!

It was vital to me to survive to tell the world what these people were capable of doing. I received my strength from my strong faith in G-d. There were so many times when I came so close to death and somehow my life was spared.

A Hungarian woman with two daughters had a piece of wax that they used to liquify every Shabbat night and all the girls with her would pray saying, "G-d, please let us see another Shabbat with our families."

We lit the lamp inside the block, it was just a symbol of Shabbat, it was the only thing we had and everybody would cry. We knew when it was Rosh Hashana and when it was Yom Kippur we fasted, we did not have much to eat but still we fasted. We did not pray, we did nothing.

We would sleep, eight or ten girls on a bunk. The girls would fight for the blanket. Others would cut up small pieces to make some underpants. Among ourselves there was stealing; the girls who had arrived before us were very experienced. They had no pity for us and generally gave us no advice or help or compassion. People who could not work were sent to the sick bay and were never seen again. Looking healthy was vital! I remember once I had a terrible pain in my leg and a girl whom I had befriended, a Belgian nurse, gave me an injection to relieve the pain. Unfortunately, the needle was infected and I developed a huge abscess. Luckily the German who saw that I was absent from roll-call came to ask me what my problem was. I told him that I had scraped my leg on a rusty nail in the kitchen so he sent me to the doctor so that I could receive proper care.

One day I saw my 16 year old brother crying because he was so hungry. He said he was going to die here, he had nothing to eat. I consoled him and promised to take care of him and bring him a blanket for he was so cold. I tried to organise something for my brother. A German caught me and they made me stand outside the entrance holding four bricks in my hands outstretched over my head, I thought I was going to collapse but I held on. Luckily another officer came past and and said,

"What are you doing here?"
I said, "I don't know what I am doing here" so he said, "Raus, Raus! Go to your block."

It was a miracle that I came back to the block alive. No one could believe it! I heard that later when my brother was working in the coal-mine he ate a piece of charcoal which poisoned him.

I remember one day they took us to a place where there had been a bombardment and we had to remove all the things from the mess. It was a terrible day in November and it was dark with fog, I don't know how many kilometres away from Auschwitz this place was, perhaps five. Nobody could take a tool in her hand it was so foggy. I saw a stable for horses nearby and I said to my friend,

"Let's go there. At least it will be warm and the Germans can't see us in this fog."

Four of us went inside and we saw a little German boy with two goats. His mother saw us from the window and she sent the little boy with bread, potatoes and salami saying, "My mother sent you this. Don't tell anyone we gave it to you."

We ate and then put our coats back on and went back. That was the only time I thought of escaping but we realized that when they counted us and found some missing, they would come with dogs to find us. But I shall not forget that kindness.

We were one of the last wagons that arrived at Auschwitz. Soon after our arrival the crematorium stopped burning. I was so scared that I might be sent there because I was getting thinner and thinner that I would rub some beetroot on my cheeks to appear healthy and strong. In Auschwitz, after one such selection we were sent to another camp, a small camp, Lager VII. We were given coats in the train because it was freezing. We grabbed them only to realise that they were riddled with lice and fleas. On arrival we went straight to the disinfection.

Lager VII had only two hundred prisoners and no crematorium just a communal fosse. The commander was very good. Fortunately I was sent to work in the kitchen cleaning pots. I had enough to eat and enough to bring to my friends and cousin. It was the first time that I began to feel like a human being again, with hope of surviving this ordeal. No longer did I have to carry bricks from A to B, or to remove the rubble from bombings, or clean railway tracks all day long. Prisoners were the cheapest form of labour! The work itself was not unbearable but the conditions and treatment we endured in the camps were.

One day I saw a cart being wheeled in with five Rhodesli girls on it, totally emaciated and on the verge of dying. Over a short time I managed to steal quite a lot from the kitchen and they gradually recovered. One day it was one potato, another time beetroot. Once when I came out from the kitchen I put a piece of meat in my trousers and a SS man said to me,

"Where are you going?"
I said, "I am going to the toilet."
He said, "OK, go quickly."
If they had found me with a piece of meat in my pocket I would have been killed.

Today, most of these girls are alive and well.

As we approached the end of the war they sent us on to Lagers XII and V, and the camp organisation began to deteriorate.

One evening in one of the camps where we arrived, a young girl saw her mother in another section behind barbed-wire and ran to talk to her. They were so emotionally involved that they did not hear the whistle for roll-call. The Germans felt nothing and ordered their electrocution through barbed-wire.

At the very last camp, I remember that we lived with the uncertainty of what they would do to us. One night, the Germans told us that as the Americans were arriving they were going to set the whole camp on fire. We waited anxiously, knowing that there was no escape from this situation.

In the early hours of the next morning, we heard SS commands to hurry up and get on the road. For three days and three nights they led us walking. Allied planes would fly over us, and not bomb us as they could see by our uniforms that we were prisoners. Finally, we arrived at Dachau. Although there were no more selections, people still continued to die of hunger, sickness and fatigue.

One morning we woke up to a deadly silence outside. We went out and saw the Americans arriving. It was the Liberation! They brought an enormous amount of bread; unfortunately the starving prisoners attacked the food like flies. Many ate so much that they actually exploded. That was to me the worst thing. After all that suffering, the nightmare wasn't over; people were still dying from sicknesses like cholera, typhus.

After the Americans had arrived, I did everything in my power to get out as soon as possible. They had told us that Italians were to be repatriated last and I just could not wait any longer. I managed to get out with the Belgian group of prisoners. When they found that I had never been to Belgium, they sent me to Paris to the special camp for survivors. After I sent a cable to my brothers in the Congo I met some families from Rhodes who had emigrated to Paris who welcomed me into their homes. Life began to smile at me again. After eight months during which I was well taken care of, I was re-united with my brothers.

That reunion was something very special and emotional. When the plane landed I was so excited and overwhelmed that my dream was coming true that I could hardly walk off the plane.

There are some nightmares that haunt me and will continue to haunt me for the rest of my life. Those scars are forever! However, there are survivors who have come to appreciate life so much. The life that I lived after the Holocaust in the Congo with my friends and family who spoilt me, was for me like having been born a second time. It was like going from hell to paradise!

I have asked myself what was all this suffering for, was it worth anything? I have never looked back, I just wanted to go forward. However I am not ashamed to say that I cannot be with Germans. I simply cannot erase all that happened to me and my people.

SARAH JERUSALMI nee Notrica was born in Rhodes Island in 1920 and went to school at the Jewish Alliance Francaise and trained as a typist. She survived Auschwitz and Dachau from where she was liberated in April 1945. She moved to the Congo, arriving in South Africa in 1974. She married Gabriel Jerusalmi.

ASHER VARON
Rhodes Island, Auschwitz, Shalogububa, Mauthausen, Linz

I was born in Rhodes Island. My Father worked in the clothing department of a departmental store. I had two brothers and two sisters and went to the government school run by priests until the Fascist Laws came in when I had to go to the Jewish School.

In 1943 the Germans took over the island. In June 1944 everything changed and all the Jewish men were called to the army camp and the next day they called the mothers, the wives with the children. We spent a couple of days in that building and then they took us to the docks where two or three ships were waiting, coal ships like tugs.

We were taken to army barracks in Greece not far from Athens called Haidari where we spent a few days and there I started to see dead people. For a child of 14 to see dead people was not pleasant. We slept on the floor and they used to bring us honey, water, not too much water.

Then they took us to the railway station and put us in the cattle trucks, sixty to eighty people were in each truck, standing and lying down and we went to the North. We did not know where we were going. We knew nothing about what was cooking in Europe. Some times we would see pictures of anti-Semitism in the newspapers but in general we knew nothing of what was happening to the Jewish community in Europe. Even during the journey from Greece to Poland it was hot in the truck. They used to stop once a day to give us water or open the doors to take out the dead people.

After four or five days we reached Auschwitz. There were some people who spoke our language who told us not to panic but to get out of the wagon and stand in line, the women and children on the right, the men on the left. We stood in line and marched to the gates where there were some SS people. Some young people in

their 20s who looked ill because of the journey were selected, as were the women who carried children in their arms. They went to the left. We went to the right. So did my uncles and my father. My mother and sisters were in the other line. My mother who was old, and a younger cousin of mine were selected to be gassed. My sisters went to the workline.

Then we walked to the showers of the camp where we were shaved. We were naked and they took us to the showers. Many hours later they took us to the barracks. I think it was Birkenau number 2, where we stayed for a few months.

Practically three times a week we had a selection - I think I saw Mengele selecting people. We would stand naked in the yard and they would pick out the people who were not strong and fit for work. Oldish persons or sick persons and those who had diarrhoea. The age that was of use to them was from twelve to thirty or thirty five. If you were to take a summary of the survivors that are here the majority were young up to 20, the rest were a few aged 40, maximum age 50. I do not recall anyone over 50 who survived.

In Auschwitz we were sent to build, to mix cement with sand or go to the station to empty the trucks of bricks or sand. They showed us no mercy for the weather, or whether it was day or night. Sometimes we would come home to the barracks around 11 or 12p.m. in the pitch dark and if it was raining we would return wet like fish. We wore a jacket with a pair of trousers. Some days if we were lucky we had a shirt and wooden boots with our feet covered with paper or pieces of rags. We were never shown compassion by the Nazis.

One day when I was returning to the barracks I made a joke to a kaffir. (A kaffir was a political prisoner often not Jewish who was placed in the camps to supervise us.)

Sometimes they were worse than the Germans. There were some Jewish kaffirs too. They were the survivors that used to do anything to survive themselves.) It was not really a joke. I said,

"It was a lovely day today!"

The answer he gave me was a rubber stick in my neck.

We would sleep five or six in a wooden bed with no mattress about one metre wide. It was possible to sleep because we were so tired. If somebody died during the night there was more space. We got a little bread and the last person to eat from the soup drum got a little bit of cabbage or thick soup but the first people had mainly liquid. In the morning we had something like tea or coffee but it was not like tea or coffee that you have today and a piece of bread, the same at lunch and in the evening. After we ate we went to work. We used to be up at least 16 hours a day and had about 6- 8 hours to sleep if we were lucky between getting up in the morning, working and appels. We had roll calls every day in the morning and in the evening, and if someone was missing they would search for him and give punishment to the whole block. Once someone who was working in the kitchen, took a cabbage, potatoes or something and the guard shot him.

Sometimes there was punishment for somebody's mistake or negligence and then we all had to run; everybody was punished. Escape was out of the question - we had no knowledge of the language of the country, no knowledge of the country and on top of that we had to wear these striped uniforms.

The women were in camp no 1, separated from us by the electric wire. We used to try to help each other, like before emptying bricks from a truck we used to slap each other for warmth and used to be together in harmony. On Yom Kippur in Auschwitz about 40 of us held some prayers, not in public and tried to avoid punishment.

We were moved from Auschwitz to the Charlotte Gruppe coal mine nearby at Shalogububa, in Poland where we worked. It was hard work, long hours but we had better food - there the soup was thicker, they used to give us two slices of bread a day and sometimes a spoon of jam and a piece of cheese. That was a luxury for us because the food was supplied by the mine. I was there with my brother and my uncle - my other brother and my father had been selected in Auschwitz.

We saw some people kill themselves, like jumping down the lift shaft, perhaps they realized that their family had died or something. One chap tried to escape and hid himself in the latrines where there was a little space to hide but they found him and killed the chappie. There was no time for collective punishment, however, because the Germans were then in retreat and the Russians began advancing from the East and we had to leave and walk for many, many days, I think to Czechoslovakia, and suddenly they put us in empty open railway trucks with other prisoners and we arrived in Mauthausen.

I must say it was thanks to the dead people that I managed to remain a survivor, still alive, because I was hiding in the truck, covered by the dead bodies, dead from the cold and from starvation. When they emptied the truck they took me out still alive; we went to the showers, then to appel, and then to the barracks.

When I was in Mauthausen I worked outside cleaning buildings, all sorts of work and suddenly I caught this scarlatina infection, a skin disease. The Germans were scared of disease or anything contagious and they used to either kill or look after you. They put me in this epidemics department where I stayed for a few weeks in the skin-disease barracks. We were not working but we were also not killed. There were no doctors, no medicine, nothing. They gave us a blanket, a bowl of water with some skins of potatoes or piece of something. This was in January 1945.

About the 10th March we were moved from Mauthausen. It was a death march. Many people died. We were in rags and would take anything to put on our bodies, letters, cement bags. If someone died and they saw you try to take his jacket they would shoot you, you were not allowed to take anything. We walked, sometimes we would come to the same place a second time - we would go towards Denault, then would go back and then return again. We would walk from early morning and during the night we would stop somewhere and sleep. If someone left the column during the day to try to pick something in the field, grass, carrots, potatoes, he would be shot. No prisoner was allowed to get out of the road. We did not walk on national roads but on secondary roads. There were about 150 soldiers posted all around us to supervise us - there were thousands of us.

One day I told my uncle that I would like to rest and rejoin him when I got some strength back and I sat down with other prisoners. When all the prisoners had gone past the Germans who were behind us forced us to stand up. There were about fifty of us but only about ten or fifteen stood up. I got up. Once we were up they did nothing to us but we had to walk. The rest were killed. I saw a few being killed, shot not in the chest but in the head.

Then we reached Linz in Austria where we stayed in a barracks for a week or so and did not work. We did nothing because there was no more organisation among the Germans.

One day around lunchtime we heard shooting and a few hours later some more shooting. Then some prisoners and ex-soldiers came running inside saying that it was the end of the war.

It was the 5th May. I was more dead than alive. I was lying among other soldiers, prisoners. My uncle was nearby and I could not walk. My weight was 23 or 28Kg - when they put me on the scale I could not make out the exact number. The Americans sent me to an ex-German army hospital. At first after the liberation the Americans had given the survivors a lot of food and they had died. With us they had very strict rules, they used to feed us like babies, a lot of food but in small quantities; at 6 'o clock, 9 'o clock, 12 'o clock, 3 'o clock, 6 'o clock, 9 'o clock.

It took me three months to come right. I was still with my uncle. Then I went to Italy where I saw my brother's name on the list of survivors. I found my younger sister in Murano in North Italy to where she had come from Russia and my older sister in Stockholm.

I stayed alive to survive, to live. We were thinking only of being able to live and eat better.

Some people think that the second generation of Germans is better than the first generation. For me a German is always a German. We Jews must be strong and united and able to fight.

Asher Varon was born on Rhodes Island on 21.5.1928. He was transported by the Nazis to Auschwitz and from there to forced labour in the Charlotte Gruppe coal mines and then to Mattthausen. He was Liberated near Linz on 5.5.1945. He moved to Rhodesia and then came to South Africa on 11.2.1971.

DIAMANTE FRANCO
Rhodes Island, Auschwitz-Birkenau

From Rhodes we were sent to Auschwitz-Birkenau. After 40 days quarantine a selection took place during which I was separated from my parents and my younger sister. I remember my separation from my mother. That was a real problem! I kissed her, and my little sister. I shouted for my mother. A German was hitting me with his batton. She turned around and said,
"My darling, don't...".

It was terrible! My other sister Rachelle and I remained together and the only luck we had throughout this awful nightmare is that we stayed together until the end. During the quarantine, I was totally exhausted, I could not handle the cold and I pretended to be sick - "Le malade Imaginaire". One morning after the doctor's rounds, I jumped into the line where sick people with temperatures were standing. We did not then realize where that line was heading. Only now do I realise what a great risk it was to pretend to be sick and what a great miracle it was that I was not sent to be killed.

When we arrived at the "Revier" or infirmary, I complained of a headache. They found that I actually did have a temperature! They took me to the hospital. There we saw some of the Rhodeslis who had been taken sick before me, like Allegra Levy from Kos, and Regita Binou. Allegra invited me to share her bunk with her, third level, and told me that she had typhoid fever. Her temperature was more than 40 degrees C and she was delirious. Beneath her was the sister of Rebecca Menashe, Sylvia, just as sick. The nurse came twice a day to hand out pills. I used to hide the pills under the mattress. The nurse would mutter to herself in German as if to say "what on earth are you still doing here alive?" I did this for five or six days.

Rachelle tried to visit me. The only way for her to enter the hospital was to put a square of white fabric on her head so that she could pretend to be a nurse. She came to warn me that very soon they were going to transport the men elsewhere and that we would no longer see our father and brother. She urged me to get out of hospital.

The following morning was Yom Kippur. I got up and went to block 20 to rejoin the girls I had been with. A few hours later I saw the men leave. My sister and I shouted good-byes to my father but he never saw us. All of a sudden, a German lady guard came calling a number (We had become mere numbers by then). It was my number! I got up. She seemed to ask me who gave me permission to leave an infection area to come and infect this block. I could not figure out what she was asking me. She grabbed me by the ear and threw me hard from one side of the block to another. My head hit the fire place and I subsequently got a huge infection there. I had a very high temperature. I developed an infection in the ear with lots of pus coming out and had to return to the infirmary to show the nurse. They took toilet paper and bandaged it, that was it! The infection disappeared all by itself. From then on I never left the block. I pretended to be sick all the time and never went to roll-call.

All the time that I was in the camp I managed to keep my old blue cardigan. When it was the call-up, I always had to remove it or they would have taken it away from me. I would hide it! It was covered with body lice all the time. This blue jersey kept me alive. Those lice would suck my blood when I had the jersey on, but kept me warm. There was never time to remove them so I just left them on. Hygiene was such a terrible problem! There was a room with a large hose pipe with a few holes every here and there and that's how we were expected to remain clean; no soap, no towels. (My sister still has today a soap that she stole there, with three initials on it which stood for - PURE JEWISH FAT. I just do not know how she can bear to look at it). I remained there from August to January until the Germans abandoned us.

After eight days they came back. We learnt later that they had dug a huge ditch planning to kill us all in order to destroy any evidence. Our luck was that the Russian troops approached the place where the ditch had been dug between Auschwitz and Birkenau. The Germans put the sickly in the jeeps and forced all the others to walk. All those who were unable to handle the walk were shot dead. Rachelle and I were at the very end of the line. My sister who had always done much for me was totally discouraged. She sat on the side of the road and said,

"Diamante, you go on. If you see our parents tell them that you had to leave me because I just could not go anymore, Go on!"

How could I leave her behind? I decided to stay with her. The German guards would in these cases come near the sufferer and count up to three. If by then the person did not get up, they would shoot her in the head. When one of them came to me and did this, I did not get up in order to give Rachelle a fright and make her get up. She did not want me to die so she got up just in time and then I did also.

After a while, afraid to be captured by the Russians the Nazis simply abandoned us in the middle of the road. We did not know what to do. Rachelle was really weak. We saw a barrack in the distance and headed for it. It was a big building which served as a hotel for the Germans. There we found coal which saved us. There were eight of us girls. The next morning we saw a Hungarian doctor coming out of one of the rooms. He spoke a little Italian and a little French and said,

"Brothers and sisters, we are approaching the liberation! Don't be discouraged now. The Russians will liberate us soon."

We stayed there for three days. Rachelle would go outside every day with a bucket to fetch snow so we had some water. We also had a little bread that we had kept which we shared among us. That is what saved us once again from death.

On the third day, Rachelle went out when the bombardment stopped and saw the first Russian. She tried to alert us that "the Russ..". From the excitement, she fainted. He tried to tell us that he would not harm us. He took some sugar cubes out of his pocket and gave them to us. We ate and stayed there waiting. All the places nearby were liberated: the sick were taken to hospitals and the others were taken to Auschwitz. We were stupid, we refused to go with them, afraid that we would then become prisoners of the Russians. We stayed behind for 21 days eating rubbish left over by the sick at Birkenau.

Each day when we hid in the building two of the girls went out to "*organize*" i.e. steal some food at the old Birkenau blocks. One day, Rachelle returned with a piece of mirror. She asked us to look at ourselves. I looked at myself, I saw ugly hair sticking up untidily. I asked her jokingly to find me a clip now that she had made me look at myself. Believe it or not, she brought me one!! A miracle! Another day I asked her for a piece of fish, for a change! She said that I was pushing my luck, we were nowhere near the sea. The next day, as she was on the hunt for food, she found a little fish hidden under the snow! I ate it raw, without the head. We were far from the sea; how did this fish land up there?

One day the girls met Simon Hasson the first cousin of one. He said he was looking for his wife, Rosa, whom he believed was with us. He was going from block to block and asked us which was ours. We explained that we stayed elsewhere. He said that we were silly and should rather join up with the other prisoners. The next day, we arrived at the gates of the camp. We could not go in. A Russian stopped us and forbade us to enter. We showed him our numbers. He said,

"We have been here for three weeks- Where have you been?".

They thought that we were German partisans. It was mid-February. It was cold. We were stuck! All of a sudden, four trucks arrived. One of the men there, an interpreter for the Russians, heard us speak French and asked us our story. When we explained, he promised to help on condition that we went to the end of the road to join the Serbs. He said that he would try to bring us some food. We went there and found an empty building in which we settled. At night he came with three German prisoners who brought us some food: bread and honey. We just could not believe that this was really true!!!

He told us that to be safe we would have to be quiet and put out the candles at night. But there were mattresses there, we had food, we were protected from the cold - so we started to have a party!!! At about 2.00 am, a Russian arrived and tried to throw us out. We begged him to wait till the morning. The next day, the interpreter arrived and was cross when we told him the story. He told the Russians that we were prisoners of the Nazis, just like all the others. They eventually agreed to let us into Aushwitz on condition that we worked in the kitchen peeling the potatoes. So we did.

The German prisoners would come in to clean our room two or three times a day. We were given cigarettes, tobacco and paper. I never smoked and so I accumulated quite a lot. One day, I thought I would give some to the German cleaners. A Russian saw me and could not believe his eyes. He grabbed me and said,

"Mama caput! Papa caput!!."

He could not believe that I could be kind to the people who killed my parents.

There were Poles and Hungarians with us. The first time that we met up with Rhodeslis was in Bologna. After the war, all the countries were trying to repatriate their citizens who had been taken prisoners. Italy was the last. Once we returned to Italy, we went with the Italians to Bologna, to a DP camp where everyone was redirected to their home towns. We were standing in the food queue in the evening, chatting in Ladino. Someone heard us and when we said that we were waiting to be sent back to Rhodes, we were told that we would be there a long time.

We escaped the next day to find the Jewish community of Bologna. We were directed to a place out of town; it took us two hours on foot. We were directed to the third floor of a building. We saw some of the people we knew from Rhodes. We started to ask news about our relatives. We were invited to stay there and we were very well taken care of, fed and lodged. That is why I always say that I have eaten charity food and so I will never refuse to give food to someone else, so much did I appreciate it. One lady living there, Marie Gandos, an ex-Rhodesli was married to the very religious Jewish engineer who came to Rhodes to build the famous bridge. Her family managed to escape. On the eve of Rosh Hashanah, she came to say good-bye to the refugees and give them a little money. She saw us and later on sent us money through her daughter. Thus the first money we touched after the camp was from that lady who had found out who we were. All of us were debating seriously what to buy first. What beautiful charity! Next, we received money from an American society, UNRRA, who gave us 3000 lirettas every month and a voucher to eat at "Mezza populare", a restaurant for workers, until the time when they could repatriate us.

We were put into contact with people from Elizabethville and there we joined my two older brothers and my husband of one day who was in Abuta. I had not expected him to have waited for me. He did wait!

DIAMANTE FRANCO was born in Rhodes Island in 1920 and educated there. She survived Auschwitz-Birkenau and was liberated on 27.1.1945. Before coming to South Africa in 1978, she lived in Italy and the Congo. She married Bension Franco and has a child

Chapter 7

LIFE IN RESISTANCE

MIKE BRESLIN
Mir, Nalibocki forests

I was born in 1924 in a small town in White Russia called Mir. I was the youngest child of Pesha and Morris Breslin, a polony maker who had moved to Mir from the town of Slonim. Mir had about 4000 inhabitants, **more than half of whom were Jewish. Jews were first mentioned as living in Mir in** the seventeenth century and were credited for turning it into an important commercial centre. Besides being merchants and skilled craftsmen, the Jews of Mir were also scholars and had established a yeshivah that attracted students from far and wide. The Jews lived in relative harmony with the Byelorussian peasants and the Poles, who formed the nobility, the intelligentsia and the administrators, although the 1920s had seen an upsurge in anti-Semitic feelings including attacks on Jews and their property by the Polish army and the local populace.

Mir and its surrounding lands belonged to Prince Swiatopol Mirski whose castle was a landmark. He died two years before the war and a Rumanian nephew took over. He was arrested on 17th September 1939, the day Communist Russia occupied the town, and disappeared.

Swiatopol had another nephew Prince Wassily, a playboy who was not trusted by his uncle and had friends within the Jewish community. He was not arrested by the Communists but managed to escape to Germany. The next time we saw him was when he arrived as a lieutenant in the occupying German army. He visited his erstwhile Jewish friends. After the liquidation of the Mir ghetto the tailor and one pharmacist, Mrs Chaimowitz, had been allowed to survive and continue their trade as they were useful to the Germans. Prince Wassily warned Mrs Chaimowitz of the final liquidation order against her and she managed to escape in time. She worked in the partisan hospital which is where I met her and learnt her story. She told me that Prince Wassily had told her that he had in fact worked not for the Germans during the war but the Russians.

Prior to the German invasion, I went to a Hebrew and Polish school, but now I went to a Russian school. The Soviets tried to politicize the region and eliminated or exiled their opponents. This phase stopped when the Germans attacked Russia on 22nd June 1941. I was in the 7th grade at school. On this day our fate was sealed.

The Red army retreated from the Germans in great disorder, many of the inhabitants ran eastwards into Russia but most remained, not accepting the unbelievable stories of German bestiality. In the early hours of the 27th June the first German detachments arrived and the first thing they did was to go from house to house setting them on fire.

Soon there was nothing left of our homes but a heap of ashes. These acts of terror were not aimed specifically at the Jews but at the inhabitants of Mir because it lay on the road from Berlin to Minsk. However, gentile gangs used this opportunity to break the windows of Jewish homes and terrorize us and we realized that there was no one to whom we could turn for protection. Soon after the SS arrived and arrested these gangs - not for attacking us but for acting without authorization. They threatened to shoot these hooligans but did nothing, deciding they could be useful.

On the 19th July another section of the SS arrived and visited all surviving Jewish homes. All men between the ages of 15 and 60 were chased to the market place. The SS demanded that we supplied them with certain goods and although difficult to find we got together what they wanted. After a terrifying few hours, the SS fired some shots in the air and ordered us to disperse and return the following day wearing yellow stars.

The next day we were again chased into the market place and 19 people were selected and buried alive in the nearby forest. The same day the SS ordered the formation of a Judenrat whose function was to act as a go-between. They sacrificed themselves for us as they were given terrible decrees to execute, each one more frightening than the next.

On the 9th November 1941 a number of cars filled with Germans arrived. They surrounded our little town on all sides and began a slaughter of the Jews which lasted the whole day. They murdered young and old, little children and adults; the majority of the Jewish population was killed. The Germans murdered fifteen hundred of the two thousand three hundred Jews who had lived in Mir. The streets and houses were running with blood and filled with corpses.

My father was amongst those murdered that day.

The remaining Jews were herded into what was known as 'The Jewish Quarter'.

I escaped because I had been staying with my married sister in a small town near Slonim called Kozlowczyzna. My parents came from Slonim and their family was well known there - my uncle was a printer and as a child I used to play with his machines. My sister and her family went into hiding on a farm near Slonim and were hidden by the farmer throughout the war.

I refused to go into hiding with her. I was fifteen and did not believe the ridiculous stories that the Germans planned to kill every Jew and make the area Judenrein. I had a rude awakening. Soon the killing started in Kozlowczyzna. I ran into a cellar and hid.

That night I went to Slonim. I arrived in Slonim in the middle of an 'aktion' and I saw the Germans taking 9 000 Jews packed on lorries into the forest. I removed the Magen David from my arm and walked through the streets. A German stopped his car and asked me the way to Lida. I was too afraid to answer in case he realized from my accent that I was Jewish, nor did I know the way there. To my relief the German drove away after having sworn at me for my ignorance. That same day they erected a ghetto there.

I found my aunt but unfortunately my uncle the printer had been one of those murdered.

I decided to return home to Mir. I had to go a roundabout route as most of the surrounding areas were now Judenrein. I walked seventy kilometres in that one night - fear lent wings to my feet. Although it was freezing and I wore out the soles of my shoes. I was aware of neither. I went to an uncle in Nowogrudek and stayed with him for a week. He was a religious man who woke me one morning and told me that he had had a bad dream and I must leave immediately. He hired a man to smuggle me out. On my way out of the town I saw the Germans arrive and begin another 'aktion' and I saw them shooting the Jews.

My uncle was one of those killed.

I made my way to Mir by going around instead of through villages. My brother, Leizer, sent someone to find me who brought me home. I returned to Mir in December and found only my mother and Leizer alive. Only eight hundred Jews still remained in Mir, mainly those selected as workers or people who had managed to hide during the aktion.

A ghetto was established consisting of a quadrangle with a number of small side streets with peasant huts into which the surviving Jews were packed in great congestion. The terrible conditions and inadequate hygiene in which we lived are impossible to relate.

Photo taken by a German of the Judenrat in the Mir Ghetto 30.12.1941 My brother Leizer is 3rd from the left without a hat, standing next to Rabbi Eliahu Baruch, Judenrat Chairman, in the long coat. They are wearing yellow stars.

All Jews between the ages of 15 and 60 had to work and for this each received 125 grams of bread a day. I started to work for a German as a signwriter going out of the ghetto each day. We had to change the street signs from Russian to German letters. That winter was very cold with sleepless nights and constant terror.

Serafimowicz

The German Chief of Police, Meister Hein, with a guard from the Waffen SS and a Byelorussian called Serafimowicz, arrived to establish a gendarmerie to be in charge of the town. Serafimowicz (later regional police chief) was a brutal murderer who had been responsible for many killings.

One day he gave me a beating because I had painted a poster advertising the 1st May holiday for him but had not painted a frame because I had no varnish. Fortunately Meister Hein intervened.

German policy also aimed at eliminating the Polish elite. One spring night twenty five of the Polish intelligentsia from Mir were arrested. These included my school principal, Mr Balicki, and the priest who lived near us, Father Mankiewicz. They were transferred to the Koldyczewo concentration camp where they were all gassed in special trucks.

One day a friend, Berel Reznik, an electrician was sent by the Germans to fix some wires at the police station. While he was there he recognized a friend called Oswald Rufeisen. He was about 21 years old, came from an observant Galician family and like Berel had been active in the Vilna youth movements although Oswald belonged to the political Akivah and Reznik to the socialist Hashomer Hatzair.

But what a change! Now Oswald was wearing German uniform and standing in a group of SS thugs! He looked gentile, spoke perfect German, Polish and Russian and had managed to pass himself off as a Volksdeutsch (a local German) and had

become a translator for the German gendarmerie. He was even living with Serafimowicz as a guest and was later appointed Town Commandant of the German Occupation Army in Mir!

Oswald recognized Berel. They looked at each other in silent tension. Oswald signalled to him to meet him outside and left the room. They then arranged to meet that evening in a side street - the ghetto was not yet enclosed. Oswald approached him and said,

"Shalom Berel. How is my friend Shlomo Charchas?"

He offered to help the Jews as much as was possible on condition that his secret was kept. His identity would be revealed only to two other men in Mir who had been in the Vilna kibbutz with him - Israel Reznik and Shlomo Charchas, one of the Hashomer Hatzair leaders. Berel gave him the names of trustworthy intermediaries who could deliver messages - some were office cleaners, others worked in the Police stables.

After that Oswald would come to the ghetto to deliver things needed there as well as information about plans to destroy the ghetto. He managed to arrange for some of his old friends to get work that would bring

Oswald Rufeisen, aged 17

them into contact with him without arousing suspicion. In this way they were able to smuggle revolvers, bullets and grenades into the ghetto. The rifles Oswald himself would bring in. He would drive up to the ghetto about midnight and hide the rifles between the bushes. We would carefully retrieve them and smuggle them into the ghetto. This was very dangerous and we had to be careful that the Judenrat Police did not find

Mir Castle

out although some of the Police were active members of the Resistance.

The peasant owners of those huts who were now within the ghetto were compensated with the few Jewish homes not destroyed by the fire. They were not satisfied so they approached the Provincial Governor in Baranowitz, Commissioner Werner, who agreed to return their houses to them. In the spring of 1942 we were transferred from these huts to a very small crowded ghetto in the mediaeval castle which had belonged to Count Swiatopol Mirski.

The castle consisted of five towers, each five storeys high joined by thick stone walls with deep cellars underneath. We were each alotted a small space. The narrow, congested conditions created new problems. The only well had insufficient water for the eight hundred Jews crammed between the castle walls. Rumours crept in about the liquidations of the other ghettos, about the formation of partisan troops deep in the nearby forests. My friends and I began to hear about a secret organisation operating in the ghetto. My brother Leizer was one of the leaders of the underground movement in the ghetto and he persuaded them to let me join even though I was only 15. Our ghetto in Mir seemed to contain the last outpost of Jews in the area. We began to realize that our days were numbered.

One day early in August 1942 Oswald entered the office to overhear Meister Hein talking on the phone. He realized from his subservient "Yes, Sir. Of course, Sir." that it must be to someone of high rank. He heard Hein say "I have the date. Thirteenth August will be the total liquidation. The date is fixed. Jawohl."

Oswald and his friends decided not to divulge the date generally but to make plans for our escape. We felt that if the Germans were going to massacre us, at least we wanted to have the opportunity to defend ourselves and die like heroes. We felt that as the ghetto was a fortress we might have a chance to defend it for a while. We hoped that before our deaths we might be able to inflict losses on the Germans with the arms Oswald had provided us. The idea of death and struggle were dominated by a desire for revenge.

Oswald felt that the only chance some of us would have to remain alive would be by escaping from the ghetto and he gradually convinced us to give up the idea of fighting within the castle and plan instead for a mass exodus from the ghetto. Oswald would join us and form a Jewish Partisan Unit.

Oswald planned to bring the German police force to the forest on the pretext of attacking the partisans. He led them to believe that on the night of August 9th, a large armed band was expected to pass through one of the forests about a half day's march from Mir.

The months went by. We planned and waited. We knew that the massacre was to take place in August. Oswald had told us. He began coming to the ghetto more frequently. He said we must be patient as he was still waiting for the orders to make Mir "Judenrein." Werner, the Commandant of the Baronowicz area, a notorious mass murderer, was supposed to be in charge but had not yet issued the order. Oswald told us to be ready because Wilhelm Kube, the Commissar-General of White Russia and Hitler's adviser, had decided that the whole of White Russia was to be made "Judenrein." (In September 1943 Kube was killed by a bomb placed under his bed by his servant, a girl working for the partisans, who managed to escape to a nearby Soviet Partisan group.)

On Friday morning 7th August 1942 Oswald came to the ghetto and told us that the orders had come. We were all to be murdered on the 15th August. He told our group to escape from the ghetto on the Sunday night. Our group under Berel Reznik and Shlomo Charchas began to finalize our plans. On Sunday the Judenrat called a special meeting. Shlomo told them that our destruction was inevitable and that everyone who did not want to go to their deaths meekly should try to escape. Our group was told to escape from the ghetto and take revenge.

At midnight on Sunday 9th August two hundred young Jews left the ghetto. My brother, Leizer, and I were amongst them. I can remember the scene as clearly as if it were in front of me now. The gate was closed, the guard was missing, and people were crawling out through the holes in the walls. There were terribly heart-rending scenes as children parted from their parents, sisters from their brothers, husbands from their wives. Even today I can still hear the sounds of the weeping that accompanied us as we left the ghetto.

When the escape became known, a Jewish informer betrayed Oswald. When the Chief of the German Police learnt that he had organized it, he summoned Oswald before him. Oswald realized that he was trapped and that there was no escape. He said, "I am a Jew and I will die as a Jew!" The Chief would not believe this. "I had total trust in you," he said, "And I am leaving you the only way out."

He then left the room pretending that he was going to call the guard but Oswald realized that he was being given the chance to take his life. Instead he managed to escape through a window. It was getting dark and he evaded the police, hid between sheaves of corn and made his way to a cloister where some nuns hid him for a time until he was able to join our partisan group where he distinguished himself as a hero, blowing up many bridges.

When Meister Hein learnt about the escape he ordered the castle to be surrounded so that no more could escape. On Monday at 4 p.m. the ghetto was encircled by a heavy cordon of police and Germans with machine guns. Those left behind were doomed to their fate. They began to destroy their remaining possessions - their food, leather and clothing - by pouring petrol over it so that the Germans would not profit by it. Some poisoned themselves. At 4 a.m. on Tuesday the German police entered the ghetto.

As Oswald had warned, the rest of the Jews in Mir, including our friends and families, were massacred.

My Mother was one of the victims.

When we got to the forest near Mir we formed groups. Leizer and I managed to get arms for our group as I knew where some had been hidden by gentiles and we arranged to buy them. This area became dangerous so we moved deeper into the forests where we established family camps. There were about 2 800 Jews in the Bielski and Zorin camps - each surrounded by a ring of fighting groups. Our aim was to protect all Jews regardless of age. Oswald joined us.

It took us time to be accepted into Russian partisan units as fighters. Only in 1943 did the Russians show an official willingness to accept Jewish fighters. Our job was primarily to destroy bridges. Some of us died fighting, some were shot either by Germans or by anti-Semitic partisans, and only a fraction made it to the end of the war.

There were about 360 000 partisans in white Russia. We even had our own underground newspaper which was circulated to the local populace with news dictated to us over the Russian radio. The Russians gave the partisans a printing press and as I had printing experience of a sort, because of my childhood visits to my uncle, I became the printer. A Russian Jew, Boris, trained me. Because of this I was transferred from the Stalin Brigade to the Comsomolsky Brigade.

Many of the Polish partisans were themselves strongly anti-Semitic. In 1943 an ex-Polish Lieutenant Milaszewski organized a separate fighting group which identified itself with the Polish home army underground and under his leadership the Polish fighting group grew to several hundred men. When a fighting group of twelve Jews from the Zorin camp came to the forest from the Iwienies region, they were attacked by the Polish partisans and all but one was killed. They also ambushed another group of Jews on their way to collect food. These killings were in direct opposition to the policies of the Russian command and by order of General Panimarenko of the Russian partisan headquarters in Moscow this group was disarmed. A secret order was given to certain partisan camps to surround these Polish partisans at night. In the early hours of the morning they were taken prisoner without a shot being fired.

I was the man who printed these orders.

When the other Polish partisan groups heard what had happened to this group for killing Jews, they united with the German anti-Semitic, anti-Communist and fascist underground group and fought against us.

I was in the forest for two years until June 1944. Mir had already been liberated. About 110 partisans from Mir returned. In August 1945 I went to Lodz, Poland, where I found my sister and her family. There the Poles arrested me. There had been pogroms by the Polish underground and our Jewish partisan group was arrested. They kept us overnight and told us to leave Poland as they did not want Jews there and threatened to kill us if we stayed. I felt that it would be better for me to leave Poland and its anti-Semitism completely. Together with my sister and her family we went to a Displaced Persons' Camp in Munich in the American zone of Germany. I remained in Munich until 1951 when I left for South Africa and settled in Cape Town.

My sister settled in Switzerland. My brother went to Palestine with Aliyah Bet in 1945. Shlomo and Berel also settled in Israel, and so did Oswald. For sixteen months after running away from the Germans he had been hidden by nuns and he had been thoroughly indocrinated by them. He later became a Carmelite monk and lives in Haifa where he has become well known as Father Daniel - particularly after challenging the Israeli Law of Return in court. I visit him when I go to Israel and we talk about our days in the forest.

For many years I felt uncomfortable talking about what I saw and experienced during these years. Recently, however, in 1992 and 1993 I had visits from officers from the Scotland Yard Crime Division who flew out from England to interview me. They had also interviewed Brother Daniel - Oswald. They were investigating allegations against the man responsible for the deaths in Mir, Serafimowicz. He had been discovered living in Surrey. Unfortunately despite substantial evidence against this war criminal, the case has gone no further. This is a great pity as I have always wanted to see this beast brought to justice.

Because of this I believe that my story is still relevant today and I have a duty to record what happened so that it will never be forgotten.

Mike Breslin was born in Mir, Poland in 1924 and was educated there. The war years he spent in the Mir ghetto and as a partisan in the Nalibocki forest in White Russia. He was liberated in June 1944 and after staying in Munich he emigrated to South Africa in 1951. He is married to Dora and has two sons, Maurice and Steven.

JACK FRIEDMANN
Stax, Tunisia

As one of the many young Jews in South Africa eager to combat the Nazis, I enlisted in Johannesburg shortly after the outbreak of hostilities. In due course I found myself in North Africa as Assistant Adjutant of No.2 S.A.A.F. Fighter Bomber Squadron. One day I was ordered to proceed with an advance party to arrange for the occupation of an airfield, recently vacated by the German forces. The date according to my diary was 12 April,1943. The location of the airfield was near the ancient town of Stax in Tunisia.

We had now reached the final stages of the campaign in North Africa with the Nazi forces desperately clinging to shrinking areas of territory, harassed by the Allied Air Forces which had now established air superiority. Squadrons were leapfrogging their way in the pursuit of the enemy, as the ground advance continued, taking over airfields deserted in some haste by the Germans whose rapid departure was evidenced by lack of booby traps.

Soon after Stax fell to the Allies, we were installed at the nearby airfield. To us, used to desert conditions, it was an idyllic new environment. We saw real grass, there were trees dotted around and to complete a pleasant picture, waving wheatfields surrounded the airfield.

I did a brief tour of inspection of the outer perimeter of the airfield, where the squadron's camp would be dispersed, and noticed that there were areas reflecting bombing attacks by Allied bombers. Pockmarking some areas were large craters where the bombs had fallen. Next to one of these I noticed something sticking out of the sand and debris, which included some twisted metal thrown up by the explosion. It was a piece of parchment.

I bent down to look at the parchment and was amazed to see that it was covered with HEBREW letters. It did not take me long to identify the parchment as part of a Sefer Torah.

But how did it get there?

An obvious starting point was to ask the local residents if they could throw any light on the matter. There were some homes and farmhouses in the surrounding areas and the Italian occupants - or at least some of them - helped to provide a solution.

I was informed that there was a synagogue in Stax which had been desecrated by a group of Nazi soldiers. They had taken a number of scrolls of the law as booty. These they had torn up and used for purposes one could only associate with the mentality of persons totally steeped in Nazism and its creed of blind hatred of Jews.

I learned that a German anti-aircraft gun crew had apparently been part of the raiding party who had desecrated the synagogue in Stax. They had brought back a Sefer Torah - or parts of it - to their gun emplacement at the landing field we were now occupying.

Shortly after they returned to their posts, the airfield was subjected to an Allied bombing raid. One of the bombs dropped scored a direct hit on their gun emplacement, sending into oblivion those responsible for, or associated with, the dastardly act.

Was it Divine wrath for desecration of the Holy Word?

In a disused military office, I found a date stamp with the word `Stax' on it, so, to record the area in which I had found the piece of parchment as well as the date, I impressed this information on a small corner of this fragment which contained a portion of Bereshit.

I then posted the parchment to my father, Capt. Aron Friedmann, in Cape Town, who mounted it in a suitable frame. Strangely enough, the rubber stamp impression on the parchment fragment disappeared completely after a short period of time and no trace of it can be seen today. Yet the original hand lettered characters forming part of the section of Bereshit commencing with the words,

"And the Lord G-d said it is not good for man to be alone"
are as clear as the day on which this portion of the scroll was found.

On my return home from active service Up North I followed the injunction in this parsha *"to find a helpmeet"* and married within a few months. My dear wife, Freda, and I have now been married for more than fifty years.

Ultimately the Sefer Torah was passed on to me and remained in our home for close on forty years. Concerned about the possible fate of this historic and holy relic, I decided to present it to Temple Israel in Wynberg.

The dedication ceremony was attended by Jewish ex-servicemen who helped to destroy the cult of bestiality engendered by the Nazi regime, and signified the end of thousands of miles of travel in war-time, from North Africa to a final resting place in Cape Town, of a fragment of what is so central to Jewish life - **the Torah**.

By coincidence the parchment was dedicated on the 23rd October 1991, the anniversary of the battle of El Alamein.

An even more amazing coincidence occurred in 1986 when Freda and I went to Melborne to celebrate the barmitzvah of our grandson Dion. At the barmitzvah I was called up to the Torah. What was the portion being read at that moment?

"And the Lord G- d said it is not good for man to be alone."

The identical portion to that in the scroll which I had found in North Africa in 1943, 43 years earlier.

Jack Friedmann was born in the Transvaal in 1915. Like many other South African Jews, he joined the South African armed forces and served in North Africa and Italy, the latter part as a war correspondent attached to the South African Air Force. He has a wife, Freda, a daughter, Renee, a son, Bennett, and grandchildren.

175

Concentration and Extermination camps
The Holocaust; The Falsehood and The Facts by Arthur Suzman

Chapter 8

LIFE AS A DISPLACED PERSON

MATILDA HASSON
Rhodes, Haidari

~~~~~~

I was born in Seattle, America. This was to save my life. My parents did not like the American weather and returned to Rhodes Island where I grew up and married. In 1938 I tried to get into America but I could not find my birth certificate and by the time my cousin in Washington managed to get me immigration papers, war had broken out. However I did receive papers which showed that I was an American citizen. When the SS arrived to arrest us, there were some Turks with them to whom I showed these papers. Later the Turkish consul came and freed the Turkish citizens. The SS said that we could not stay here but must be sent as political prisoners to Greece. My husband Albert, my daughter Stella and I were packed into the boats from Rhodes along with my parents and the other Jews.

They were sent to Auschwitz but we were separated and sent with other prisoners to the Haidari Camp in Athens. When I arrived there I said,

"I am not an Italian, I am an American citizen."

We were placed with the other foreigners who included Turks, Russians, Argentinians, Spaniards and people who had mixed marriages. The men were separated from the women. When Albert tried to tell them that he was an American citizen, he was beaten.

"You are not an American. You are a Jew!"

!! POW !!

So he had to keep quiet.

Stella and I were sent to a big building with about two hundred people in a room. She was to celebrate her second birthday in this room. She became very sick with pneumonia, coughed all the time and could not sleep. She had constant diarrhoea and I had no medicine to give her. I did not sleep for a month. We stayed in Haidari for about three months.

Every time one German was killed, the Nazis would line us all up, take fifty at random and kill them in revenge. First they made us dig a ditch, line up, take off our clothes and then would shoot us. One day in 1944 the SS called out my name and that of a lady from Cos, Juliette Menashe, with her two children. We thought that it was our turn to be selected to be killed. We cried and cried. A nice young lady tried to comfort me, telling me not to worry, I would be freed. (Some time later we saw each other in the street. She was very glad and embraced me - she had wondered what had happened to us.)

I discovered that my husband and Mr Menashe had also been selected. To our surprise they took us and put us outside the camp. We said,

"Where are we going to go? We have no money or anything." Everything had been taken from us - our money, our gold, our rings. Only one street led from Haidari and as we walked up it a lady saw us and called,

"Have you come from Haidari? Women with children? Come and spend the night with us."

We learnt that the tide of war had turned, the Germans were retreating and the Russians were about to land in Greece from Yugoslavia. The Germans had decided to set the foreign citizens free - the others remained in Haidari. I do not want to talk about what they did to the others. That night all the Germans flew out of Athens.

We spent the night in that woman's house. A man arranged for a truck to fetch us to take us to the Red Cross who would house and feed us in the morning and at lunch. They put us up in a school where we settled down on the floor.

We had nothing. No mattress, no covers, nothing. We were displaced persons. We stayed there for a few months. The children had lice, there were bugs. It was awful.

In Haidari we had met Mr Profetta, a rich Jew married to a German. He was one of the first to be released - his wife had paid a lot of money to get him out. He came to the school and when he saw the conditions under which we were living, he found us a cheap hotel and paid for us. Later when we returned to Rhodes we repaid everything he lent us.

We did not like the food that we got from the Red Cross. We were not used to that sort of food. My husband sold the food and in this way we got a little money. We kept the bread but used the money to buy butter or oil which we would eat on a slice of bread - it was better than their meat .

Then the Civil War started. Unfortunately our hotel lay in the middle between the Communists and the Royalists. They would fire at each other and hit the hotel. A man looked out of the hotel, was shot in the stomach and had to be taken to hospital. Another woman was cleaning the window and while she bent down to pick up the cloth, a bullet passed over her head. She was lucky. The Communists came and searched under our mattresses for arms - but we had nothing. Our room did not even have a closet. This went on for over a month and we suffered a great deal.

At last Hitler was defeated and the World War came to an end but we were still displaced people, and a long way from home and its comforts. There was no oil, and no water, no electricity and no power. It was winter by now and I was sick in bed. The Red Cross had stopped giving us food because they thought we were Communists. A teacher we knew spoke to them and told them that we were not Communists but were from Rhodes, and had been in Haidari and begged them to continue giving us food parcels. In the meantime the next door building was bombed. Albert went there to pick up scraps for firewood. I used to make a fire in a small room on the roof of the building to cook the little we had.

One night while I was trying to cook, I fainted and fell on the floor as though dead. My sister-in-law's brother, Albert Franco, who was also with us pulled my ear to revive me. I woke up to find many people surrounding me looking at me. They put me to bed. I could not move. I did not have the strength to comb my hair or put something on. Albert sold something and used the money to buy me an egg. One egg. We boiled the egg. Stella sat there looking and looking at the egg, so I said'
"Okay,we shall split the egg - half for you and half for me." There were so many things

available; chicken, oranges, apples, lots of fruit but we did not have the money to buy anything. We could only look. I was so weak, I was dizzy and could not go out by myself.

After a year we met Reuben Hasson from Rhodes who had fled to Turkey and joined the Greek navy. He told Jacques Israel who worked for the Alhadeff Company about the existence of our little group of Rhodes Island Jews - Albert Hasson, Albert Franco and Moshe Menashe. Reuben Hasson would visit us in the hotel and wrote to my brother in the Congo who sent us Egyptian money. Now we could buy something to eat. We also wrote from the Red Cross to my brother in America telling him what had happened to my parents and to ourselves. They sent us money and a parcel of clothes. The latter never arrived. We now moved into a house outside Athens with a man we had met in Haidari. There was no furniture but we bought a mattress and moved in.

In September 1945 Menashe met a Greek man who had a little boat who agreed to take them home to the island of Cos, from where we could go on to Rhodes. However when we tried to get a permit to leave, this was refused. The English authorities said that we were Communists. Apparently there was an Albert Hasson from Salonika who was a Communist spy, and they mistook my husband for him. Although my husband said that he was from Haidari, they refused to believe him and claimed that he had borrowed some money to get a permit for Cos.

The English knew, I do not know how, that we had decided to leave Athens without a permit to go back to Rhodes. We stopped at a few islands on the way but when we got to Cos, the Greek police were waiting to arrest 'Albert Hasson'. They threatened to put us in gaol unless we left and went to Rhodes. We sailed for Rhodes together with Albert Franco but when at last we arrived home, the English put my husband in gaol along with the other men. They wanted to put Stella and me in gaol also but people recognized us and said,
"Leave the woman; they are good people; they are businessmen; they are not Communists".

The men stayed in gaol for two nights in a cell with another man who was put there in the hope that they would reveal information so they were careful what they said to each other. When they were released, we were told that we were to be deported from the island!

The Germans had deported us from our homes in Rhodes to Athens and now that we had at last managed to return to Rhodes after suffering terribly, the English were doing the same thing.

In order to return to Rhodes, we had to get a permit to go to Athens. Then we had to return to Athens.

Then we had to get a permit to go to Rhodes, Only then could we go home.

By this time we had some money. We had given some gold jewellery to good Greeks in Rhodes before we left and we had managed to get some of it back. The rest of it the Greeks claimed had been given to the Germans to save themselves from being killed; they made up some stories. We now had to pay the man who had the boat to take us back to Athens.

It took us FIFTY days to get to Athens.

We needed a permit to go there. We went from island to island trying to get one. As we had been deported, each island refused to give us a permit. In addition it was dangerous to sail around the islands because mines still surrounded the entrances.

"Be careful, don't go this way. Be careful, don't go that way!" we would be warned. We had constant anxiety. The motor of the boat was broken so we could only use the sails. Finally we met a nice man on one of the islands who took pity on us and gave us a permit to go to Greece. Moshe Menashe had also been deported from Cos and had also had to return to Athens to get a permit to return to Cos. It only took him one day to go - it took us fifty!

After a few weeks in Athens we got the permit and boarded a boat again. The boat was halfway out to sea when the police stopped us and called,
"ALBERT HASSON! MATILDA HASSON! COME BACK!!
Take your suitcases and everything out of the boat with you!"
I sat on the pier and cried!
"What is going to happen to us now!"

We went with the policeman - he was a nice person.
"Why are they doing this to us?" we asked him.
"We are not Communists. The Germans took us all away from Rhodes and imprisoned us in Haidari."
He said. "Go! Go to your place!
Go to Rhodes!" and he took the permit.

We arrived in Rhodes on Rosh Hashanah. We went to my aunt who was at shul. Can you imagine the excitement when she returned home to find us there!! As our house had been destroyed, she invited us to stay with her.

We never heard from my parents. They were probably killed in Auschwitz.

Our shop had been taken over by someone else. All our goods had been confiscated by the Germans. What had remained had been put in a warehouse but these goods could only be claimed if the owner's name was on it. We managed to find a few things with our name and we were given a damaged shop which my husband fixed. We sold all the unclaimed goods from the warehouse on behalf of the Jewish Community and the money was given to the community. With the devaluation of the drachma we had very little. I became very ill and was taken to hospital in Rhodes. I thought I was going to die. While I was in hospital the American immigration papers arrived.

In 1948 we went to America but we were not happy there and moved to Zaire. Recently we settled in Cape Town.

When we returned to Rhodes and found that everything of ours had been destroyed and that we had nothing, my aunt said, "What does it matter if you have lost everything!
You are alive. That is enough. Thank G-d."

Today I have two lovely children and grandchildren. We are alive. Thank G-d.

MATHILDA HASSON was born in Seattle, America in 1912 and educated at Rhodes Island where she trained as a dress maker. She was taken to the Haidari Camp outside Athens until liberated on 11.9.1944. She then lived in Athens until allowed to return to Rhodes, and moved to New York and Kinshasa, Zaire. She came to South Africa in 1974 with her husband Albert. She has a son Ikey and a daughter Stella.

MENDI SOFFER
Bucharest, Place Tradati, Koenigsdorf, Marseilles.

We lived in Bucharest, Rumania, in a small wooden house which had an oven in the middle. My father was a very poor and very religious shammas and cheder teacher from a well-known Talmudic family. He was very kind and would often bring guests home from shul and although we had nothing, we would share the little nothing we had. I had to leave school early to go to work as we were running out of bread.

I was about 11 when the war broke out. There was always a lot of anti-Semitism in Rumania and I remember being beaten up at school by two bigger boys who said, "There's a Jew - let's beat him up."

The Poles were rotten but the Rumanians were not much better. We knew very little about the Germans. We were totally ignorant. We did not know what was taking place on the outside. My first experience with Nazis was when a German came into our house to take my father away. My mother stood in front of my father and refused to allow him to go and then the Nazi left. My mother was thrilled.

There were no ghettos in Bucharest because it was an industrial city and General Antonescu kept the Jews because he was good and because he could use their factories for the war effort but he had an anti-Semitic rival, Horisima, who wanted to destroy all the Jews. Between the 19th and 23rd January Horisima's forces massacred about 50 000 Jews as well as many Rumanians.

Some were taken to the abbatoirs and were hanged by the neck and called "kosher meat", others were executed by firing squad. We saw many dead people all over the show. Fortunately Antonescu's faction came out victorious and he decided that, as so many Jews had already died, he would spare the Jews of Bucharest.

We lived there throughout the war. Using an assumed name, I would go out to work building wooden boxes in an ammunition factory.

I also used to stand in queues, long queues, to buy paraffin to sell on the black market. Standing for paraffin in weather fifteen degrees below zero was no joke and many people would pay anything to get their paraffin without queuing. I would stand in the queue for the whole night and sell the can for a few extra cents.

Later when Bucharest was bombed by the Allies I became a carpenter and would fix the shops that had been destroyed. Jews were also killed in the bombing. I did anything as long as I could make a living.

Because of my father, we would sometimes get kosher meat even though it was prohibited for Jews. People would bring him meat to slaughter and cut up in our cellar and we would get the bones and maybe a little meat.

My sister had joined the Communist party and went to Russia and was sent to a concentration camp there but by some miracle I knew someone who was going there. We gave him some money and he managed to bring her back from Russia.

My father, my brother and I used to do forced labour. We would be taken into the forest and made to do all sorts of things like digging trenches and would return home at night. Many of the people would never come back. It was a question of luck.

When the war finished I decided to leave Rumania. I took a train to the border, crawled across it into Hungary, and from there I wandered around Vienna and Munich through Germany. I passed Bergen Belsen and then saw what had been going on. There were no people in the camps, just ruined buildings although I met many survivors with their marked arms who had been in the camps.

I joined a Dror Habonim kibbutz and everything went fine until Aliyah Bet started. They tried to smuggle the survivors into Palestine despite Britain's blockade. A big contingent was brought from Strasbourg and I joined the convoy hoping to get to Israel with them, but when we got to the border the English prevented the convoy from going by shooting against the wheels. We were forced to return to the same place in Austria called Wiesenhof on top of a mountain.

They sent a group from Italy and I was one of the very first to open up a way for the people to cross the border there moving illegally from Austria into Italy on the way to Palestine. For six days each week I used to smuggle 40- 50 people across the mountains, hand them over to people on the other side and come back alone. At that time I knew the mountain very well. We opened up six different routes. We knew exactly where the borders were, and when the guards changed. When the guards were at the bottom we would be on the top and they wouldn't bother to climb up.

Then I decided to go to Israel and went to a place outside Italy called Place Tradati that had been Mussolini's castle. It was now a religious kibbutz affiliated to Mizrachi. The madrich who had commanded me to open the border across the mountain would not take me to Israel but sent me back to the border.

I refused and instead went around Germany and landed up at the main school of madrichim in a place called Koenigsdorf hoping to go to Israel. That night one of the barracks burnt down and I called the fire brigade. I didn't know that they had grenades and all kinds of things hidden under the floor, and that there was a haganah school in the centre of this kibbutz. They made such a fuss because I had called in the fire brigade that I left the kibbutz.

I wandered around all over the place until I landed up in Marseilles in the Exodus camp but they wanted money to have my name placed at the top of the list. I refused and went to Paris where I got a job and settled down. Later I came to South Africa as a stowaway. Most of my family moved to Israel. My parents went to Bnei Brak, my brother and sister lived around Petach Tikvah. My brother now lives in Cape Town.

Mendi Soffer was born in Galatz, Rumania on 15.2.1928. After the War he stayed in numerous Displaced Persons Camps including camps in Vienna, Saltzburg, Innsbruck, Vienna, Koenigsdorf, ending in the Exodus Camp in Marseilles. After staying in Belgium he moved to South Africa in 1950. He is married to Hannah Rabinowitz and has two sons, Ivan David, and Selwyn and a daughter Linda.

FREDA GLEZER
Namangaan, Bratislava, Wechsler

(Continued from chapter three)

When the War finished I decided that I was going to go where the rest of the refugees wanted to go, to Palestine. I was not going to go backwards, I was going to go forwards.

Before I left Namangaan I got married. Wulf was from Vilna and had lost his whole family. He was a quiet, kind, sensible man who had been part of the group of ten who had been with me there. I got married because I was terrified to travel by myself. I was goodlooking and it was inadvisable for a girl to travel alone.

We returned through the Polish organization to Poland with a group of several hundred. We prepared bread for the trip because the train was supposed to take three weeks. Instead it took us two months to come back in those trains.

The Haganah were already in action and were expecting us and they promised that somehow they would get us into Palestine. We had to go through Czechoslovakia - we walked the whole way. We hid in the day and walked by night.

The war was finished but we did not belong anywhere.

We had no papers. We had no passports. We were stateless.

We had nothing to say where we were from or where we were going and the Haganah warned us not to say anything, but just to go.

We came to Bratislava. There were hundreds and hundreds of us and the Haganah organized the whole thing. They told us where to go, where to hide, what to say. We were hiding from the Russians who had taken Czechoslovakia and would have wanted to know where we were going - we could have been arrested.

We walked from Bratislava to Austria. Sometimes we went a little way by train. In Austria we were surrounded by the American army who were afraid that such a large crowd of refugees would bring them health problems and they sprayed us with disinfectant. They kept us for six weeks surrounded by barbed wire and gave us a little food.

Then I got diphtheria and was taken by ambulance to a German hospital. I was terrified. I did not want to speak to the Germans, I did not want to tell them my name.I did not know what to do. If the group left without me, how would I get to Palestine alone? I was very frightened and decided to run away. I was in hospital for three days. The doctor said to me in German,

"I want to help you, but how can I help you if you do not want to communicate with me?"

I was so frightened of him - I knew that the Germans did not like the Jewish people and I did not know what was going on At 5 o' clock when the gates were opened, I ran away and managed to find my way back to the refugees.

The Haganah in Munich had discovered that we had been surrounded with barbed wire and they brought a lot of food from the American Joint and distributed it. Some people were so desperate to get food for their children that they fought over it. I was not going to get myself killed fighting for food, and I did not take part. They noticed this and gave me a pound of butter.

Then we were taken to D.P. Camps in Germany, a train a day. We went to Wechsler, the third station from Gressen. We stayed in the military barracks - five people to a room - this was luxury accommodation. The D.P. camps had a committee to run them and arrange everything. There were 1 500 of us. The U.N. were there to help people to emigrate to other countries. One country would say: "We shall take three families."Transports would go all over

They needed someone to work for them and they chose my friend and me - we had been separated in different sections of the camp. We worked for the U.N. helping with cooking and making things - this was my best time - I had food, I was paid, I had some clothes. I could go out to town. I met a Dr Kaplan at the Joint. He had come from Warsaw and he was very nice to my friend and me. He knew we had lost everything and wanted to make up for this and offered to help me get to America.

He said,"Freda, you have gone through such a lot and you will have such a difficult life in Palestine. Why do you want to go there? Can't I help you and take you to America?"
I said, "Dr Kaplan, I am not going anywhere else. I am going to Palestine."
He said, "Why are you so obstinate? There is fighting there. It is still not independent. We do not even know if there will be a state of Israel."
I said, "Dr Kaplan, I have made up my mind and no one will change my mind."

I worked and worked. My husband and I would travel for the Haganah, smuggling things that were going to be needed. Once a week we would go to Munich with a suitcase and buy things like binoculars. I would put the suitcase under the seat, being careful that there was no one around to see and then I would sit somewhere else watching. If the suitcase were opened, the authorities would not have realized that the contents belonged to me. I was very proud that I could do something.

The State of Israel was declared. We had a big celebration in the camp. Delegates came from Israel and all over. The whole time the Haganah would say,
" If they try to persuade you to go to Sweden or anywhere else, don't! Don't put your name down!" But some people did.

I spent two and a half years in the D.P. camps and I managed to buy a lot of things because I worked. I prepared myself to go and at last at the end of November I was able to travel illegally to Israel with Aliyah Bet.

First we went to France, and for three weeks we hid in Marseilles while waiting to get onto a boat. The State of Israel had already been declared but Britain was still in charge. We hid 40 people in a room. We could not sit down, only stand. Then we emigrated and after three weeks we came on the first Israeli ship, the *Negba*. There were 500 people and the boat could only take 150-200 and we lay like herrings. After two weeks we arrived in the night in Israel.

I went to Netanya. We came to the Ma'abarot. On Friday I decided I wanted to see my sister. I had written to her from Germany that she must not worry, that I did not know when or how I should get to Israel, but I would come and would communicate with her the first opportunity I had.

I went to a taxi and I told the driver that I wanted to go to my sister, that I had not money but that I had 10 dollars. The driver laughed and said that he was glad to be able to help me. He took me to Rishon Le Zion. My sister was so pleased, she fainted. I was so happy to arrive in Israel. My only regret has been that we left to come here.

FREDA GLEZER was born in Poland in 1920 where she was educated. She spent the war years in Russia and afterwards was in displaced persons camps in Poland and Germany before going to Israel , arriving in South Africa in 1952. She is widowed and has a daughter, Batya.

MINNA LEVITAS
Belsen, Hamburg, Paris

I came to Belsen in 1946. Bergen-Belsen had been liberated by the British under Major Cloete, a South African.

The former SS Army barracks had been encircled by the new barbed wire fencing of the liberators. Inside were the hundreds of stateless survivors still virtually prisoners. They stayed in the comparative comfort of the SS quarters, were clothed by British Jewry, were being fed on the meagre post-war rations and cared for kindly by the British but it was a prison nevertheless. They were not allowed out of the guarded gates.

The Zionist Organization wanted the survivors to be allocated to Palestine. The British were equally determined not to permit this, so they were virtually kept hostage to the ongoing political struggle between the Zionist body and the British Government.

I went as a volunteer worker, the first of about 20 South Africans who had answered an appeal by the American Joint Distribution Committee through the Jewish Board of Deputies for funds and help in the enormous task of assisting the Jewish survivors of the Holocaust. I was to be the liason officer interviewing people for the end purpose of emigration within the bounds of the sorely restricted annual quotas for Jews which each country had imposed.

Some of the American volunteers returned home almost at once, unable to cope with their reactions to the chaos and the nature of our own task. The week before my arrival a member of a British Parliamentary Mission to the Camp had committed suicide because he could not accept the horror of what he had been confronted with.

When I first arrived in Germany I was issued with American Army uniform and was escorted by Herbert Katzki, the Director for the A.J.D.C. in the British Zone, to meet the U.N.R.R.A. heads. I was witness to the remains of the original camp of Belsen which with its terrible evidence had been burnt to the ground by the liberating British army. In a corner of a desolate empty field the crematorium structure remained. A disintegrating skeleton of a human being had been kept nearby as a dreadful monument to indescribable inhumanity. The soil was a mixture of ash and sand. Strewn in an adjoining field were pathetic material remains of metal buttons and buckles which had survived the fire.

All that was left of what once had been clothed living human beings.

My memory of the time I worked in Belsen seems always to be Grey. The colour of perpetual mourning. People, faces and events connected with that time still emerge and retreat.

I recall a blonde Jewish boy pacing the passage way of our office. He had survived the years sheltered by a German family. His parentage had now been revealed to him. He was to choose whether to remain German with his foster parents or to return to Judaism. I have a clear vision of this young boy deep in thought and I still sometimes wonder what he decided to do.

I remember being taken by a Palestinian, formerly German, worker called Kurt Leving to visit a hidden camp on the outskirts of Hamburg to meet a group of Polish Jews who had been repatriated to Poland from Siberia. Following renewed pogroms they had decided to try to emigrate illegally to Palestine.

This hide-out was a stage en route to Palestine in the "Secret Roads" mentioned in Kimche's book. In memory I stand there with him in this camp surrounded by a group of these men and women who were overwhelming us in Yiddish with their saga of hardship and suffering. I pay homage to the memory of Kurt Leving who some years later was appointed Israel's Ambassador to Germany.

Another memory is of going early one evening to a "community" meeting in the

185

This photograph was taken in Germany in 1946 on a Sunday expedition out of Belsen at Hann Munden. I am 3rd from left

long shed that served Belsen as an assembly hall. A listlessness pervaded that gathering. Only twenty people were there, including us workers and those carrying on their left forearm the branded number of their martyrdom and in their eyes, as indelibly, the suffering of those years. A black curtain had been drawn across the small stage.

When the curtain opened Yossele Rosensaft, a small man with bowed head, stood before us on the stage and delived a fiery oration in Yiddish, filled with indignation at the British blockade of Palestine and the infamous "Exodus" story. I was to encounter him again in 1959, now a wealthy New York art collector and communal leader, as the guest speaker at a Belsen commemorative gathering in Toronto.

From Belsen I was sent to administer a Children's Rehabilitation Centre housed in a former Rothschild mansion on the Elbe near Hamburg in Germany. I supervised this home for children survivors found in the forests or gathered up from their war time hiding places. Two Palestinian girls, formerly from Germany, were in charge of the home and their refusal to communicate in English was an expression of their resentment to the resistant attitude of the British Government.

Later I was seconded back to the Emigration Headquarters of the A.J.D.C. in the Rue Cambaceres in Paris. We were besieged daily by a flood of anxious would-be emigrants and tried quite desperately to cope with the confusion, the endless delays, the red tape and the frustration.

Amongst leaders of the South African Jewish community who at this stage were arriving to examine and report on the future of the survivors was Nicolai Kirshner. He would sit day after day amongst the waiting people weeping unashamedly, shaken to the depths by the lamenting voices and the reiterated stories, listening quietly and intently. Shaban and Kentridge were other notable visitors. Back in South Africa, Simon Roy with much difficulty begged and received permission to bring 80 Jewish survivors to their relatives in South Africa.

1947 was a bitterly cold winter and in the scarred and hungry countries of Northern Europe food and fuel was scarce. A.J.D.C. would charter ships, usually Greek, which often failed to materialize. After reports received by the A.J.D.C. on the problems encountered with the shipowners, I was sent to Genoa to escort a party of embarkees to South America. When we crossed the border to Italy the train ran out of coal and rattled to a halt. It was dawn before we could resume the journey.

Our promised ship - as was often the case at that time - was a week overdue in Genoa. Frustration and anger flared into fisticuffs between our officials and our group in the office of Hebrew Immigrant Aid Society in Rome.

"You promised us a ship! You promised us a ship!!"

They were angry and afraid that they would be returned once again to a repetition of the past. In all this time it seems to me that I met no Displaced Person who was not consumed with utter desperation to escape the past.

We witnessed the immense repercussions

and the implacable force of Jewish history asserting itself. There was a sense of awe and privilege of being a witness both there and later in August 1947, en route home, in Israel, itself, to the last violent phases which led to the proclamation of the Jewish State the following year.

And in 1948 I was privileged indeed to attend the massive historical event in Madison Square Gardens, New York, with Ben Gurion himself, reading the historical declaration - the new birth of Israel - the Jewish Nation.

But these are other memories.

Minna Levitas was born in Libau, Latvia and was brought to South Africa as an infant by her mother Ada. Her father Benjamin Dwor/Dorfman was an experienced tanner and pioneered the Swartkopsriver Tannery in Uitenhage, probably in 1915. She served amongst the volunteers under the American Joint Distribution Committee in Belsen and in Paris. Her only son died on Kibbutz Revivim in Israel, leaving two children, Tal and Erez.

JANE HERSCH
El Shatt, Egypt

I trained as a social worker at the London School of Economics and in 1944 volunteered to work for SAVE THE CHILDREN'S FUND. The War was still on in Europe and we did not know where we would be sent. I went by troop ship to Cairo where I sat around and did little so I went to the UNRRA Office and asked to be given a job. They sent me to a refugee camp in the desert on the west bank of the Suez Canal.

El Shatt was home to thirty thousand refugees divided into five camps. Six thousand refugees lived in each camp, thirty per marquee. The camp was run by the British Administration and was well organized by British and South African Officers. It was clean, well run, and had no flies. I was to be the social worker.

When I arrived, I could not get much information about the camp from the previous social worker, an American, so I decided to go around to each tent with an interpreter and introduce myself. I discovered that El Shatt housed Serbian Communists from Yugoslavia, confident Titoists, happily awaiting the proud future they forsaw for themselves after the war, a new era without their king and with Tito as their leader. They would hold concerts where they would sing songs, the only word in which, it seemed to me, was the name of Tito. They were well organized, controlled and confident.

I went from tent to tent introducing myself as
"Miss Cohen, the social worker."

In the one tent this produced an excited gasp, the delighted recognition of a fellow Jew. I discovered the existence of a Jewish island among this sea of Serbs. This was a group of one hundred Austrian Jews, most of whom came from Vienna. They had fled Hitler, had managed to get into Yugoslavia and from there onto the last ship to leave the country before the Germans invaded, along with many fleeing Yugoslavs. They

had landed here in Egypt under Allied supervision and had been in El Shatt for some years. There were about thirty couples in each spotlessly clean tent and they appeared cheerful and uncomplaining.

They were a totally different community to the Serbs. They were fed and watered, and physically cared for, but what about their future? There was nothing for them to do in the desert, but to sit around their tents. The Serbs were happy and confident - a glorious future was before them. But the Austrian Jews were different.

They were strangers among thirty thousand Serbs. Because of language difficulties there was very little communication between the groups. Their future could only be an upheaval. Their pasts had been wiped out, their present was one of marking time and their future was unknown and impenetrable.

As the Serbs did not need me, I spent most of my time with these Austrian Jews. With their school English and my school German we were able to communicate. They were delightful educated people. There was no time for individual stories, it was practical help that was needed.

One spring day when everyone was sitting outside in the pleasant desert air, I noticed a man inside the marquee lying on his bed. They explained to me that he had a spinal injury, was unable to move and had to be carried everywhere. I contacted the Red Cross in Cairo and within a few days had arranged to get him a wheelchair. What a difference it made to him and his wife; independence, the greatest gift anyone could have given them. He was now able to move around or sit outside with his friends.

By Pesach 1945 the end of the war was approaching but it had still not ended. Some wealthy Egyptian and American Jews arranged for Pesach seders for these refugees - matzos, meal and chickens galore arrived with a rabbi from Cairo. What happiness, what excitement - something to look forward to, something to do. For the women there was now a purpose to their week, as they bustled about preparing everything. A special marquee was set aside with white sheets for tablecloths. The officers were invited to join them.

I went to the kitchen marquee to see if there was anything they needed.

"Could you get us some leaves to decorate the tables?" one woman asked me. I looked around at the desert sands and my heart sank. Where did one find leaves among the sand dunes but I had been taught,"

If you don't ask, you don't get."

I borrowed a truck and drove to the Canal and went across on the ferry to Port Tufique where before the war the rich Egyptians had kept their yachts and their summer houses. There were still a few splendid houses with expensive gardens and I knocked on their doors. The servants helped me load the truck and I returned to the camp triumphant. I had become so accustomed to seeing sand, sand and more sand, that green gardens and leaves had become a dream.

When I returned with a truckload of greenery, the delighted women asked me what was my favourite part of the chicken. I told them it was the pupick. I explained the meaning of the seder to the Major seated next to me. When the meal arrived, a happy woman came to me with a plate piled high with the pupicks from all the chickens.

"For you, Miss Cohen."

The Major next to me thought this was another one of our strange customs.

There we were celebrating the Seder in a country which had been cursed until they had to release us from slavery. The Haggadah recalled what had happened to our forbears in the very same country which now gave us asylum at the request of the Allied Armies. Never had I felt so close to my ancestors as I did that night.

When the war ended, several of the Austrian refugees opted to go to live in what was then Palestine. The others preferred to return to Austria. At the end of 1945 when I was working in Greece, I managed to get three weeks leave and hitched from Piraeus to Alexandria on a Greek L.S.T. (Landing Ship Tank) and on arrival in Palestine visited several of the refugees who had been settled in small villages. They appeared to be happy and all seemed to be adjusting well to their new surroundings. The villages, small as they were, had several cultural activities which helped to make them feel at home. They were thankful to have a new life in peace where they could be Jews.

When I was sent by UNRRA to work with displaced persons in Greece, I met Mike, a naturalized South African, who had been born in Russia. He had been a prisoner of war in Italy and Germany and had volunteered, as a Russian speaker, to go to Lithuania for UNRRA in the hope that he would thus be able to track down his family. Unfortunately his whole family had been wiped out with the exception of his sister, who is living in Israel. The Russians did not want foreigners in Lithuania so he was sent to Greece. We married in the British Consulate in Athens and I came with him to South Africa in 1946 and settled in Thaba 'Nchu before retiring to Cape Town.

Jane Hersch was born in London in 1911 and was trained at the London School of Economics as a social worker. She was the first Jewish probation officer in London. She volunteered to join the Save The Children Fund in 1944 and was posted to Egypt where she worked in a refugee camp. She married Mike and came to South Africa in 1946. She has a son David and a daughter Ruth.

HOLOCAUST EXHIBITION

זכור

COMMEMORATING THE
40th ANNIVERSARY
OF THE LIBERATION OF THE
NAZI CONCENTRATION CAMPS

CULTURAL HISTORY MUSEUM

ADDERLEY STREET, CAPE TOWN

17 APRIL – 15 MAY 1985

OPEN DAILY 10 a.m. – 5 p.m.

SUNDAYS 2 p.m. – 5 p.m.

★ LECTURES (EVENINGS)

★ FILMS (LUNCH TIMES)

SEE PRESS FOR DETAILS

'LEST WE FORGET' - זכור

THE EXHIBITION IS PRESENTED BY THE JEWISH COMMUNITY OF CAPE TOWN

PROGRAMME — First 2 Weeks

Date	Subject	Speaker
Monday 22nd April '85	A Judaica Tour 'through a Philatelic Holocaust Collection	Mr Benzion Surdut
Tuesday 30th April '85	The Nations and the Jewish Question: 1933 – 39	Prof Bernard Steinberg
Wednesday 1st May '85	Social and Political Background to the rise of Nazism	Mr Harry Schwarz, MP
Monday 6th May, '85	Panel Discussion "What is the Holocaust to us"?	Father Roger Hickley Dean L. King Rabbi E. M. Kaye Chair: Rabbi D. Sherman

Details of further lectures will be announced in the May Issue of the Jewish Chronicle

All lectures are at 8.15 p.m. sharp and will be held in the Lecture Hall, SA Cultural Museum, Adderley Street, Cape Town. Seating is limited — come early.

Lunch-time lectures and films will be held — watch Press for details.

Additional suitable memorabilia is required for the Exhibition. Please contact 24-5020 exts 17 or 37.

Chapter 9

LIFE IN CAPE TOWN

BONNY FELDMAN

In the years following the destruction of the Nazi war machine, Jews who had survived Hitler's carnage wandered around Europe, seeking both relatives and homes. For many, the only prospect of life in the future was one far from the killing fields of Europe. Among many other places, Cape Town became a haven for a fairly small number; their ranks grew over the years when, for instance, some who had settled further north in Africa made their way south following political upheaval in their adoptive countries.

The local community has paid homage both to the survivors of the Holocaust and to those who were murdered during the dark days of the War. Over the years since the late 1940's, various commemorative functions and educational programmes have been organized in Cape Town by, among others, the local Jewish Board of Deputies, religious bodies, educational institutions and She'erith Hapletah (the organization representing survivors).

A major undertaking was the assistance to survivors resident in South Africa to lodge claims for compensation for the loss of property and possessions against the government of West Germany. This work was undertaken by the Restitution Office established by the South African Jewish Board of Deputies (on a national level). Locally, in Cape Town, many claims received attention through the extensive efforts of Advocate Dr Erwin Spiro, in particular.

As regards commemorative events, the major one has been the annual Yom Hashoa Vehagevura observance: the day commemorating the Holocaust and Heroism. In recent years the event has been under the auspices of the Jewish Board of Deputies and the United Council of Orthodox Hebrew Congregations. The programme has reflected the special features of Cape Town Jewry in that there is both a religious and a Zionist

element to the proceedings; there is full participation of the Reform Congregation; the Ashkenzi and Sephardi communities are represented equally in the commemoration readings and scholars participating in the programme have been representative of both the Jewish day schools and the government schools.

Since 1976 the commemoration service has taken place at the Pinelands No.2 cemetary and has been attended by between 1000 and 1800 people annually. An important element of this event is the keynote address, and, over the years, there has been an impressive array of speakers including both overseas and local academics, communal leaders and religous leaders from all sectors of the community.

In 1985, to mark the 40th anniversary of the liberation of the concentration camps, an exhibition was mounted at the prestigious SA Cultural History Museum which included stories and personal memoribilia of seventeen Holocaust survivors who resided in Cape Town. The exhibition drew large crowds and was extended from four to seven weeks.

Recognizing the need for intensified awareness and education, it was decided in 1986 to establish the Cape Town Holocaust Memorial Council (a joint project of the Jewish Board of Deputies (Cape Council) and the Western Province Zionist Council in association with She'erith Hapletha) to co-ordinate and promote Holocaust commemorative and educational programmes and projects within both the Jewish and wider community.

Over the years a number of significant events and projects have been undertaken. Highlights have included the 50th anniversary in 1986 of the arrival in Cape Town of the "Stuttgart" a ship carrying refugees from Germany, the 50th anniversary in 1988 of Kristallnacht, the 50th anniversary in 1993 of the Warsaw Ghetto uprising.

The international exhibition "Anne Frank in the World" which recently toured South Africa was mounted in 1994 at the SA National Gallery for a six week period drawing record attendances including thousands of school children from all sections of the wider community. An ancillary programme of theatrical and musical events, films, lectures and symposia also attracted much interest.

Other projects undertaken by the Holocaust Memorial Council include exhibitions, lectures, a promotion to encourage the lighting of Yarzeit candles in the home on the eve of Yom Hashoa, special Holocaust education programmes for high school history students studying World War II, video interviews of survivors, a study group and the publication of this book.

In addition to impressive annual Yom Hashoa services on all their campuses, the United Herzlia Schools have an intensive Holocaust study programme in the Middle and High Schools. A special scholar-in-residence programme, funded by a leading member of the community, has brought a number of Holocaust educators from abroad to lead this programme. Jewish Studies teachers have attended the summer course at Yad Vashem in Jerusalem and high school students have participated in the "March of the Living" tours to Poland and Israel. A number of adults have also participated in these tours.

The Jessie and Isaac Kaplan Centre for Jewish Studies at the University of Cape Town facilitates the provision of undergraduate credit courses in Holocaust studies. Visiting overseas academics have included leading scholars such as Dr. David Bankier, Prof. Zeév Mankowitz and Prof. Steven Katz, who have also been made available for public lectures.

The SA Union of Jewish Students (SAU-JUS) on the university and technikon campuses have conducted their own annual Yom Hashoa functions and have also had an opportunity for very meaningful study of the Holocaust through the Student Holocaust Interview Programme (SHIP) which began its work in 1981.

The Jacob Gitlin library has an extensive and impressive collection of Holocaust literature and audio-visual material. Regrettably efforts to establish a permanent Holocaust Resource Centre has, to date, been unsuccesful.

Cape Town, like many centres of Jewish settlement, will ensure that the world will, indeed, NEVER FORGET.

Bonny Feldman was born in Bulawayo on 4.4.1963. Her late father, Phillip Feldman, was born in Alytus, Lithuania and fought as a partisan in the Ponari forests. The family moved to Cape Town in 1968. She studied history, education and law at the University of Cape Town

XAVIER PIAT-KA

In the summer of 1952, some Holocaust survivors from Johannesburg came to Cape Town on holiday. Nohum Zolin decided to hold a meeting to welcome them and introduce them to the Cape Town survivors. The latter included Peggy Berolsky, Mike Breslin, Chaim Chayet, Rabbi J Dushinsky, Cantor Jacob and Miriam Lichterman, Henry and Mita Knopf, Dr Isak and Sima Kaplinsky, Leib and Gita Markman, Xavier and Chayela Piat-ka and Joseph and Lottie Tarko.

This was the beginning of the She'erith Hapletah, the Association of Jewish Holocaust Survivors (1939-1945) in Cape Town.

An Ad hoc committee was established with Nohum Zolin as the organizing secretary. They advertised through the Jewish press for survivors to join them. The aim of this newly founded association was to promote social and cultural ties amongst the survivors and the community, to involve them in the affairs of the community, to render assistance to members when required and to participate in all aspects of historical research and testimony on the Holocaust.

However, the fifties was, for the survivors, a decade of new beginnings, of establishing new lives, of starting new families. Professions were changed, businesses were established, babies were born. The Association's activities centred mainly on private socials on week-ends and holidays with those befriended. During the sixties and seventies the organization was not very vibrant although contacts were established with the Israel Remembrance Authority, Yad Vashem and the Claims Conference regarding compensation and material help. Members of She'erith Hapletah would take part in the annual commemorative memorial evenings at the Zionist Hall and in pilgrimages to the Pinelands No 1 cemetery where the Holocaust Menorah was inaugurated. Mr Zolin arranged for several smaller replicas of that six-branched menorah to be installed in synagogues as a permanent memorial.

The Weekend Argus published a double-page article about the Nazi terror in the Vilna Ghetto written by Xavier Piat-ka in May 1976 to coincide with Remembrance Day - Yom Hashoa. In subsequent years he contributed many such articles to the local press to keep the memory of those tragic events fresh in the public's mind, both as a reminder and as a warning.

When Yad Vashem, Jerusalem, in 1977 initiated the "Pages of Testimony" project to record for posterity the names of all the Jews who had perished during the Holocaust at the hands of the Nazis, the She'erith Hapletah was involved in collecting the names known to relatives in the Cape.

In February 1984 a new executive committee was elected with Lucien Feigenbaum in the chair, Leon Borstrock as treasurer, Xavier Piat-ka as secretary and PRO and Miriam Lichterman and Asher Varon as committee members. Nohum Zolin was awarded Honorary Life Presidency of the She'erith Hapletah at a special banquet for his thirty years devoted service to the Association.

The Association now grew in numbers due to the enrolling of Sephardi survivors from Rhodes Island who had a special representative on the committee. Contact was established with the American Federation of Jewish Fighters, Camp Inmates and Nazi Victims, New York as a result of which our members receive a bi-monthly publication "Martyrdom and Resistance" together with the Association's local newsletter.

An era of activity followed when the Student Holocaust Interviewing Project (SHIP) began in 1983. Teams of Jewish students under the leadership of Dora Wynchank tape recorded testimonies from the survivors. In 1984 Prof Martin Gilbert, a Holocaust historian, was the guest speaker at the Yom Hashoah ceremony and met with several of our members. He later included his interviews in his book "History of the Holocaust."

In 1985 with full participation of the members of our Association, a commemorative Holocaust Exhibition was held at the Cultural History Museum in Adderley Street, Cape Town attracting large attendances and much interest

Cape Town survivors at opening (l-r): Violette, Lucia, Leon, Bella and Mathilde.

By 1976 the number of members had grown to 46 and two representatives were actively involved in the establishment of the Cape Holocaust Memorial Council by the Cape Jewish Board of Deputies. Several members of the She'erith Hapletah participated in the World Assembly of Survivors held in Israel in May 1985 together with Johannesburg members. This was held to commemorate the fortieth anniversary of the Liberation from the camps and the defeat of Nazi Germany.

The She'erith Hapletah was also very concerned that the remembrance of the experiences of the survivors during those tragic times should be perpetuated and that the Jewish community and the outside world should have a better understanding of those nightmare years. A proposal was put forward to collect into a memorial book the memoirs of those residing in our area. In 1988 a plan of action was submitted to the Holocaust Memorial Council and the result, after a lot of hard work by many people, is this book.

The Association is deeply grateful to Mr and Mrs Korzuch and their Wellington friends for the assistance rendered in this project.

Mr Feigenbaum resigned as chairman in December 1989 and Mrs Violette Fintz was elected in his place, representing the majority of members who are of Sephardi origin. The committee now consisted of Mr X. Piat-ka as secretary/treasurer, Mr L. Feigenbaum, Mrs M Lichterman, Mr M Breslin, Mrs C Soriano and Mrs L Borstrock.

The Association approved a design submitted by Hillel Turok, a well-known architect, at the request of Mr Markman, for a Holocaust Monument to be built in memory of the Six Million victims of Nazi slaughter at the Pinelands No 2 Jewish Cemetery opposite the Tahara House. Subsequently Mr Turok arranged for sponsorship for the project and the donation of materials, and directed the erection of the monument which was subsequently awarded the 1990 Fulton Award by the Concrete Association in the Sculpture Category. He was co-inaugurator with the writer at the dedication ceremony of the monument held on Yom Hashoah on 22nd April 1990.

In recent years we have invited to our annual Yom Hashoah lunches the children and grandchildren of the survivors in Celebration of Surviving, and of Living. Invited guests are also hosted. Members of the Association are on call for a variety of meetings organised by different organisations, schools and colleges, where we serve as "living witnesses" of the Holocaust, recalling for them our past experiences. Our association has also initiated renewed activities of the "SECOND GENERATION" club, which consists of the children of our members. Recently members of the community who have a special interest in the Holocaust have formed a supporting group called "FRIENDS OF SHE'ERITH HAPLETAH" to assist with the needs of the association.

These off shoots and this book are proof of our continued growth as an organisation. Fifty years on we have survived and can look back with pride to the achievements of our association, both personally in the emotional support and friendship it has given to its members, the survivors, and generally in the educational support and asssistance that we have given to the wider community to ensure that the Holocaust will never be forgotten. This book is an example of our commitment to this aim. May it also serve in memoriam to all our family and friends who did not survive.

May their memories be blessed for ever.

IN MEMORIAM

MRS. S. BERRO.
LEON BORSTROCK,
HAYIM CHAYET
RABBI E.J. DUSCHINSKY
PHILLIP FELDMAN
WELVEL GLEZER,
HENRY KNOPF
DR ISAK & SIMA KAPLINSKY,
RAY KETELLAPPER
ELISABETH KORANSKY

CANTOR JACOB LICHTERMAN
MIRA LASER
MRS JOHANNA LINSSEN
LEIB & GITA MARKMAN
CHAYELA ROSENTHAL-PIAT-KA
GABY ROSE-KOVES,
SYBIL SHEIN
JOSEPH & LOTTIE TARKO
NACHUM ZOLIN.

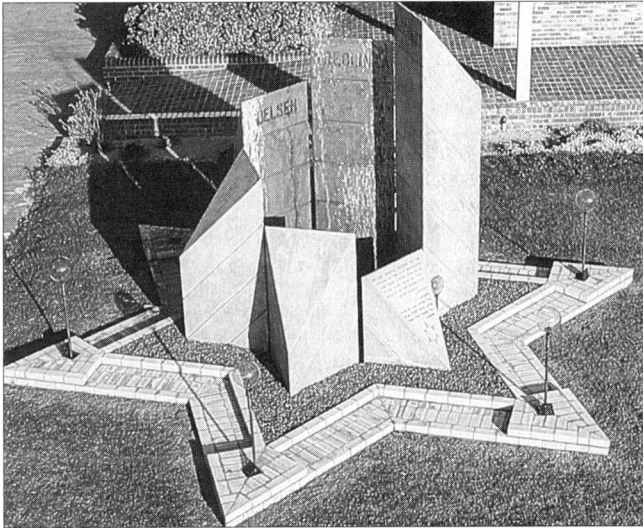

Monument for the Six million victims

"FOR THESE I WEEP, STREAMS OF TEARS FLOW FROM MY EYES BECAUSE OF THE DESTRUCTION OF MY PEOPLE" (Lamentations.)

This inscription is affixed to the monument which was designed by Hillel Turok as a powerful sculpture creating an atmosphere of brutal starkness and monumental simplicity.

The monument is based on the Magen David whose six equal triangles represent the six million Jewish victims. Each triangle is a precast concrete column inscribed with the name of a notorious concentration camp. These columns, separated from each other and rising at half metre intervals, have their tops chamferred to indicate an indiscrimate termination of life and stand around a hexagonal pool with a central water jet representing the tears and sweat of the concentration camp inmates.

The podium of white bricks is shaped like a Magen David with a recessed border of black stone aggregate representing the ashes of the gas ovens. In the extreme points of the Magen David gas lamps have been inserted. These are lit each year on Yom Hashoa by children of the survivors.

SOLLY KAPLINSKI

Extracts from LOST AND FOUND - A SECOND GENERATION RESPONSE TO THE HOLOCAUST.

My parents, who were constantly in danger and on the run when they were Partisans in the forests of Poland and Russia for five traumatic years, rarely spoke of their experiences or those of their families who were murdered by the Nazis. In an attempt to protect us, they seldom referred to the Holocaust, if at all, on the intellectual level. There was almost a sense of denial operating in our household.

Emotionally, of course, they carried the scars and were often prone to bouts of anxiety, panic and depression.

I, in my own way, tried to protect them and myself by avoiding references to their past; and in that sense I was an emotional cripple. My trip to Poland in April of 1988, however, as part of the "March of the Living" experience, was a cathartic moment for me: it released a gush of hitherto repressed and unabridged emotional responses (as reflected in these pages) and allowed me to express my mourning and come to terms with the death of my parents (*Zichronam Livracha*) both of whom passed away in 1987, within six months of each other.

It is to their memory that I dedicate this "stream of consciousness".

SOLLY KAPLINSKI was born in Cape Town on 26.6.1948. His late parents, Dr & Mrs I Kaplinski, were Holocaust survivors. A clinical psychologist, a professional teacher and former Headmaster of Herzlia High School in Cape Town, he now lives in Toronto where he is the Executive Director of the United Synagogues Day Schools. His poetry has been featured in several publications. An anthology LOST AND FOUND – A SECOND GENERATION RESPONSE TO THE HOLOCAUST was published in Cape Town in 1992. He is married and has three daughters.

Illustrator: LIORA GLAZER

TO GO HOME?

I owe it to you Mom & Dad
even tho' you rest in the earth
to go home

I owe it to you my bobbas and zeidas[1]
whom I never knew
who could never spoil me
and who were shoved
alive
into a mass burial-pit
in the Ponary Forests
to go home

Home conjures up images of
warmth, familiar smells
laughter
security
and peace of mind

Poland may've been home then
but it's really hell on earth
It's evolution in reverse
It shakes you to your very core
It makes you fear for man

So why go back you may ask

To remember
to bear witness
to be the link
to pay homage
to take care of the past.

----

[1] grandmothers and grandfathers

POLAND — SOME HOME TRUTHS

Clutching my Gilbert
close to my chest
I travelled through Poland
hoping to gain
a new understanding

His well-thumbed Atlas
(my Bible)
filled in some gaps
provided the detail
gave me fresh insights

posed many more questions.

I still could not fathom
the silence of my parents
why they rarely spoke about
It.

I'd always known
they were different from others.

The nightmares, the screams
the pain-filled recurring dreams
the fear of the doorbell
the panic at the shrill telephone ring
the never-ending paranoia and mistrust
the obsession with the ein hora[1]
could never quite cover up
the games they played
to over-protect my brother and me —
neither could their oft acted-out anxieties.

And then one day
walking through a cast-off street
of Warsaw
seeing all those tell-tale signs
of once sturdy Mezuzot[2] on ancient door-frames
and feeling a bitter rage
at the gouging out
of the very heart of Judaism
in this now 'ghost city'
some truths
were revealed to me
about my home secrets.

What is there left to say
to innocent children
when the very centre of your gravity
has been cruelly dislodged
when you've been denuded and deflowered
and utterly robbed of all your dignity
and all that remains
is a permanent scar on the heart?

Isn't it easier to play make-believe?
and yet:
so many things
left unsaid
unexplained
unexpressed
unshared.

I couldn't even get a foot in the door.

---

[2] prayers from the Bible written on parchment, placed in a case and attached to the doorpost

IN THE SHOE SHOP

I went to a shoe shop
today
in
Majdanek
800 000 pairs on display
but
no
body
to fill them

How easy it must've been
to be ambitious
in
those days

It didn't take long
to fill a dead man's shoes.

EPILOGUE: THE BOTTOM LINE

How many times must we stand up for the rights of others?
We must — to the nth degree
and yes
let's proclaim it to the world
(they always want proof)
but it's still not enough.

How many injustices must we confront
on behalf of others?
We must — to the nth degree
and
let's shout it from the barricades
but it's still not enough.

How many banners must we hold up
and how many miles must we march
for the dignity of others?
We must — to the nth degree
but it's still not enough.

They know
yes they do
when the crunch comes
we always stand up
to be counted
but it's still not enough.

So let me ask you
very tentatively
with tears in my eyes
will it be enough only
when we turn the other cheek?

IN MEMORIAM

THE FOLLOWING PERSONS HAVE MADE A CONTRIBUTION TOWARDS THIS PROJECT IN SACRED MEMORY OF THEIR FAMILY MEMBERS WHO PERISHED IN THE HOLOCAUST (1939 - 1945)

Families **ANGEL. RESTIS, SHA'ALTIEL**
of Milnerton,Cape
in Sacred Memory of Reyna,widow of Bension Levy and children,
Jacques, Rachel, Esther, Jeanette, Eliakim and Gioia
of Rhodes Island, Italy.

JACQUELINE AVZARADEL
of Sea Point, Cape Town
in Sacred Memory of my father-in-law Joseph, of Regina, Allegra
and Stella Avzaradel
of Rhodes Island, Italy.

HANA BENJAMIN
of Gardens, Cape Town
in Sacred Memory of my parents Emil and Regina Oberndoerfer
of Fuerth, Bavaria, Germany.

ROGER M BRANDT and family
of Cape Town
in Sacred Memory of Leopold and Betty Brandt
of Berlin, Germany.

LILY BORSTROCK
of Sea Point, Cape Town, **JEFFREY BORSTROCK**
of Camps Bay, Cape Town and **MILTON BORSTROCK**
of Los Angeles, U.S.A.
in Sacred Memory of Late Leon Borstrock's parents Jacob Levi and
Alida Borstrock, his brothers Jules and Henri, his children
Frederika and Jacques Borstrock,
all of Amsterdam, Holland, and of my uncle Isak and Esta Zakheim
and family of Warsaw, Poland.

MICHAEL and **DORA BRESLIN, MORRIS, REBECCA,
NATHAN AND STEVEN BRESLIN**
of Sea Point, Cape Town
in Sacred Memory of parents Morris and Pesha Breslin
of Mir, and brother Shamai, his wife Feigel and Abram,
Solly and Chaya their children
of Novogrudek, Poland, Belarus.

LEA-LUCIA CAPELLUTO-HABIB
of Sea Point, Cape Town
in Sacred Memory
of Reyna, Rachel and Mathy Capelluto
of Rhodes Island, Italy.

NOAH CHAIT, HILDA KISNER
of Highlands Estate, Cape Town
in Sacred Memory of Sheina and Abba Gillman
of Shaulai (Shavel), Lithuania
and of Meyer and Masha Chait
of Yanishik, Lithuania.

MATTEO CHARHON and family
of Sea Point, Cape Town
in Sacred Memory of my Mother
Lea Emmanuel Charhon,
and my Uncle and Aunt Rahamim and Flore Cohen
of Rhodes Island, Italy.

EVA BEN-MELEH DAVIS
of Welgelen, Parow, Cape
in Sacred Memory
of Father Yusef (Joseph) Ben-Meleh
of Athens, Greece.

SHULAMIT DERMAN and RUTH JOWELL
of Sea Point, Cape Town
and EMANUEL DERMAN
of New York, U.S.A.
in Sacred Memory of our grandparents
Rivka and Nachum Zvi Sapirstein,
our aunt Paye Sapirstein and uncle Leibel Sapirstein
of Brest-Litovsk, Poland,
and our uncle Yisroel Dereczynski
of Slonim, Poland.

JUDY DIAMANT
of Claremont, Cape Town
in Sacred Memory of Sally and Lily Fanty
of Ostrava, Czechoslovakia.

BETTY DIAMOND
of Oranjezicht, Cape Town
in Sacred Memory of Chaje and Chiam Allon,
children Rochel, Leibe, Berke and Nachame
of Jasvionia, Lithuania
and of Sarah and Chiam Fine
and Gusta, Gita, Hinda, Chena, Simon Jankel,
Beinez and Feiga, their children,
of Yelock, Lithuania.

LUCIEN AND SHIRLEY FEIGENBAUM
of Wynberg, Cape
in Sacred Memory of Leon, Zofia and Hania Feigenbaum
and the Feigenbaum,
Brochis and Gesundheit Families
of Warsaw and Lodz, Poland.

SEVVIE FELDMAN and Daughters of Orangezicht, Cape Town
in Sacred Memory of Phillip Feldman (survivor), Aaron Feldman,
Noah and Bonah (nee Feldman) Slutzky and daughter,
Judith of Alytus, Lithuania.

VIOLETTE MAIO-FINTZ and NISSIM ITZHAK FINTZ
of Sea Point, Cape Town
in Sacred Memory of Yaacov Maio, Rahel,
Yehuda-Leon and Mirjam
of Rhodes Island, Italy.

H.M. FLORENCE
of Sea Point, Cape Town
in Sacred Memory of my Parents Rabbi Moshe Zelig and Mire
Florence,
Brothers Kalman Shlomo and Smere Leizer,
Grandmother Taube Shapiro
of Lygumai. Lithuania
and of Sister Sore Leah (nee Florence) and husband N Bloch
of Shaulai (Shavel) Lithuania.

DIAMANTE FRANCO-HOUGNOU
of Sea Point, Cape Town
in Sacred Memory of Ishak, Perla, Aaron, Yaacov
and Fortunee Hougnou
of Rhodes Island, Italy'

PERCY AND CLARA GERSHOLOWITZ
of Vredehoek, Cape Town
in Sacred Memory of my mother Rachel and my sisters Berta Lifshitz
and Chaya Brestowitzki and her husband Jacob
of Baranowicze, Poland.

LINDA GLAZER
of Clifton, Cape Town
in Sacred Memory of Sanyi (Josef) Glazer
of Budapest, Hungary.

FREDA GLEZER (nee Szteyn)
of Vredehoek, Cape Town and BATYA of Johannesburg
in Sacred Memory of my mother Batya and brothers
Moshe and Ruben Szteyn and sister Ida and Josef and Ester Sitman
of Dubno, Poland.

BLANKA HARITON
of Sea Point, Cape Town
in Sacred Memory of my Sister Rosa Lowinger
of Berlin, Germany.

JACQUES NATHAN HASSON and family
of Constantia, Cape
in Sacred Memory of my parents Nathan Gabriel and
Sarina Hasson and sisters Laura, Jeanette and Zaphira
of Rhodes Island, Italy.

MATHILDA ISRAEL HASSON and Family
of Sea Point, Cape Town
in Sacred Memory of my parents, David and Bulissa Perla Israel,
and of my parents-in-law, Esther Ishak and Jacques Hasson,
Marco Scemaria, Mathilda,
Esther and Jacques
of Rhodes Island, Italy.

RIVA HURWITZ (nee Chatzkel) and her children HELEN BERGER, LILY BECKER, MAX HURWITZ AND ROCHELLE MAISEL
of Cape Town
in Sacred Memory of Mordechai and Hinde-Rashel Hurwitz
of Kamai (Rakashik), Lithuania,
Sorrel Chatzkel, Bassa, Leah and Zelik Chatzkel,
Zalman and Feige Chatzkel
of Ponodel, Lithuania.

RAPHAEL AND MARTINE ISRAEL and Family
of Sea Point, Cape Town
in Sacred Memory
of Celibi Raphael,
Lea, Mathilda, Rachel and Samuel Israel,
and Miriam Sigoura
of Rhodes Island, Italy.

SARAH NOTRICA JERUSALMI
of Sea Point, Cape Town
in Sacred Memory
of Rosa and Mazliah Notrica
and Salvatore Yehoshua Notrica
of Rhodes Island, Italy.

LATE JANKEL AND SONIA KATZEFF'S CHILDREN
c/o DR.H.R. SANDERS
of Bantry Bay, Sea Point
in Sacred Memory of
our grandparents Moishe and
Gasse Katzeff and Shroel and Blume Peitz
of Mazeikiai, Lithuania.

ISRAEL KETELLAPPER
of Wynberg, Cape Town
in Sacred Memory of my Mother Raatje Ketellapper-Drukker
of Amsterdam, Holland,
and Parents of my late wife, Ray Ketellapper (Survivor),
Hartog and Bessie (nee Goldstein) Van Der Kar
and her Brother David
of Amsterdam, Holland.

DAVID AND ETTIE KORZUCH,DAUGHTERS
BARBARA BONT AND BEVERLEY LYONS
of Wellington, Cape
in Sacred Memory of my parents, Josef Boruch and
Blime Rykil Korzuch, my Brothers Israel,
Abram Leib and Alter Simon,
my Sisters Chana, Ester and Gitel
of Strzemieszyce, Poland.

MIRIAM LICHTERMAN
of Sea Point, Cape Town
in Sacred Memory of my Parents Jacob Joel and Pearl Teitelbaum,
my Brother Israel and my Mother-in-law, Bela Lichterman, all
of Warsaw, my Uncle Moshe, wife and daughter Ana
of Chmielnik, Poland,
Uncle Aron Rotman, his wife and four children
of Kolnam Rhein, Germany,
Victor Rotman and Hadasa of Blonic and Yakov and Sara Rotman
of Skierniewicze,Poland, Family Weinfeld
of Koprzywnica, Poland,
Hannah, Hershel, Carol and Rose Shabman
of Warsaw, Poland,
Aunt Henia and Walter Srebrnick and children Rosa and Leo
of Dortmund, Germany,
and other close members of our family in
Warsaw too numerous to mention.

LOTTE LIEBRECHT
of Muizenberg, Cape
in Sacred Memory of parents Albert and Franziska Levy,
Sisters Lore and Renate, Grandmother Marianne Bucky
of Altenburg, Thueringen, Germany.

PESLA LIS
of Sea Point in Sacred Memory
of my Parents, Abram Abish and Ryfka Fajgla Lewenstein,
my Sister Dorothy, my Brother Josef, Uncle Jakob Kaminski
and daughter Hanka
of Koszyce, Poland,
of Cousins Jakob David and Sara Lieberman and daughter Ada
of Warsaw, Poland, and my Uncle Leib and Aunt Golda Prajs, sons Abel
and Perec Prajs and families
of Busko Zdroj, Poland.

FREDERIQUE C. MARCUS
of Cape Town in Sacred Memory
of Baruch and Greta (nee Rosenthale) Marcus
of Berlin, Germany.

DAVID AND ELSIE MENASCE
of Bantry Bay, Cape Town in Sacred Memory
of Mardoche, Rebecca and Rachel Menasce
of Rhodes Island, Italy.

EGON MENDEL
of Kloofnek, Cape Town
in Sacred Memory of Hermann Mendel of Rocken-Hausen,
Siegbert and Johanna Mendel
and their children Helga, Ernst, Ruth and Sonja
of Koln, Germany,
and Heinrich and Elizabeth Kallmann
of Sobernheim, Germany.

SARA MERGIAN
of Sea Point, Cape Town
in Sacred Memory of my parents Avram and Rebecca Galante,
my sisters Rosa, Juana and Mathy
and of Elia, Gioia and Mazaltov Mergian
of Rhodes Island. Italy.

VIOLETTA HASSON-MIZRAHI
of Sea Point, Cape Town
in Sacred Memory of Mazaltov, Behor, Jeanette, Esther and
Jacques Hasson, Rebecca Mallel and
children Nissim and baby daughter
of Rhodes Island, Italy.

CHARLES ODES of Fresnaye and **JANICE BLOCH**
of Kenilworth, Cape Town
in Sacred Memory of their grandmother Pese Eta Odes
and her four children
of Plunyan (Plunge) Lithuania.

XAVIER PIAT-KA of Sea Point, Cape Town and **NAAVA LEVITT**
and **ZOLA SHUMAN** of Boston, Mass. U.S.A.
in Sacred Memory of my Mother Vava (nee Goldman)
of Paris, France, my Father Zachary Jutan,
my parents-in-law, Nochum and Fruma Rozental,
my brother-in-law Leib Rozental, Uncle Samuel and
Asya Jutan, Aunt Sonja, Reeva and Tzire-Leah, Aunt Rachel Tunkel all
of Wilno, Poland.

BELLINA ALMELEH-RAHMANI
of Sea Point, Cape Town
in Sacred Memory of Parents Raphael and Rosa Almeleh
and Grandmother Ricca Cohen
of Rhodes Island, Italy.

CHAYA MAOZ and SARAH REIFER
of Israel and son **AARON SHANDLING**
of Three Anchor Bay, Cape Town
in Sacred Memory of Grandmother Frieda Lang,
Parents Avraham and Ella Scheindling,
sisters Feige and Esther
and brothers Joseph, Myer and Shalom
of Shkood (Skoudas). Lithuania.

SALLY ROBINSON (nee Berman)
of Green Point, Cape Town
in Sacred Memory of my uncles Alec, Morris and
Israel Behr-Berman and their families
of Plungyan (Plunge), Lithuania.

HENRY ROSENBAUM
of Oranjezicht, Cape Town
in Sacred Memory of David Rosenbaum,
Jacob and Flora Grande
of Berlin, Germany,
and Willi Marcus
of Oberkotzau, Germany.

ILSE ROSENBAUM
of Green Point, Cape Town
in Sacred Memory of Sister Nelly Hirsch (nee Rosewitz)
and her child Ellen
of Muenchen Gloudbach, Germany.

PAULINE SCHKOLNE
of Sea Point, Cape Town
in Sacred Memory of Sheva Chana
and Arye Leib Schkolnik,
daughter Bassa Leah Epstein and Family
of Chweidan, Lithuania.

SELMA SEGAL, MOIRA SELIGMAN and EVELYN SHEMER
of Sea Point, Cape Town
in Sacred Memory of Sarah Seligman and family
of Janiskis (Yanishok) Lithuania.

LEON AND CLARA SORIANO of Sea Point, Cape Town
in Sacred Memory of Baruh and Esther Avzaradel and
Regina Renata Avzaradel,
and of Yakov and Bulissa Tarica,
Bulissa Aslam Soriano,
Moshe and Yohevet and Giacomo Soriano, and
of Boaz and Rebecca Israel,
Giuseppe and Moshe Israel, Semah
and Shemayah Israel,
Susanna and Isaac Avzaradel (nee Israel),
Sarah and Regina Israel
of Rhodes Island, Italy.

BELLA VARKEL of Sea Point, Cape Town
in Sacred Memory of my Mother Mania,
my Sister Miriam, Brother Nochum Rudaszewski,
Cousins Rachel and Leiba Bretzki
and Aunt Olga Mozes
of Wilno, Poland\Lithuania.

INDEX

CONTRIBUTORS LISTED
ALPHABETICALLY

R.A.

LUCIA AMATO

LEON BORSTROCK

MIKE BRESLIN

ALIDA COHEN

GIUSEPPE CONE

HELENE CZERNIEWICZ

EVE DAVIS

LENIE DE JONG-SANDERS

MENNO DE JONG

JUDY DIAMANT

BETTY DIAMOND

LUCIEN FEIGENBAUM

BONNY FELDMAN

VIOLETTE FINTZ

DIAMANTE FRANCO

JACK FRIEDMANN

FREDA GLEZER

RUTH GREEN

IRENE GROLL

SYLVA GUTTMANN

MATHILDA HASSON

JANE HERSCH

SARAH JERUSALMI

HELENE JOFFE

HANNAH JOLES

SOLLY KAPLINSKI

SHMUEL KEREN

ISRAEL KETELLAPPER

RAE KETELLAPPER

DAVID KORZUCH

KARL LANGER

MINNA LEVITAS

JACOB LICHTERMAN

MIRIAM LICHTERMAN

LOTTE LIEBRECHT

PESLA LIS

SIPPORA LOCKITCH

ZOFJA LURIE

MARTHA MANNSBACH

JONY MARKMAN

CHANA OBERNDOERFER

SANTA PELHAM

XAVIER PIAT-KA

A.R.

CHAYELA ROSENTHAL-PIATKA

HENNY SAUER

MENDI SOFFER

LOUIS THEEBOOM

KLARA VAN KLEEF

BELLA VARKEL

ASHER VARON